DEMOCRACY

AND THE PUBLIC SPACE
IN LATIN AMERICA

Leonardo Avritzer

PRINCETON UNIVERSITY PRESS

PRINCETON AND OXFORD

Library of Congress Cataloging-in-Publication Data

Avritzer, Leonardo.
Democracy and the public space in Latin America / Leonardo Avritzer.
  p. cm.

ISBN 0-691-09087-4 (alk. paper) — ISBN 0-691-09088-2 (pbk. paper)

1. Democracy—Latin America. 2. Collective behavior—Political aspects—Latin
America. 3. Political culture—Latin America. 4. Political participation—Latin
America. I. Title.
JL966.A99 2002
321.8′098—dc21   2001051035

British Library Cataloging-in-Publication Data is available
This book has been composed in Sabon

Printed on acid-free paper. ∞

www.pup.princeton.edu

Printed in the United States of America.

10 9 8 7 6 5 4 3 2 1

10 9 8 7 6 5 4 3 2 1
(Pbk.)

CONTENTS

જી

ACKNOWLEDGMENTS

එ

This book was written during a one-year stay at the Department of Political Science at MIT. I am very grateful to Joshua Cohen for his support during this period and above all for his wonderful job as a commentator on the manuscript. Many friends and colleagues commented on several different versions of the book. Among them I would like to single out my lifelong friend and collaborator, Alberto Olvera, whose help made possible the fieldwork on Mexico. I am also indebted to many other people who have commented on different parts of the manuscript or on my previous work: Enrique Peruzzotti, Jose Mauricio Domingues, Sérgio Costa, Sonia Alvarez, Evelina Dagnino, Myrian Santos, Antonio Mitre, Luis Roeniger, Claudia Feres Faria, Brian Wampler, Ilse Scherer-Warren, Andrew Arato, Alberto Melucci, Jose Casanova, and Timo Lyyra. Many state and social movements activists helped me develop the book's fieldwork. I would like to mention only a few: Luciano Brunet and Jose Utzig in Porto Alegre; and Hugo Almada, Jesus Cantum, and Ernesto Isunza in Mexico. James Ingram did a great job helping me to improve the English of the manuscript. I would also like to thank Ian Malcolm at Princeton University Press and two anonymous reviewers for their contribution to the final format of the manuscript. I would finally like to thank my wife, Ana, for her love and support of my work during all these years.

DEMOCRACY

AND THE PUBLIC SPACE
IN LATIN AMERICA

INTRODUCTION

☙

This is a book about democracy in Latin America and democratic theory. It tells a story about democratization in three Latin American countries—Brazil, Argentina, and Mexico—during the recent, "third wave" of democratization.[1] This story emphasizes the role of popular participation through human rights organizations, groups devoted to a more just distribution of local resources and groups in charge of electoral monitoring, during the process of democratization.

My analysis of Latin American democratization challenges an assumption that lies at the heart of conventional theories of democratization: that all processes of democratization must cope with anti-institutional mass mobilizations of a kind that led to the breakdown of democracy in Europe during the first wave of democratization, and that the only way to produce stable democracy in the face of those mobilizations is—as in Europe after World War II—to narrow the scope of democracy to the selection of elites through periodic elections. This theoretical approach is known as democratic elitism. By showing how democratic collective action in Latin America opened a space for popular participation and transformed traditional (hierarchical and clientelist) understandings of politics, I hope to demonstrate the limits of democratic elitism as a general theory of democracy. Instead of applying an elitist framework derived from the particulars of European experience to Latin America, I use Latin American experience to support a more generous and hopeful understanding of democratic possibilities.

The recent wave of Latin American democratization marked a significant departure from the region's long-standing lack of civic activity. In

Argentina, for example, democratization was connected to the growth of a human rights movement that insisted on democratic politics and a moral commitment to life and physical integrity as the foundation of such politics. In the wake of the authoritarian regime's withdrawal from the political scene in 1983, human rights groups marched in the streets of Buenos Aires demanding full state accountability for the fates of missing individuals. By joining a human rights program to demand government accountability, these movements sought to restore the relation between morality and political competition in the new Argentine democracy.

Democratization in Brazil also implied a broad, long-term change from the traditional lack of popular activity in the public space and the Congress's lack of accountability to societal actors. In the first months of 1984, millions of people occupied the streets of Rio de Janeiro, São Paulo, and dozens of other Brazilian cities to demand the completion of transition that had begun eleven years earlier. The Brazilian *diretas* movement occupied the streets to call for a reconnection between public opinion and a Congress accustomed to responding to pressures from an authoritarian regime and resistant to mechanisms of popular accountability. The movement sought a new democracy in which public opinion is connected to the political system and, thus, able to craft a new relation between state and society.

Democratization has just come to completion in Mexico. One novelty has already been incorporated into the country's political system: the monitoring of elections by members of the Alianza Cívica, which was created in response to citizen concerns about political fraud and the view that only a political movement could restore the moral background needed for a decent electoral process. More than 18,000 monitors scrutinized electoral districts in order to assure the cleanliness of the 1994 presidential election. Alianza Cívica changed the political landscape of the country by restoring a moral component to the process of electoral competition. In 1996, the Federal Electoral Institute (IFE), the institution in charge of organizing the electoral process in Mexico, introduced the principle of citizen councilors as the organizers and supervisors of the electoral process. In the July 2000 elections, more than 450,000 individuals participated in the organization and monitoring of the presidential elections. Democratization in Argentina, Brazil, and Mexico shows a new phenomenon in these polities: the emergence of democratic forms of collective action.

A central dimension of democratization in Latin America was the role of forms of collective action that took place at the public level. Human rights movements in Brazil and Argentina retrieved the moral component of politics just as authoritarianism was destroying the most basic bonds of solidarity. In both cases human rights activists utilized the potential for social solidarity that survived at the private or religious levels in order to publicly reclaim the right to life and physical integrity. Neighborhood associations blossomed in Brazil and Mexico during the process of political liberalization. Urban social movements raised the banner of autonomy by challenging authoritarian regimes' attempts to interfere with the daily lives of urban dwellers by relocating them or restricting their access to social services. Through independent associations, petitions presented directly to public officials, and the occupation of public space, urban movements challenged one of the region's most deeply ingrained traditions—the idea that material improvements for ordinary citizens represent favors to be delivered by elite political mediators. Electoral monitoring, as well as the political campaigns launched by Alianza Cívica, tackled the issues of the right of individuals to have equal weight in the political process and of making the law on power-holders' control effective. Again, Alianza Cívica, human rights movements, and urban social movements retrieved the moral dimension of politics by introducing public forms of collective action in Mexico, Argentina, and Brazil.

Despite this powerful presence of popular collective action at the public level, democratization in Latin America continues to be analyzed by the most well-established democratization theories (O'Donnell and Schmitter, 1986; Stepan, 1988; Linz and Stepan, 1996) as the restoration of political competition among elites. In place of the theory of transitions to democracy derived from the democratic elitist tradition, with its fundamental elite-masses distinction, I will propose in this work a conception that links the emergence of political democracy to the formation of a public space in which citizens can participate as equals and, by arguing about collective projects for society, guide formal political decision-making.[2] The public sphere lies between the market and the state and involves individual communications and deliberations through face-to-face interaction. The concept of the public allows democratic theory to overcome the elite-masses dichotomy by suggesting a new way of approaching democratization, namely through the analysis of practices prevailing at the public level. Thus, democratization ceases to be regarded simply as the institutionalization of political competition and becomes a societal practice in need of institutionalization. I will argue that democratization is the result of transformations at the public level and that full democratization is the capacity to transform new practices from a societal innovation into a public form of decision-making.

To defend this argument, I will need to establish a contrast between the central problem of the first and second waves of democratization—the contradiction between mobilization and institutionalization—and the problem for the consolidation of democracy during the third wave of democratization. When we consider formal politics in the recently democratized Latin American countries, it shows sharp elements of political continuity with the previous authoritarian period. Social movements occupied the public space at a moment when there were serious restrictions on the free organization of political parties in Brazil and Argentina and on the forms of political competition in Mexico. To be sure, the completion of democratization in Brazil and Argentina and its recent completion in present-day Mexico has lifted most of these restrictions and brought the political opposition to positions of power. Yet the arrival of the Peronistas, the Partido do Movimento Democrático Brasileiro (PMDB), or the Partido de la Revolucion Democratica (PRD) and the Partido de la Accion Nacional (PAN) to power positions did not imply the renewal of democratic political practices, or the incorporation of new practices into the political system, but an attempt to rebuild old practices that were at best semidemocratic and at worst the cause of the previous breakdown of democracy. Traditional actors brought clientelism, permanent changes in the rules for political competition, the subordination of moral issues to majoritarian considerations, and silence on former and current human rights violations back into the democratic political system.

I will argue, then, that the central challenge facing current Latin American democracies does not come from a contradiction between mobilization and institutionalization but from the dissociation between a more open, egalitarian public space and other, more traditional means of gaining control over and using the administrative state apparatus. There is now a tension between democracy as a form of societal organization that involves demands for accountability, respect for rights and democratic practices at the local level, and the expansion of political rights, and democracy as a form of organization of political competition among groups and state administration. I will call the former the political public space and the latter political society. The essential point is that the two levels may not coincide and that, in late democratization situations, tensions between an open, egalitarian public space and a more closed and hierarchical political society may endanger democracy itself.

My argument is developed in two parts. In the first part, I contrast the elitist and public-space theories of democracy and sketch some general reasons for being skeptical about the elite view and preferring the public-space theory. I argue that democratic elitism makes ad hoc assumptions about the democratic role of elites and the anti-democratic role of forms of collective action. I show that the attempt of the theory of transition to introduce the category of hard-liners as the anti-democratic members within ruling elites does not solve the issue of semi-democratic, oligarchic members of political society. It is their presence in post-democratization scenarios that poses the problem of the limits of current democratization theory. Thus, the first part of the book has two theoretical arrival points: (1) the impossibility of furthering democratization in Latin America by drawing solely on political elites; and (2) the theoretical alternative represented by an analysis of democratization based on the emergence of what I call participatory publics. The conception of participatory publics involves four elements:

- The first element is the formation at the public level of mechanisms of face-to-face deliberation, free expression, and association. These mechanisms address specific elements in the dominant culture by making them problematic issues to be politically addressed.
- The second element is the idea that social movements and voluntary associations address contentious issues in the political culture by introducing at the public level alternative practices.
- The third element involves the transformation of informal public opinion into a forum for public deliberation and administrative decision-making.
- The fourth element is that they bind their deliberations with the attempt to search for institutional formats capable of addressing at the institutional level the issues made contentious at the public level.

The second part of the book develops the case for participatory publics by examining democratization and post-democratization periods in Latin America. I show that forms of renewal at the public level such as publicly demanding the respect for human rights or rejecting political intermediation in the claim for public goods or election monitoring did not reach the political system in Brazil, Argentina, and Mexico. The moral renewal introduced by human rights movements did not quite reach the political system in Argentina and in Brazil. The demand that a moral dimension be reestablished in politics collided with political society's quest for normalization. Issues such as settling accounts with the past and respecting human rights in the present retained the support of society, but they could not make their way into the political system. Movements for social and material welfare in Brazil and Mexico met a similar fate. The autonomy of neighborhood associations and the public presentation of demands were undermined by the reintroduction of clientelism, which became one of the principal ways of building political majorities. Again, renewal had societal support but became relatively insulated at the public level. Last but not least, political campaigns and monitoring had only temporary effects on political society. They enjoyed successes such as the removal of a president in Brazil and the reduction of electoral fraud in Mexico, but they could not transform themselves into new patterns for political activity. Between political campaigns, they remained isolated at the societal level. The result was a compartmentalization of public and political dimensions. While renewal at the public level does not vanish, neither is it incorporated into political society. It is at this level that the theoretical analysis of the first part of the book (chapters 1, 2, and 3) meets the storytelling on democratization and democratic life in recent Latin America, in chapters 4, 5, and 6, generating a new understanding of the political dilemmas of third-wave democracies.

The central conception derived from the two parts is the understanding that third-wave democracies face a new consolidation problem caused by the non-overlapping between the public and the political dimensions. To cope with this problem, present even in well-established democracies, a new issue has to be faced: how to transform informal practices at the public level into forms of deliberative democracy. Because the gap between the public space and political representation is wider still in postauthoritarian countries, I argue that the central problem facing contemporary democratization theory is the transformation of democratic practices that have emerged at the public level into institutionalized relations between social actors and political society.

Based on my analysis of conflict between the public and the political, I will propose in chapter 6 an alternative form of conceiving democratic institutionalization. Based on an empirical study of Brazil, I show the scale of the changes that have taken place in face-to-face interaction and deliberation. I show how within the realm of voluntary associations, new neighborhood associations express the emergence of a new conception of autonomy for claiming material goods and establish a new moral parameter to the practice of politics. Members of voluntary associations support democratic values more than do Brazilians at large. When asked, they proclaim their preference for more direct and participatory forms of decision-making. They utilize generalizable criteria to justify their actions even when their demands are material: when asked to rank their reasons for participating in politics, they place organizational or collective aims higher than the attempt to improve their own material condition.

The empirical data on voluntary associations allow us to deepen the alternative conception of democratization advanced in this book. Departing from the stalemate between social actors and political society, I show that political society has been unable to incorporate innovations arising from the societal level, especially the reconnection of politics and morality and the disconnection of material and deliberative inequality. From this diagnosis I propose a different political problem, namely, how to bring the forms of renovation institutionalized at the public level to the political system as a whole. The main analytical and normative assertion of this work is that Latin American democratization can be broadened if public arenas that have given rise to political renewal are transformed into forms of public deliberation.

In chapter 6 of the book I take two cases, the example of so-called participatory budgeting in Brazil and the institutionalization of citizen participation in the IFE in Mexico to show the success of the attempts to integrate political innovations introduced by social movements into the process of political deliberation. In Brazil, the participatory budgeting process allowed social movements' critique of the non-public and disempowering dimension of the claim for material goods to be transformed into a public form of decision-making on the distribution of the same goods. It allowed the incorporation of patterns of publicity and equality that emerged at the societal level into the decision-making process. The result is one arena in which collective action at the public level and democratic decision-making become compatible by the introduction of a deliberative, non-administrative device. A similar case took place in Mexico with the fully *ciudadanización* (citizens' control) of the IFE. *Ciudadanización* allowed the critique of electoral fraud and informal electoral monitoring practices to be transformed into an institutional form of electoral organization with citizen participation. The result is, again, a public arena in which public action became compatible with a democratic process of decision-making. I link participatory budgeting and the IFE to the previous discussion of democratization, showing that fora capable of assimilating public forms of discussion and deliberation, contrary to the assumptions of the democratic elitist tradition, reinforce rather than weaken democratization processes.

The conclusion of this work builds on the overlapping of the theoretical concerns of the first part and the analytical conclusions of the second. It shows that the Latin American recent experience of democratization departs from the experiences that led to the consolidation of democracy in Europe after World War II. In that case consolidation was directly linked with the ability to present an alternative to the contradiction between mobilization and institutionalization. The Latin American cases point in an opposite direction: the most sensible way to further democratize state-society relations is to transfer democratic potentials that emerge at the societal level to the political arena through participatory designs. Without this second step through which informal publics become deliberative, problem-solving publics, democratization in Latin America will not be able to bridge the gap between democratic societal practices and a hybrid political society that resists its full democratization. Thus, deliberative publics become the central arena for completing democratization due to the way they manage to connect renovations within the public culture to institutional designs capable of transforming non-public and hybrid practices into democratic forms of decision-making.

The book's conclusion on the Latin American process of democratization enlightens the current discussion of democratic theory. It shows that beyond the problem of institutionalization faced by European democracies, new democracies face a different issue: How can they produce a new stock of democratic practices capable of providing specific answers to the region's cultural tradition? Unlike the second-wave democracies, the Latin American democratizations point in the direction of the rehabilitation of those traditions within democratic theory that stress the importance of participation at the public level.

CHAPTER ONE

❧

Democratic Theory and Democratization

The recent process of democratization in Latin America is part of what has been called the third wave of democratization (Huntington, 1991), a concept which involves the idea that democracy, throughout the twentieth century, spread itself across the world in three waves, each one possessing essentially the same features. Democratization in Central and Eastern Europe in the aftermath of World War I, democratization in Germany, Italy, and Japan in the aftermath of World War II, and democratization in Latin America and Eastern Europe in the late 1980s were, thus, part of the same process. Such a theoretical framework would have as its consequence the analytical assumption that the phenomenon responsible for the breakdown of democracy during the interwar period—mass mobilization of an anti-institutional type—would be responsible for the breakdown of third-wave democracies. Likewise, it leads to the assumption that the same phenomenon responsible for the endurance of democracy in the postwar period—the narrowing down of participation—would be preconditions for the success of third-wave democracies. This chapter is an attempt to show why this rationale does not help us understand the new Latin American democracies.

The hegemonic democratic theory of the postwar period, the theory of democratic elitism, assumes a contradiction between political participation and democratic governance. The origins of this contradiction can be found in the new consensus that emerged within democratic theory at the end of World War II: democracy was consolidated as the only acceptable form of government and at the same time narrowed both as a theory of popular sovereignty and as a theory of the formation of rationality through public discourse. Democratic elitism was democratic theory's response at the end of World War II to three major challenges it faced in the first half of the twentieth century.

The first concerns the degree of sovereignty that the people might have in an era of complex administration. Max Weber inaugurated one line of challenge to the concept of sovereignty hegemonic in eighteenth- and nineteenth-century political theory by criticizing the idea of sovereignty as the direct participation of the people in governance.[1] The bureaucratization of political administration, he argued, precluded both possibilities:

> [T]he separation of the worker from the material means of production, destruction, administration and academic research and finance in general, is the common basis of the modern state, in its political, cultural and military sphere, and of the private economy. In both cases, the disposition over these means is in the hands of that power whom the bureaucratic apparatus . . . directly obeys or to whom it is available in case of need. . . . Increasing public ownership in the economic sphere today unavoidably means increasing bureaucratization. (Weber, 1978, 2:1394)

Weber announced a contradiction that would cut deeply in twentieth-century political practice: between the broadening of economic regulation and social citizenship through the expansion of public services, and the exercise of popular sovereignty.[2] Beginning with a concept of means rationality (Weber, 1978; Mommsen, 1984), Weber had already at the beginning of the century deduced the difficulties involved in participatory economic administration from the contradiction between sovereignty and bureaucracy. Although he did not set out to provide an alternative democratic theory, his analysis pointed in one direction: the rule of the elites. His argument points to the inevitable replacement of collective decision-making within public and private administration with the rule of technical elites capable of applying the knowledge necessary for efficiency. Weber's work is an expression of the stalemates generated by the first wave of democratization. It gives birth to the democratic elitist tradition by assuming a contradiction between popular sovereignty and complex administration.

The second issue that became central in the interwar political debates was the transformation of rational political debate into mass irrationalism. Democratic theory emerged in association with the idea of a rationality homo politicus.[3] Since the Enlightenment (Kant, 1781 [1959]; Rousseau, 1968), the prevalence of rationality at the political level was associated with the rejection of illegitimate forms of government, a view based on the perception that rationality is the basis of individuals' primary act of authorizing government. At the beginning of the twentieth century, however, and particularly during the interwar period, the link between democracy and rationality was undermined by two parallel processes. The first was what has been called "the emergence of particular interests." Eighteenth- and nineteenth-century democratic theory understood free public debate as an intrinsic part of the formation of the general will. Yet, it failed to perceive that the path from Rousseau to Marx admits the entrance of particular interests into public debate, and thus to the triumph of particular interests over rationality. Carl Schmitt was among the first to see the consequences this development might have for democratic politics:

> The development of modern mass democracy has made argumentative public discussion an empty formality. Many norms of the contemporary parliamentary law, above all provisions concerning the independence of representatives and openness of sessions, function as a result like a superfluous decoration. . . . The parties . . . do not face each other today discussing opinions, but as social or economic power groups calculating their mutual interests and opportunities for power (Schmitt, 1923:6)[4]

Schmitt's argument carried several anti-democratic implications pointing in the direction of the substitution of public and democratic forms of discussion by decisionism, that is to say, by a process through which the rule of law and parliament are replaced by a strong executive branch that assumes most legislative duties. The case for the particularization of politics, which is in Schmitt's version explicitly anti-democratic, is also an argument for the rule of elites. For Schmitt, the need to have deliberative bodies under unified control leads to the need to guarantee the presence of elites with final decision-making capacity at the center of the state.

The third problem to emerge from the interwar political debates was the issue of mass society. Authors such as Ortega y Gasset, Karl Mannheim, Erich Fromm, and Max Horkheimer argued against the possibility of rational politics from a direction opposite from those who decried its particularization. For them, de-differentiation within the polity caused by the end of the insulation of elites (Gasset, 1932; Kornhauser, 1959) as well as by the rise of forms of cultural domination at the private level (Horkheimer, 1947; Arendt, 1951) transformed the nature of politics at the beginning of the twentieth century. This diagnosis led to a critique of democracy, according to which the preservation of values critical to democratic politics requires the insulation of those social groups which better embody such values (Kornhauser, 1959:22), meaning the insulation of the elites from the masses.[5] The mass-society argument assumes two forms. The first, like Schmitt's case against particularization, carries anti-democratic implications insofar as it assumes a fundamental contradiction between political equality and freedom. The second does not break with democratic politics. According to this version, which we can identify with the first generation of the Frankfurt School as well as Hannah Arendt and C. Wright Mills, the central issue raised by mass society is not the dangers involved in broadening participation but the transformation in how elites control the population. Forms of social control are extended from the public to the private sphere, allowing the penetration of the commodity form into the cultural realm (Horkheimer and Adorno, 1946; Adorno 1951). The dissociation of politics and rationality is understood as a consequence of the extension of domination to the private domain. The mass-society argument breaks the association between democracy and political participation because it sees broader political participation leading not to the enlargement of actors and issues in the political sphere but to the irrational pressure of the masses on the political system. Again, the consequence of this argument is rule by elites, because it is the only guarantee that cultural values not shared by the masses will be preserved.

Democratic theory by the end of the first half of the twentieth century faced three main lines of criticism, each pointing clearly toward elite rule. The first challenged the validity of the concept of popular sovereignty in light of the extension of public and private forms of complex administration. According to this argument, complex administration required the substitution of popular sovereignty by the rule of those embodying technical knowledge. The second criticism pointed out the problems caused by the penetration of particular interests into arenas designed for rational argument and the generalization of interests. Skepticism that public rules for argumentation could lead to rational conclusions led naturally to the idea of reserving decision-making for the most able, namely, for political elites. The third criticism involved the effects of mass society on political institutions, in particular the risk that mass mobilization would bypass the institutions in charge of the formation of the general will. Again, the preservation of the values of democracy was entrusted to the insulation of elites from the political pressure of the masses.

These problems received both democratic and anti-democratic political answers throughout the interwar period. But they also played a central role in the reconstruction of democratic theory after World War II. The main current of political thought that attempted to address these problems became known as democratic elitism (Bachrach, 1967). Democratic elitism was based on two main theses: first, that in order to be preserved, democracy must narrow the scope of political participation; and second, that the only way to make democratic decision-making rational is to limit it to elites and restrict the role of the masses to that of choosing between elites. These two central canons of democratic elitism have been challenged by many democratic theorists (for example, Pateman, 1970; Bachrach, 1967; Held, 1987) as both an inadequate empirical description of contemporary democracy and an untenable defense of its normative desirability. This chapter includes a critique of the democratic elitist tradition from a different vantage point: instead of searching for its capacity to explain well-established democratic systems in Europe and North America, it shows that democratic elitism cannot explain democracy in late-developing countries.

In this chapter, I develop an argument about the practical and analytical impossibility of either building or analyzing democracy in Latin America with the tools of the democratic elitist tradition. I proceed in two steps. First, I analyze the framework proposed by democratic elitism to explain the success of the democratic experiences linked to the so-called second wave of democratization. I show how Schumpeter and Downs integrated three elements—the rule of the elites, the critique of public means of generating rationality, and the materialization of politics—into one coherent framework for the operation of democracy. I argue that the same elements that might account for the ability of the democratic elitist framework to explain the consolidation of democracy in Western Europe during the second democratic wave are unable to explain the failure of democratization in Latin America during the same period. I will attribute this failure to the impossibility of contesting power or disputing material resources without a prior normative consensus at the public level on the rules of democratic contestation.

Second, I evaluate the attempt by the most well-known theory on democratization—the theory of the transition to democracy—to adapt the democratic elitist framework to the Latin American context. I will show how this theory tried to change democratic elitism's assumption about the democratic nature of elites and how it tried to introduce the possibility of a democratic role for forms of collective action. My main argument in this chapter, however, is that without replacing the elite-masses dichotomy with the concept of a democratic public space, it remains impossible to understand the recent processes of democratization in Latin America. I show that transition theory's break with the democratic elitist tradition has been incomplete because it has retained the differentiation between mass and elites and assigned the latter a superior role in the process of democratization. These two elements account for its inability to explain Latin American democratization and for its recent rift on the definition of consolidated democracy. I argue that this rift turns on different conceptions of the nature of the public sphere and cannot be resolved within the transition theory framework. I propose an alternative framework based on the formation of a democratic public space, which will then be utilized in the later chapters to analyze the current dilemmas of recent Latin American processes of democratization.

From Schumpeter to Downs, or the Emergence of Democratic Elitism

The reconstruction of democracy and democratic theory in the postwar period involved the attempt to transfer the center of both democratic practice and democratic theory from Europe to North America. Joseph Schumpeter occupies a special place in this process from both the biographical and the theoretical point of view because he lived through the political turmoil of the European interwar period and responded directly to it in his work. His move to the United States, whose political practice inspired his proposal for restructuring the democratic system, involved an overlap of biographical and theoretical concerns. The elements at the heart of Schumpeter's proposal for the reorganization of democracy are exactly the same as those that led to its breakdown in Europe during the first wave of democratization, namely, the issue of popular sovereignty, the role of the elites, and the problems caused by mass-politics (Schumpeter, 1942). By integrating these three elements into a procedural framework for the operation of democracy, Schumpeter renewed democratic politics. However, as I will argue, he did so at a cost.

In a fashion similar to Weber and Schmitt as well as the mass society theorists, Schumpeter took the transformations in democratic practice such as it has been conceived in the eighteenth and nineteenth centuries as his point of departure. The central idea of the section of his magnum opus *Capitalism, Socialism, and Democracy* devoted to the discussion of democracy is therefore the validity of the concept of popular sovereignty. Schumpeter challenges two of popular sovereignty's founding pillars by raising against them the same issues raised by mass-society theory and by Weber's theory of increasing administrative complexity (Weber, 1978, voll. 2). Mass-society theory is addressed in order to show that the opinions of the majority are not necessarily democratic. Citing examples such as sixteenth-century witch-hunts and the persecution of the Jews in this century, Schumpeter shows that the preferences of the majority, inherent in the concept of popular sovereignty, might legitimize anti-democratic attitudes sanctioned not by rational political actors but by the irrational masses (Schumpeter, 1942:242). Thus, in order to uphold the concept of popular sovereignty it is necessary to indicate clearly "how" and "by whom" decisions are to be made (Schumpeter, 1942:248).

Schumpeter challenges a second element of the concept of popular sovereignty by picking up an issue already raised by Weber: how it is possible for the people to govern? His answer to this question is that if we understand sovereignty in a broad sense as the formation and determination of the general will, it is impossible for the people to govern. For Schumpeter, to make the concept of democracy useful it is necessary to separate it from the pursuit of a substantive notion of the common good, transforming it into a process for the choice of governing bodies: "Democracy is a political method, that is to say, a certain type of institutional arrangement for arriving at political—legislative and administrative—decisions and hence incapable of being an end in itself." (Schumpeter, 1942:242)

His solution to the problem of sovereignty seems clear: in reducing the scope and meaning of the concept of sovereignty, it is transformed from a process of forming the general will into a process for authorizing the exercise of power by members of representative political bodies. This move allows Schumpeter to bring to the interior of democratic theory two concerns up to that point alien to democratic theory and promoted only by its detractors: a theory of elites and of mass society.

By accepting a narrow concept of sovereignty, Schumpeter makes democratic theory compatible with a theory of the role of the elites in the political process. Elite theory had initially rejected democratic politics because of its belief that elites would rule regardless of the form of government. The central tenets of Pareto's historical and ontological justification of elites are not contradicted by Schumpeter but harmonized with democratic theory. He accordingly reconceives democracy as a method for ensuring the turnover of elites in positions of political power. Thus, the gap between democratic theory's self-understanding and the use of categories that deny the very possibility of democracy is closed by the special role assigned to elites within the democratic system. Reducing the scope of sovereignty allows Schumpeter to limit the role of the people to producing governments, that is to say, to choosing the particular group among the elites that seems most qualified to govern. Through this operation the people remains the ultimate arbiter of democratic politics in only one capacity, as the arbiter of competing elites.

This reduction of the scope of the concept of sovereignty simultaneously implies a change in how the relationship between democracy and rationality is conceived. For Schumpeter, as political elites join a competitive system of representation, the access of the most qualified to positions of political leadership is guaranteed (Schumpeter, 1942:280). This is advanced as a new solution to the problem of democracy's inability to generate rationality. For Schumpeter, the idea "of the human personality that is a homogeneous unity" cannot resist the teachings of Le Bon and Freud, who called attention to the extra-rational or irrational components of human behavior. These components are present at both the economic and the political level. Even in their role as consumers, modern individuals are unable to form their will without regard for the mechanisms of persuasion. However, within the political field the tendency for the rational individual to become a member of a crowd displays itself throughly:

> [E]ven if there were no political groups trying to influence him, the typical citizen would in political matters tend to yield to extra-rational or irrational prejudice and impulse. The weakness of the rational process he applies to politics and the absence of effective logical control over the results he arrives at would in themselves suffice to account for that. . . . Human nature in politics being what it is [allows groups] to create the will of the people. And often this artefact is all that in reality corresponds to the *volonté générale* of the classical doctrine. (Schumpeter 1942:262–63)

What is surprising in Schumpeter's construction is less his repetition of the most well-known mass-society arguments than his capacity to make them compatible with democracy. As long as the exercise of sovereignty is narrowed to a process of elite selection, it is not susceptible to the risk of irrationality inherent in mass society. In this way, his theory does not represent a denial of irrational impulses but an attempt to insulate politics from them. The central point for democratic politics is that such impulses should not express themselves directly in politics. Instead, they should remain latent for a long period until a democratic leader manages to process and insert them into the competitive bid for popular support (Schumpeter, 1942:270). What makes the democratic system unstable is not the existence of irrational impulses but the direct use politics might make of them. Once their expression through elites is guaranteed, there is not much problem in making democracy and mass society compatible.

A consideration of the contribution of democratic elitism to the reconstruction of democracy in the postwar period reveals a contradiction between a positive element that contributes to democratic engineering and two gaps that remain unsolved by democratic theory. Positive elements include the broad consensus built around the desirability of democratic political systems and a consensus facilitated by the possibility of integrating the charges made against democracy in the interwar period into the framework of democratic theory. Yet, Schumpeter's attempt to reconcile democracy with the power of elites within mass society led him to adopt problematic positions on two issues.

The first concerns the relationship between normativity and the common good. Schumpeter's critique of the idea of the common good from the perspective of the plurality of individuals advances a position that has become a general consensus in recent ethical debate.[6] His solution to this problem, however, ends up throwing out the baby with the bath water by assuming an irresolvable opposition between realism and normativity.

This perspective is unable to grasp the ethical formal consensus upon which democracy is founded.[7] Such an inability, as I will show, is particularly problematic when constructing democracy in the context of a developing country.

The second problematic assumption made by Schumpeterian democratic engineering has to do with how it conceives the relationship between individual and general rationality. The author of *Capitalism, Socialism, and Democracy* takes for granted all the assumptions of the irrationality of individual behavior in contemporary societies. For him, the twentieth-century individual is an irrational consumer as well as an irrational citizen because he or she allows the influence of manipulators to determine his or her preferences. By adhering to one of mass-society theory's most extreme formulations, Schumpeter generates a logical inconsistency in the structure of his argument based on a contradictory understanding of mass irrationality. On the one hand, he seems to argue in favor of the democratic system's capacity to guarantee the production of rational results by assigning elites the role of formulating political proposals, a conception that assumes the capacity of the masses to choose the best political offer in a competitive political market. On the other hand, he adheres to the mass-society postulate that the masses are likely to adopt purely irrational stands on political matters. Schumpeter does not resolve the contradiction between his theory of individual irrationality and his assumption that the results produced by the democratic system, where individual choice plays a central role, will be rational. In the postwar period, democratic elitist theory attempted to solve this contradiction within the framework of a theory of elites.

ANTHONY DOWNS, OR
THE ECONOMIZATION OF POLITICAL RATIONALITY

Capitalism, Socialism, and Democracy can be considered a transitional work because of both the problems it deals with and the influence of European interwar politics in generating these problems. The central place of the problem of irrationalism in Schumpeter's theoretical framework and the formulation of the central problems within democratic theory as related to the contest between capitalism and socialism, as the title makes clear, are both signs of the central role played by interwar European issues in Schumpeter's work. Anthony Downs's *Economic Theory of Democracy*, in contrast, completes the transfer of political and theoretical debate about democracy from the European to the North American context. After the publication of this book, issues such as mass society or the problem of irrationality no longer occupy a central place within democratic theory. Downs added two new elements to the democratic elitist approach. The first is the issue of apathy, which changes the way the whole problem of masses and elites is discussed. Downs no longer regards the masses as irrational and willing to exert collective pressure on political institutions; in his framework, the masses become rational citizens who have reason to be apathetic. Elites are no longer conceived as authoritarian, nor are they concerned to exclude the masses from politics; they are active minorities willing to elaborate proposals to be picked up and decided by the masses. The core of the Downsian reformulation of the democratic elitist tradition is his reinterpretation of the relation between elites and masses in terms of a theory in which both sides of the equation behave rationally: for Downs it is as rational for the elites to participate as it is for the masses not to participate. Democratic elitism thus becomes a theory of the different roles of participating elites and non-participating masses in the production of a rational democratic system.

Downs approached the problem of constructing democracy from a point of departure very similar to Schumpeter's: the unreasonableness of approaching rationality from a generalizing perspective. For Downs, the only element of rationality that can be evaluated is the different means individuals use to maximize the utility generated by their actions. His strategy is to narrow the Weberian concept of rational action to transform the utilitarian evaluation of the means to be employed to reach ends into rationality per se.[8] The rational individual is defined by Downs as having five attributes:

- the ability to decide when confronted with alternatives
- the ability to rank his alternatives and his preferences
- the ability to make his preference ranking transitive
- the ability, when confronted with different alternatives, to choose the one at the top of his preference ranking
- the ability, when faced with the same alternatives, to make the same choices (Downs, 1956:6)

The concept of the rational individual introduced by Downs de-psychologizes the political attitudes of the common individual within a framework very similar to the one proposed by Schumpeter. The common individual is not charged with elaborating political proposals, but only with making a hierarchy of preferences on given proposals. In this sense, Downs sticks to the different roles Schumpeter assigns to the masses and the political elites. Downs's disagreement with Schumpeter is limited to a series of criticisms directed against the idea of mass society. These criticisms arise from Downs's attempt to salvage the concept of individual rationality for democratic theory. He shows that Schumpeter failed to distinguish between attitudinal mistakes and irrational behavior. For Downs, individuals are always at least hypothetically capable of reflecting on their mistakes. Thus, irrationality cannot be postulated in individual terms but only in global or general terms. Still, in order to pursue the irrationality argument, it would be necessary to have in mind the rational benefits of those who profit from the irrationalities of the political system:

> If a significant section of any body politics becomes irrational in its behavior a different problem is posed for the man who does not. What is the best course for a rational man in an irrational world? The answer depends upon whether the irrationality he faces involves predictable patterns of behavior. If so, rational action is still possible for him. And because almost no society can survive for long if no one in it is efficiently pursuing his goals, there is usually some kind of predictability in the political system. Citizens who behave irrationally do so partly because someone who stands to gain thereby urges them so. (Downs, 1956:10)

Downs's approach to the problem of irrationality in politics offers internal coherence to the elite model of democracy by introducing individual rationality into its interior. Thus, irrationality is reduced to an episodic result provoked by a provisional incompatibility between what some individuals might think is rational for them and an irrational general result. Downs's theory of democracy does not limit itself to reintroducing individual rationality in the process of political decision-making; it goes further by seeking to connect the principle of utility maximization with the general functioning of the political system. Two elements play a central role in this process: first, an egoistic definition of human nature leads the author to assume that an individual will opt for his or her own happiness without regard for the happiness of others; and second, both individual self-interest and the functioning of the political system are narrowed to the strictly economic. In his role as citizen, the rational individual simply chooses among different proposals those he deems likely to increase his share of material public goods. Hence, Downs's model for the functioning of the political system incorporates criteria of individual rationality:

> By comparing the stream of utility income from government activity he has received under the present government ... with those streams he believes he would have received if the various opposition parties had been in office, the voter finds his current party differentials. (Downs, 1956:49)

Downs transforms the individual's attempt to maximize material benefits into an ontological condition shared by all individuals, which allows him to give logical consistency to the concept of rationality employed by democratic elitism. The idea of competition among elites is supplemented by a rational element that applies to both the elites and the rational citizen. In regard to the elites, Downs can stick to the Schumpeterian analysis by assuming a process of selection, which leads the best to occupy the highest places. The electoral system constitutes such a process which, according to Downs, can be reduced to the offer and selection of negotiable public goods. Democratic elitism is also, according to Downs, rational in a second sense: the process of rationally selecting elites complements the process through which the rational voter opts for those public goods he places at the top of his preference ranking. Thus, individual rationality becomes fully compatible with global rationality.

Democratic elitism can be defined as a restrictive conception of democracy based on three points. The first is the reduction of politics to the operation of a political body formed by the members of political elites. Thus, for the elitist conception of democracy narrowing down the places where politics takes place as well as the numbers of participants in the deliberative process is the main act required to make democracy a stable form of political rule.

The second is the transformation of elite theory into a central component of democratic theory. Democratic elitism defines democracy as a system in which the government is in the hands of active minorities (Sartori, 1987, 1:147). Making elite competition the central element of democracy entailed overcoming the anti-democratic trends within elite theory but also incurred a cost: neglecting the formation of public opinion. The public domain is dissociated from democracy in two senses: elite rule makes public opinion formation unnecessary, and within the system of government one no longer needs public debate to achieve political rationality. The substitution of the periodic selection of elites for public debate leads to a deep transformation in the self-understanding of democratic politics: it is stripped of its horizontal elements, which are replaced by the political authorization of elites through elections.

Third, democratic elitism also reconciles mass society with democracy. The acknowledgment that mass behavior does not represent an obstacle for the functioning of democracy, as interwar political theorists had argued, makes democracy compatible with the presence of irrational elements in mass behavior. The democratic elitist solution to the problem of mass society is to reduce the scope of participation from mobilization to voting. However, this reduction led democratic elitism to narrow all forms of collective action to participation, and to narrow collective action itself.[9]

By reducing the individual to a maximizer of material benefits and politics to a system of distributing public goods, democratic elitism also implies the materialization of democratic politics. Materializing politics meant that the idea of consensus built in public, an idea that had been preeminent in democratic theory since the eighteenth century (Mansbridge, 1990), was replaced by conflict over the distribution of material benefits. The democratic elitist conception of democracy leaves behind the idea of a search for consensus on the public good and starts to deal with the self-interested individual trying to appropriate the largest possible share of negotiable public goods. Again, by moving in this direction democratic elitism bypasses the idea of a public consensus prior to the distribution of material goods.

The consolidation of democratic elitism as the hegemonic democratic theory in the postwar period implied strengthening the material and instrumental dimensions of politics at the expense of its public dimension. It is beyond the aims of this work to discuss how democracy could consolidate itself in Europe based on such assumptions, although there is strong evidence that a new consensus on the rules of the democratic game (Bobbio, 1987) and on the desirability of democratic institutions arose simultaneously with democratic elitism. However, the lack of any consensus on the desirability of democracy associated with the lack of a public dimension did not lead to the consolidation of democracy in Latin America, but instead to its breakdown.

The Contradiction between the Foundations of Democratic Elitism and Late Processes of Democratization

Democratic elitism became entrenched as the hegemonic democratic theory in the period usually called "the second wave of democratization." Yet, at the very time of this entrenchment the theory was confronted with a paradox it was unable to solve: the consolidation of democracy in Europe was simultaneous with its permanent crisis in much of the rest of the world. To be sure, the second wave of democratization (1943–62) was highly successful in regard to the implantation and consolidation of democracy within Europe, in a form very similar to the prescriptions of Schumpeter and Downs. In the most important cases of newly consolidated democracies in this period, particularly Germany, Italy, and Japan—countries that had broken with democratic practices as a consequence of the conflicts of the interwar period—a restricted conception of sovereignty followed the reintroduction of democracy after 1945. On the other hand, if we look elsewhere we immediately perceive a different phenomenon: the attempt to extend democracy to Latin America, Asia, and Africa in the same period was a complete failure. By the mid-1970s, one-third of the world's thirty-two previously active democracies had reverted to some form of authoritarianism, forming what has been called the "second reverse wave of democratization."[10] In 1973, only two Latin American countries had democratically elected presidents (Huntington, 1991).

An analysis of the sources of the breakdown of democracy in Latin America reveals two facts, each equally problematic for the theory of democratic elitism: either the most important democratic elitist assumptions, such as its analysis of mass society and the rationality of elites, were clearly contradicted, or they were at least unable to explain the so-called second reverse wave of democratization. What seems to be at the root of the different failures of democracy in Latin America between 1964 and 1973 are the contradictions intrinsic to the model of inter-elite competition, a model that led to a broadened exercise of sovereignty by the elites themselves.

The predominant mode of democratic practice in postwar Latin America was democratic populism.[11] This form of democratic practice followed at least two of democratic elitism's primary prescriptions: inter-elite competition and restricted political participation of the masses. Competition among elites was articulated with a form of mobilization that did not seem to contradict democratic elitist assumptions because the question of self-government or broad sovereignty was never really posed in the political arena. Popular mobilizations in Latin America were mobilizations in favor of different development projects proposed by local elites (O'Donnell, 1973). Thus, two characteristics of democratic elitist theory seem from the very beginning not to operate in Latin America.

First, the elites' presumed adherence to democratic values, an ad hoc assumption derived from the conservative version of mass society theory (Kornhauser, 1959), was unable to explain the instability caused by inter-elite disputes in Latin American democracies. Elite attempts to reverse the results of democratic elections were responsible for the breakdown of democracy in Argentina in 1966, Brazil in 1964, and Chile in 1973, among other cases. Second, the role of mass mobilization in this period must also be readdressed. Mass mobilizations sought in most cases to secure the rules of the game for inter-elite competition. Thus, there seem to be two gaps in democratic elitism's approach to democracy: first, its failure to reflect on the difference between democratic and non-democratic elites, a gap filled in a very structural and problematic form in the work of Almond and Verba at the end of this period; and second, its inability to understand mass mobilization. There are two different types of mass mobilization. The first, studied in depth within the democratic elitist tradition, is an anti-institutional mobilization that can eventually disrupt the political process. A second type, however, consists in forms of collective action within voluntary associations, social movements, and other fora of participation. Much of the political activity in Latin America fit into the second category and anticipated an approach developed later by social movements theorists to the possibility of democratic collective action (Tilly, 1986; 1990; Cohen, 1985). By assuming a priori a direct relationship among mass mobilization and democratic breakdown, democratic elitism missed the possibility of collective action in favor of the maintenance of democracy.

Democratic elitism's evident inability to explain Latin American authoritarianism using the tools it developed to analyze democracy in North America and Europe led some of its representatives to explain this failure through the introduction of a third element, an economic variable able to explain what its theoretical assumptions could not. In the midst of the so-called second reverse wave of democratization, an economic approach to democracy emerged emphasizing the correlation between economic development, distribution of wealth, and democracy. Lipset (1959) introduced an empirical correlation between variables such as education, wealth distribution, urbanization, and the existence of democracy, showing that the countries with a highly educated, predominantly urban population and a favorable distribution of wealth were most likely to be democratic, whereas countries with the reverse profile were likelier to slip back into authoritarianism. Lipset's empirical correlation led to a theory according to which the breakdown of democracy could be attributed to the inability of recently constituted political systems to cope with the conflicts generated by the uneven distribution of wealth (Lipset, 1959). It should be pointed out, however, that this correlation is merely empirical and has been unable to generate either a theory of democratization or an explanation for different cases of democratic breakdown.[12]

In the postwar period, particularly through the "second reverse wave of democratization," democratic elitism failed to elaborate a theory of late democratization or re-democratization. There were four major reasons for its inability to do so.

First, it was unable to add elements to the elitist conception of democracy in order to point out the specific ambiguities, divisions, and disputes among particular groups. It therefore lacked a theory of the factors that could make inter-elite competition problematic, which could have explained democratic breakdown in some Latin American cases.

Second, democratic elitism was unable to relativize some elements of its mass-society theory in spite of strong empirical grounds for doubting their effectiveness (Weffort, 1979; Ianni, 1970). Mass mobilizations characteristic of the populist period in Latin America anticipated an important tenet of new social movement theory, namely, the inappropriateness of declaring mass participation anti-democratic, ad hoc, and ex ante.

Third, it is worthwhile pointing out the complete absence of the institutional question in democratic elitist approaches to democracy. The only exception would be Huntington's attempt to associate mass society with de-institutionalization:

> In a highly developed political system, political organizations have an integrity which they lack in less developed systems. . . . In every society affected by social change, new groups arise to participate in politics. Where the political system lacks autonomy . . . the political organizations and procedures are unable to stand up against the impact of a new social force. (Huntington, 1969:20–21)

Thus, for Huntington the problem involved in the late construction of democracy is the insufficient institutionalization of conflicts, an approach that has the merit of connecting democracy and institutions. Yet, he deals with the institutional arena through the uncritical acceptance of the postulates of mass-society theory, precluding his theory from bridging institutionalization and democratic participation.

The fourth element that did not allow democratic elitist theories to provide a model for the late construction of democracy was the uncritical transfer of the idea of conflict over negotiable material goods from the North American to the Latin American context. Authors such as Downs stressed the conflictive dimension of democracy at the expense of the normative consensus on which democracy is based. Transferring this framework to later democracies was disastrous: the conflict to appropriate material goods in the absence of a normative consensus on democracy allows the economic "losers" to propose a rupture with the democratic system (O'Donnell, 1973). This was the main reason why democratic elitism could not transform an empirical regularity—the correlation between democracy and economic welfare—into a theoretical conception of how to construct democracy.

These four theoretical failures point in the direction of the inadequacy of the conception of democracy proposed by democratic elitism. The theory proposed by Schumpeter and Downs sets aside the normative foundations of democracy, assuming that by getting rid of normative imperatives one can transform democracy into a realistic political arrangement. It is important to understand what realism means for the democratic elitist tradition; for Schumpeter, Downs, and Sartori, realism entails renouncing any attempt to add a programmatic or substantive element to the concept of popular sovereignty. The mistake involved in this operation lies in its assumption that in order to dissociate democracy and normative imperatives, realism has to banish all forms of normative justification and any potential broadening of political sovereignty. In the next section of this chapter I will show how the theories of transition to democracy make central changes with respect to all four points in order to make democratic elitism compatible with the construction of democracy outside Europe and North America. However, I argue that transition theory's rupture with the democratic elitist tradition was partial because it retained the assumption of an elite-masses distinction. I also show how the partiality of this rupture prevented transition theory from fully understanding democratization due to its inability to approach political change through an analysis of the characteristics of the public sphere.

THE THEORY OF THE TRANSITION TO DEMOCRACY

Theories of transition to democracy represent a double rupture with the above-described scenario, which has led to the second reverse wave of democratization. On the one hand, from a purely analytical perspective transition theory acknowledged the responsibility of elites for the existence of authoritarian regimes in Latin America. It began from the crystal-clear assumption that Latin American elites' anti-democratic or semi-democratic convictions combined with economic conflicts to undermine the region's democratic systems. Thus, the evaluation of the democratic or anti-democratic nature of elites represents one of the fundamental elements of transition theory. On the other hand, from a theoretical point of view, transition theory also acknowledged that democratization does not consist in a set of variables to be empirically identified, but in a long process in the course of which there is the possibility that circumstances will force, persuade, or even fool non-democrats into assuming a democratic attitude in relation to democratic political institutions (Rustow, 1970:344–45). Thus, Rustow proposes neither accepting nor ignoring elites' anti-democratic convictions but instead thinking about a process through which it will be possible to transform non-democratic elites into democratic elites. Such a process encompasses an institutional dimension.

Building on Linz's assumption of a relationship between the role of democratic and non-democratic actors in the decision-making process and the possibility of consolidating democracy, transition theory understands the breakdown of democracy throughout the "second reverse wave of democratization" as an inability to build satisfactory institutions.[13] In this sense, the institutional dimension constitutes an inherent concern of transition theory from the very start. Transition theorists believe that "institutions have an impact upon outcomes of conflicts" and that "institutions that would provide the relevant political forces with reasonable security can be found under some circumstances" (Przeworski, 1988:66). This discussion allows a definition of transitions: they represent a period of time in which an institutional arrangement aiming at the reestablishment of political competitiveness between democratic and authoritarian political actors is reached. In the course of this process, institutional arrangements as well as mutual trust are built in such a way that at the end of a period of transition, authoritarian political actors withdraw from the political scene (O'Donnell and Schmitter, 1986). This definition, which constitutes the core of transition theory's conception of democratization, is fully compatible with the democratic elitist understanding of democracy: both share the view that democracy is dependent on the institutional rules for competition between elites. To adapt this feature of democracy to late-developing contexts, however, transition theory introduced four changes to the democratic elitist conception of democracy.

First, it renewed democratic theory by problematizing the convictions of political elites. For transition theory, elites do not a priori possess democratic values. Transition theory assumes the possibility of different types of actors within the political system. There are those whom it calls hardliners: those who "believe that the perpetuation of authoritarian rule is possible and desirable, if not by rejecting outright all democratic forms, then by enacting some facade behind which they can maintain inviolate the hierarchical and authoritarian nature of their power" (O'Donnell and Schmitter, 1986:16). Next, there are the *blandos*: those who believe that authoritarian regimes should make use of some form of electoral legitimation in the near future (O'Donnell and Schmitter, 1986:16). Finally, there are those defined as the democratic opposition: those who advocate a full return to electoral competition but accept the need to negotiate the rules of competition with authoritarian power-holders. Thus, from the point of view of political elites, the process of transition is both a restricted form of electoral competition between the authoritarian power-holders and the electoral opposition and, at the same time, a negotiation of the rules under which this competition will take place.

Transition theory represents an important advance in the analysis of democratization because it manages to integrate the various political actors and their beliefs into the democratization equation. However, an important ambiguity remains in the transition approach: it fails to problematize the political beliefs of the democratic opposition. The transition theories make an important mistake in this respect: they assume that authoritarianism constituted a brief entrance of authoritarian power-holders onto the political scene, thereby missing the structure of political society or what Tilly calls the dominant "repertoire of political action" (Tilly, 1986). Thus, transition theory's break with democratic elitism is partial because it never places societal practices on the same level as elite practices. In the Latin American case, re-democratization shows not only the ambiguity of authoritarian political actors in relation to democracy but also the ambiguity of the actors who participated in the democratic opposition.

The second element of democratic elitist theories reevaluated by transition theory is the nature and form of mass participation. In their seminal work, O'Donnell and Schmitter (1986) argue that the dynamics of transitions involve the entrance on the political scene of social actors capable of changing the precarious equilibrium between political elites as well as the configuration of the public sphere.

> [O]nce the government signals it is lowering the costs for engaging in collective action and is permitting some contestation on issues previously declared off limits . . . former political identities and others appear ex-novo to expand beyond anyone's expectations (O'Donnell and Schmitter, 1986:48–49)

The mobilization of social actors promotes the diversification of the political opposition. Groups and identities for whom the political system was considered off-limits enter the political arena, leading to the further democratization of both society and politics. Again, transition theory's approach to mass mobilization is ambiguous, to say the least. On the one hand, it breaks with the democratic elitist assumption that mass mobilization is anti-democratic by noting that collective action might strengthen democratic values. On the other hand, it still conceives mass mobilization within the broader framework of an elite-masses relationship: mass mobilizations do not play a democratizing role per se, but rather an adjuvant role in the internal process of negotiation among elites. Thus, transition theory's rupture with democratic elitism is partially due to its inability to understand fully the role of social movements in Latin American democratization.[14]

The first two critiques taken together show the limits of an approach based on the differentiation between masses and elites. Transition theory acknowledges the existence of non-democratic elite practices as well as democratic mass practices. However, the dichotomy between masses and elites precludes a proper approach to democratization by assigning an ontological superiority to the practices of the elites. Transition theory lacks analytical instruments to deal with the problem of the renovation of societal practices. This leads it to assume that the forms of occupation of the public space throughout Latin American democratization, such as those introduced by human rights movements in Argentina or urban movements in Brazil, were only alternative forms of pressure for the restoration of political competition. (I analyze both movements in chapter 4.) Thus, it cannot properly analyze the formation of democratic public spaces that took place during democratization. Instead, it sees these phenomena as provisional and assigns political society the capacity to incorporate the changes at the public level (O'Donnell and Schmitter, 1986:8–10).

The third change introduced by transition theory is a reevaluation of the role of political institutions. Although, with the exception of the above-mentioned generic explanation provided by Przeworski, transition theory did not initially offer a full reevaluation of the role played by political institutions, it moved rapidly in that direction. In their discussion of democracy in Latin America, Diamond et al. (1989) acknowledged the primary importance of the region's early choice of an institutional model derived from Western constitutionalism: the rule of law, representative institutions, political freedoms, and so on (Diamond, Linz, and Lipset, 1989:19). Nonetheless, the framework applied by the authors to approach the institutional question immediately raises the question of the relationship between institutions and political behavior. If institutions are understood as a regular pattern of interaction known and accepted by the main political players (O'Donnell, 1995:10), their relation to political behavior arises as an analytical and theoretical problem. We can identify two forms of institutionality in Latin America, one informed by the institutions that organize political competition and the other informed by the practices and ways of dealing with social and political issues. In this regard, Diamond and Linz are absolutely right to call attention to the fact that no alternative political institutionality has ever been proposed in Latin America. Elections and the rule of law have been the horizon of elite practices. At the same time, it must be noted that this does not exhaust the concept of institutions. Between the two conceptions of institutionality lies a problem which has characterized the Latin American scene: the open possibility that members of the elites might interact according to standards different from the legal ones (Rosenn, 1971; Morse, 1989). The problem is not merely heuristic: how we understand institutions influences the direction of institution building, an effort that has to take into account the concrete problems derived from the existing cultural tradition and the strategies available to deal with them.[15] Here, although transition theory has raised a problem ignored by the democratic elitist tradition but central to democratization—the specific institutional designs capable of contributing to the broadening of democracy—the problem remains insufficiently elaborated.

There is far less agreement on the fourth and final element reevaluated by transition theories: culture. The introduction of this element by transition theorists has been highly controversial. On the one hand, O'Donnell and Schmitter (1986) completely ignore it in their seminal work on transitions. This omission was probably motivated, as Moisés (1995) has argued, by their willingness to avoid structural elements in the analysis of democratization and, thus, stress the negotiation component. This led them to deny the role of political culture as a structural element capable of explaining democracy's endurance (Tiano, 1986) as well as to draw a distinction between long- and short-term elements within a particular political culture. Diamond, Linz, and Liput (1989) acknowledge the role of structural elements of a cultural nature in the process of construction of democracy, arguing that "those countries that have been the most strongly and stably democratic systems also appear to have the most democratic values and beliefs" (Diamond, Linz, and Liput, 1989:17). By calling attention to culture, these authors seem to be in tune with a literature that is gaining importance for the analysis of political phenomena (Huntington, 1991; Putnam et al. 1993; Fukuyama, 1995; Verba et al., 1995). Diamond and Linz provide us with the most advanced formulation on political culture in the transitions literature. However, their approach is an indication of the limits of this literature because it fails to bind changes in the dominant pattern of collective action with short-term transformations within a particular political culture. (I will come back to this point in chapters 2 and 3).

Taken together, the third and fourth critiques of transition theory's innovations show an additional analytical shortcoming arising from its insufficient break with democratic elitism: its inability to bind cultural traditions to democratic design. Institutional designs are reduced to institutional emulation and completely insulated from the capacity to be self-conscious in relation to a given cultural tradition. Thus, the theory of transition lacks the tools to understand how a cultural transformation of an instrumental tradition in relation to democracy needs to be supplemented by institutions capable of strengthening innovation. It also misses the fact that the renewal of a given political culture takes place at the public level. This leads it to take for granted what is not guaranteed, namely that cultural innovation at the public level is incorporated by political society.

The theory of transition to democracy thus constitutes an attempt to make minor changes in the democratic elitist framework in order to adapt it to Latin American reality. Its core idea is to keep the elite-masses dichotomy as its central focus of analysis, conceding, however, the existence of non-democratic elites and democratic forms of collective action. Yet, this move was not sufficient to construct a viable analysis of the processes of democratization in Latin America. The distinction between democrats and non-democrats was conceived exclusively in terms of the position of each member of political society in relation to electoral competition, instead of taking into account their opinions and practices regarding democracy as a collective form of public decision-making. Transition theory introduces the idea of non-democratic elites and democratic actors only at the level of political competition, thus, ignoring the positions of such actors on issues such as human rights or forms of distribution of material goods. There is a second arena in which the dispute between a democratic and non-democratic culture arises: the level of practices. A democratic political culture has to be open to changes in behavior and beliefs regarding such issues as social autonomy, political morality, and participation. As I will show in chapter 4, it was at this level that the most important changes in Latin American political culture took place. The ontological superiority it assigned to elites prevented transition theory from looking for long- and short-term changes in social actors' political practices. In short, the elite-masses dichotomy led to too thin an approach to address changes in practices at the public level. This problem became central in the discussion of the nature of new Latin American democracies.

The third wave of democratization that began in southern Europe in the mid-1970s reached South America in the early 1980s, leading to the restoration of political competition and elections in most of the countries in the region (Huntington, 1991; O'Donnell, 1996). Very few Latin American countries did not make some form of transition to a competitive electoral system during the third democratic wave; even the octogenarian Mexican authoritarian regime moved in this direction, which led to the electoral defeat of the Partido Revolucionario Institucional (PRI) in the 2000 elections (Olvera, 1995, 2000). Yet, side by side with the restoration of competitiveness, several issues emerged, posing serious problems in characterizing the emerging democracies. The continuous presence of non-democratic actors on the political scene (O'Donnell, 1992; Hagopian, 1992), the increase of economic inequality (Przeworski, 1995), deep political instability (Mainwaring and Scully, 1995), and continuities in the political culture (Moisés, 1995; Peruzzotti, 1997) served as the bases for a reflection that has led the authors identified with the transition paradigm to assume two different positions regarding the type of "post-transition" political regime emerging in Latin American societies.

A first line of analysis, which retains much of the transition theory approach, is the so-called democratic consolidation argument. Authors such as Gunther et al. (1996) and Linz and Stepan (1996) argue that democratic consolidation begins at the moment when democracy becomes "the only game in town." The most important dimension of this game lies in the fact that it is played exclusively by political actors and involves only one activity, power disputes between different political groups: "[D]emocracy becomes the only game in town when all actors in the polity become habituated to the fact that political conflict within the state will be resolved according to established norms" (Linz and Stepan, 1996:15). The problem with such a definition is that democracy cannot be reduced to a periodic game played by different groups. It also involves a set of procedures for resolving conflicts at the level of society as well as a normative consensus on the desirability of these procedures. Linz and Stepan try to integrate the societal dimension into their concept of democratic consolidation by making it an attitudinal dimension. "Democracy becomes the only game in town when, even in the face of severe political and economic crisis, the overwhelming majority of the people believe that any further change must emerge from within the parameters of democratic procedure" (1996:5). Despite the authors' intention to introduce a societal element into their analysis, they reduce it to public opinion's trust of political institutions, a variable capable of being empirically measured. Thus, the ambiguity of democratic consolidation theorists in relation to democracy stands in direct continuity with democratic elitism. They attribute to elites an ontologically superior status in relation to other social actors and try to incorporate other actors only in the de-politicized form of public opinion. Democratic consolidation theorists assume a teleological stance toward democracy by assuming that the commitment of all political actors to democracy as a method for resolving conflicts might per se guarantee the improvement of several aspects of recently democratized societies, even in the absence of political actors' willingness to do so.

A second analytical position assumed by transition theorists on democratic consolidation is defended by Guillermo O'Donnell (1994, 1996), who calls it the delegative democracy diagnosis. It is posed in direct response to the democratic consolidation argument by assuming that delegative democracies are not consolidated democracies but can nonetheless endure (O'Donnell, 1994:56). O'Donnell breaks with the teleology of the democratic consolidation argument by pointing out a gap between the norms of democratic institutions and the practices of social actors.[16] For O'Donnell, "new polyarchies do not lack institutionalization, but a fixation on highly formalized and complex organizations prevents us from seeing an extremely influential, informal and sometimes concealed institution: clientelism and, more generally, particularism. . . . I will use this term . . . to refer broadly to various sorts of non-universalistic relationships ranging from hierarchical particularistic exchanges, patronage, nepotism, and favors to actions that, under the formal rules of the institutional package of polyarchy, would be considered corrupt" (1996:40). Analysis of the new democracies leads to the widespread perception that patterns of interaction are established not only at the institutional level, but also by a set of practices that bypass the private/public dichotomy and lead to the establishment of hierarchical relations among formally equal individuals.

The problem raised by O'Donnell (1996) is intimately connected to the issue of political culture. Already in his first remarks on delegative democracy, he deemed culture responsible for what he called a caudillista tendency in the new democracies. This argument was progressively transformed into a theory of the cultural determinations of delegative democracies, an element that gives a new life to old authoritarian practices. Long-term habits such as low levels of accountability, privatization of the state, and ineffective enforcement of citizenship persist as important trends shaping the political system. The delegative democracy argument seems thereby to involve two dimensions. On the one hand, it retrieves the Huntingtonian concern with low levels of institutionalization of conflict. On the other hand, the institutions charged with pursuing the goals of citizenship are incapable of transforming these patterns of interaction. Thus, delegative democracy changes transition's point of arrival: Latin American transitions led neither to *democraturas* or *ditablandas* nor to full democracies (Schmitter, 1995; Peruzzotti, 1997) but instead to a durable semi-democratic relation between state and society, an outcome not predicted by transition theorists.

A close analysis of the debate between the democratic consolidation and delegative democracy arguments points toward a paradox arising from the lack of a theory of the public sphere—a result of transition theory's insufficient rupture with democratic elitist conceptions. On the one hand, O'Donnell seems to be right to point out the incompatibility between polyarchy and many of the dominant characteristics of Latin American political systems, such as widespread particularism (Cammack, 1990; Gay, 1994; Avritzer, 1995; Auyero, 1997), the gap between law and social relations (Rosenn, 1971; Morse, 1982; Mainwaring, 1990), the persistence of hierarchical relations, and an unaccountable political system (Hagopian, 1992; Avritzer, 1996). Yet, O'Donnnell is unable to bridge his diagnosis of these practices with the idea of the formation of a public domain. On the contrary, he limits his diagnosis to an analysis of elite practices, overestimating the continuities of non-democratic political culture due to the ontological superiority he assigns elites (Peruzzotti, 1997). The paradox is thus constituted by the fact that O'Donnell's theory retrieves a central dimension of Latin American democracies but cannot approach it heuristically because it still operates with an elite-masses dichotomy. The other side of the paradox is represented by democratic consolidation authors such as Linz, Stepan, and Diamond, who commit an inverse mistake. Despite the continuity between their assumptions and transition theory, what they call consolidated democracies have very little relation to the democracies consolidated during the "second wave of democratization," especially when the practices prevailing at the public level are considered as a political variable.

This paradox is caused by the fact that, instead of breaking with the elite/masses dichotomy, transition theory seeks to adapt it to the Latin American reality. O'Donnell's analysis of the cultural determinants of delegative democracy fails because he is unable to move beyond the culture of the elites in order to approach both deeper cultural continuities and renewal, a move that requires a conception of the public space. Linz and Stepan's insistence on political competition between elites associated with an attitudinal conception of the masses depends entirely on democratic elitism and its hierarchical conception of elites. Both the delegative democracy and the democratic consolidation conceptions are unable to deal with changes at the public level. To analyze such a dimension requires a radical break with the elite-masses dichotomy and its substitution with an analysis of practices prevailing at the public level. The construction of democracy approached as the cultivation of a democratic public sphere no longer rests on identifying virtuous or vicious actors but on the creation of a plural space in which actors present themselves in public and establish fields of conflict with the state (Melucci, 1996). The dangers to democracy are linked to the corruption of the dialogical and reflexive nature of this space; the possibilities of extending democracy are linked to its extension. The problem of institutionalizing democratic practices also finds a different solution once we adopt this perspective. It cannot be reduced to the relationship between mobilization and institutionalization but must be perceived in terms of two political logics (Cohen and Arato, 1992): the societal logic, represented by social movements and voluntary associations; and the state logic, represented by the attempt to institutionalize the delegation of power. This formulation of building democracy encompasses a different arrival point: the search for institutional designs capable of bringing new forms of participation that emerged at the associational level into the democratic arena (Cohen and Rogers, 1995). In the next chapter I present a framework for developing a theory of democratization based on the construction of what I call participatory publics.

CHAPTER TWO

ℰᴖ

Democratic Theory and the Formation of a Public Sphere

Transition theory's inability to explain processes of democratization due to the inadequate assumptions it derives from the democratic elitist tradition points to the need to look to other traditions within social theory. Three alternative traditions recommend themselves by their long-standing disagreement with democratic elitism over the ability of the elites to solve the problem of democracy: republicanism, pluralism, and critical social theory. All three also offer alternatives to transition theory's approach to democratization insofar as they agree on the existence of a space for public debate which precedes democratic institutional arrangements.

Republican political theory is based on two main tenets: the idea that politics is a community's way of life; and the idea that freedom and, thus, democracy, is a self-governing form of community organization (Arendt, 1958; Held, 1987; Barber, 1984). The roots of the republican conception of politics can be traced back to the Greek polis and the way it connected community and democracy (Finley, 1973). Transporting republicanism into the modern era leads to a very specific understanding of democracy that rejects the possibility of institutionalizing either politics or sovereignty. The rejection is based on republicanism's dissociation of politics from religious and moral order. Nicola Machiavelli was the first modern author to tackle this issue by pointing out that "there was no natural god given framework to political life. Rather, it was the task of politics to create order in the world. . . . Politics is, thus, ascribed a preeminent position in social life as the chief constitutive element of society" (Held,

1987). The problem with applying such a conception to modern politics is that it expands the role of politics and returns us to the debate on the relation between social complexity and sovereignty, one of the sources of the crisis of democracy at the beginning of the twentieth century.

A second element of republicanism is its conception of politics as the process by which a community governs itself . This process establishes a contradiction between democratic institutionalization and sovereignty. In this debate, republicans usually side with sovereignty against institutionality. Jean-Jacques Rousseau inaugurated this tradition with his remarks on British democracy:

> [S]overeignty cannot be represented for the same reason that it cannot be alienated. . . . The people's deputies are not and could not be its representatives; they are merely its agents and they cannot decide anything finally. Any law that the people has not ratified in person is void; it is not law at all. (1968:141)

The republican concept of the public leads necessarily to a contradiction between the public dimension and complexity and sovereignty. Republicanism cannot adequately address the issue of social complexity because it still operates with a totalistic conception of society that privileges the political realm, reopening the problem of the rationality of political participation. Republicanism also can only provide democratic theory with a conception of the public domain by transforming it into the only domain of the polity and assigning it an anti-institutional dimension. It retrieves the public space only at the price of reinserting into the democratic debate two elements of which it had been relieved as a result of the interwar debates, as we have seen in chapter 1. Thus, it cannot be adopted as a framework for democratization.

Despite the fact that democratic elitism itself assimilated some elements of the pluralist conception of democracy, there are many elements in pluralism that provide grounds for an alternative conception of democracy.[1] For Robert Dahl, democracy involves a set of goals to be maximized, which breaks with democratic elitist tradition by establishing a connection between the quality of democracy and the process of opinion formation among the masses. When considering which elements of democracy need to be maximized, Dahl enumerates a set of processes, some of which belong to the selection of elites and others of which belong to the process of public opinion formation within the electoral process (Dahl, 1956:70).

Dahl's central concern is how to generate within contemporary polyarchies broad political equality.[2] For him, political equality involves three different dimensions: the capacity of individuals "to formulate their preferences; to signify their preferences to their fellow citizens and the government by individual and collective action; and to have their preferences weighted equally in the conduct of government" (Dahl, 1971:2). Dahl's intention is to transform his concern about the conditions for broad political equality into institutional requirements to be fulfilled by existing polyarchies. At the level of the two principles that are related to the formation of a public domain, the level of formulation of preferences and the level of communication of preferences to fellow citizens, Dahl enumerates seven conditions to be fulfilled by existing polyarchies. Among the seven conditions, three are related to actions at the public level: the freedom to form and join organizations, the freedom of expression, and the right to have access to alternative sources of information (Dahl, 1971:3). Yet, when these requirements are seen in the light of the remaining requirements—right to vote, right of political leaders to compete for support, elegibility for public office, and free and fair elections—it is possible to note that they were conceived to play a role in the conditions to broaden the formation of political groups which will run on elections. Thus, Dahl's conditions are a list whose central concern is the process of decision-making by the citizens in the election of their representatives (Bohman, 1996:31–32).

Dahl's theory situates itself on a borderline between the public and elitist traditions. On the one hand, it is clear that both the presentation of alternatives and the evaluation of the information each individual has about them can be considered an inevitable part of selecting elites. On the other hand, both issues lead inevitably to a shift in focus from elite selection to the discussion which precedes it, a public process par excellence. Dahl's conception of the public space is derived from the latter concern. He observes that "prior to politics, beneath it, enveloping it, restricting it, conditioning it, is the underlying consensus on policy that usually exists in the society among the predominant portion of the politically active members" (Dahl, 1956:132). Dahl transforms the formation of consensus at the public level into what he calls an underlying consensus. The problem with approaching the concept of the public through the idea of an underlying public consensus is that only political parties or members of political society may draw upon such a consensus. Thus, Dahl introduces a public dimension into his conception of democracy, but does not conceive it as an autonomous political space.

Contemporary critical theory is the third line of analysis based on the concept of public space (Habermas, 1989, 1984, 1995; McCarthy, 1981; Thompson, 1990, 1995; Keane, 1988a, 1988b; Cohen and Arato, 1992).[3] Critical theory kept one positive element of the debate on democracy from eighteenth- and nineteenth-centuries: the idea of a distinction between reason and elites. Authors such as Rousseau and John Stuart

Mill attributed the rationality of democracy to public debate. The first generation of the Frankfurt School, though active in the debate on mass society (Horkheimer and Adorno, 1946), neither defended the full separation between reason and participation nor proposed their conflation. For Adorno and Horkheimer, reason continued to depend on the type of social action performed in modern societies, a conception that anticipates the debate on the characteristics of the public space. The work of the second generation of the Frankfurt School, especially that of Jürgen Habermas, has been characterized by its effort to reconnect reason and participation. Instead of entering the debate between elitist and participatory versions of democratic theory (Pateman, 1970; Held, 1987), Habermas finds a third path, which involves a different way of reconnecting reason and will, one in which reason results from public debate in a sphere located between the market and the state. An active public sphere separated from public administration becomes the place where new issues are thematized, new identities are presented, and institutional innovation emerges. It is this conception of the public space in its relation to democracy that has been lacking in the current democratization debate. In this chapter, I develop a conception of the public sphere based on three ideas: the idea of a space for face-to-face interaction in which individuals actively engage in discussion on the moral foundations of politics; the idea that this sphere is independent from the state, yet has debates connected with it; and the idea that this sphere can provide the political realm with actors and deliberative processes that can further democratize political practice.

This chapter has three parts. In the first, I sketch the main elements of the concept of the public sphere, showing how it breaks with the democratic elitist distinction between masses and elites. I show how the elitist consensus on the undesirability of participation and the desirability of the government by elites can be contrasted against the idea of a deliberative public sphere connected to an independent state administration through decision-making processes and forms of monitoring. In the second part, I address two major criticisms of the concept of public sphere—that it posits a homogeneous space and restricts social actors to defensive action—and propose two revisions. The first is an attempt to connect identity and rationality, showing that the public sphere is where the presentation of difference by collective actors takes place (Melucci, 1996). This process is central to constructing a new form of democratic politics. The second revision has to do with the possibility of non-particularistic forms of collective action providing the foundation for democratic public deliberation. In the third part, I propose the extension of understanding of the concept of the public to a form of democratic deliberation at the political level. The core of my argument in this chapter is that an alternative form of democratic politics requires the institutionalization of stronger deliberative mechanisms at the public level.

THE CONCEPT OF THE PUBLIC SPHERE: BROADENING THE DEMOCRATIC DEBATE

The concept of the public sphere is a new element in the democratic debate of the second half of the twentieth century (Habermas, 1989; Calhoun, 1992; Cohen and Arato, 1992). One dimension of the concept of the public sphere allowed it to play the role of a watershed between critical social theory critique of the Enlightenment and democracy and late twentieth-century democratic theory: its recovery in early modernity of a sphere for the free interaction of groups, associations, and movements created a third path within democratic theory beyond the debate between democratic elitism (Schumpeter, 1942; Downs, 1956; Sartori, 1987) and participatory democrats (Pateman, 1970; Held, 1987). Public sphere theory introduced the possibility of "a critical argumentative relation to the polity rather than a directly participative one" (J. L. Cohen, 1996), thereby opening the space for a new connection between rationality and participation.

In *The Structural Transformation of the Public Sphere*, Habermas laid the foundations of a new understanding of democracy based on the idea of the public sphere. He grounded the concept on a historical process—the emergence of the bourgeoisie in early modern Europe—which introduced a new claim to power: "The bourgeois were private persons; as such they did not rule. The power claims against the public authority were thus not directed against the concentration of powers of command that ought to be divided . . . the principle of control the bourgeois public opposed to the latter—namely publicity—was intended to change domination as such" (Habermas, 1989:28).[4] Thus, for Habermas, the public sphere emerges historically as the result of a process in which individuals are made equal in their capacity to demand from their rulers public accountability as well as moral justification for state actions.

The concept of publicity has two main characteristics, both connected to the debates around democracy and democratization. The first is the idea of a space for face-to-face interaction differentiated from the state. In this space, individuals interact with one another, debate the actions taken by the political authorities, argue about the moral acceptability of private relations of domination, and make claims against the state. The concept of the public space incorporates into democratic theory the republican drive for participation without making it a form of administration. Individuals within a democratic public sphere discuss and deliberate about political issues and adopt strategies for making the political authorities sensitive to their discussions and deliberations. Thus, the public space establishes a dynamic within politics driven neither by the defense of particularistic interests nor by the attempt to concentrate power with the aim of dominating other individuals. On the contrary, the public use of reason establishes a relation between participation and public argumentation. "The parity on whose basis alone the authority of the better argument could assert itself against that of social hierarchy and, in the end, carry the day, meant, in the thought of the day, the parity of 'common humanity'" (Habermas, 1989:36). This represents a major renewal within the democratic tradition: rational argumentation brings the possibility of breaking with the hierarchies of participation back into politics, substituting for them equal participation and the authority of the best argument.

The second central element of the Habermasian public sphere is the broadening of the public domain, leading to what some authors have called "politicization of new issues" (Melucci, 1996). For Habermas, the desacralization of the public sphere meant the possibility of submitting issues and problems previously approached through the interpretative monopolies of symbolic institutions such as the Catholic Church to rational argument. Thus, the Habermasian public sphere is egalitarian not only because it allows free participation but also because it allows new issues, such as the domination of workers and women within the private realm, to enter political debate (Benhabib, 1992).

The concept of the public sphere opens up a new matrix within democratic theory by breaking with two elements of the democratic elitist tradition. The first, which had its origins in Weber's analysis of the increasing complexity of public administration (Weber, 1978, vol. 2), is the impossibility of participatory forms of administration (Schumpeter, 1942; Bobbio, 1987). Habermas's distinction between the state and the public sphere changes the axis of this debate by introducing a different level of political participation. At the level of the public sphere, rationality is not linked to administration but to a space for free discussion. For Habermas, the central element for the production of rational decisions at the public level is the suspension of private interests and the possibilities for deliberation (Bohman, 1996) opened by the public use of reason.

The other element of the Habermasian break with the democratic elitism is the disconnection of the common good from the substantive means of pursuing it. As I pointed out in chapter 1, this was one of the central arguments of both Schumpeter and Downs for narrowing the scope of democratic participation. The Habermasian conception of the public sphere allows social actors to bring their struggles against various forms of private domination to public debate without having to use substantive conceptions on the common good. The public presentation of excluded identities and the public critique of exclusion become part of a process in which voicing demands leads to politicization.

The theory of the public sphere not only opens space for political participation; it also grounds participation in the process by which modern societies are constituted. In his *Theory of Communicative Action*, Habermas presents modern societies as characterized by the emergence of both bureaucratic forms of action as well as forms of action based on the possibility of reaching understanding through language.[5] Reaching understanding through language is the central feature of the process responsible for the permanent existence of a public sphere. A public space is thus made a constitutive feature of modern democracies. This move leads to an additional break with the democratic elitist tradition, without requiring us to revisit the argument around administrative rationalization. For Habermas, all actors are equally capable of mastering language and introducing arguments at the public level (Cooke, 1994; Habermas, 1995). This process, which is at the root of the generation of power, submits public authority to open criticism. At the same time, public administration is linked to a different process called complexification. By differentiating between rationalization and complexification, Habermas is able to offer an alternative to the democratic elitist and republican responses to participation. He takes from the elitist tradition its concern with the internal limits of administrative complexity and from the republican tradition its understanding of democracy as a process of public reasoning, reconciling them by separating public administration from the public sphere while keeping the two dimensions structurally dependent on one another:

> Because the administrative system must translate all normative inputs into its own language, one must explain how this system can be programmed at all through the policies and laws emerging from processes of public-opinion and will formation. The administration obeys its own rationality criteria as it operates according to the law; from the perspective of employing administrative power, what counts is not the practical reason involved in applying norms but the effectiveness of implementing a given program. . . Normative reasons can achieve an indirect steering effect only to the extent that the political system does not for its part steer the very production of these reasons. Now, democratic procedures are meant to institutionalize the forms of communication necessary for a rational will formation. . . . The more difficult problem, however, is how to assure the autonomy of the opinion and will formation that have already been institutionalized. After all, these generate communica-

tive power only ... in so far as they come about discursively (Habermas, 1995:483–84).

Habermas also reevaluates the meaning within modernity of the conflict between two different types of action coordination, one based on linguistic communication and the other on non-linguistic symbols, such as money and power. By distinguishing between these two different forms of action coordination, Habermas is able to show that bureaucratization is not intrinsic to the development of modernity but has its origins in the penetration of power into arenas in which language is the main form of action coordination. Thus, social forms of action organized at the public level can still seek to broaden democracy.[6]

The theory of the public sphere has received many critiques (Fraser, 1989; Landes, 1995; Young, 1996; Hall, 1994; Thompson, 1995). I will approach three critiques that have immediate consequences for democratic theory: first, that Habermas's theory is unable to respond to cultural difference (Fraser, 1995); second, that it is unable to think about the public sphere in its relation with the state in offensive terms, that is to say, that it is unable to redefine political democracy (Cohen and Rogers, 1995); and third, that even the most radical extension of the public sphere would be insufficient if we limit the public space to unrestricted discussions among citizens (Cohen and Sabel, 1997).

From Homogeneous Publics to New Social Movements: A Model of an Offensive Public Space

The concept of the public sphere provided democratic theory with a new alternative beyond the opposition between the republican and democratic elitist models of participation by proposing a sphere in which a critical argumentative politics becomes possible. Differentiated from the realm of state administration, this sphere allows a new connection between reason and will. Participation in the public sphere cannot be considered irrational because its results are immune to the charge of administrative irrationality. Thus, it provides a new form of thinking about the connection between reason and will.

The theory of the public sphere received important empirical criticisms due to the way it deduced its conception of rational deliberation from empirical cases in which participation was restricted.[7] The first criticisms of public sphere theory tackled the way Habermas connected his theory of the public sphere with so-called white male publics. Landes (1990, 1995) showed how "Habermas's formulation effaces the way in which the bourgeois public sphere from the outset worked to rule out all the interests that would not or could not lay claim to their own universality"

(1995:98). Thus, women and blacks have been excluded from what became known as the bourgeois public sphere. This critique has important consequences for democratic theory. If, as Habermas's critics have maintained, the concept of public is completely interweaved with white male publics, then the concept cannot be extended to other settings or cultures. Contrary to this, I will show that transforming the public space into a dialogic and interactive space and introducing social movements as its main occupants can help us to construct a concept of democratic publics.

An attempt to construct a democratic theory of the public sphere integrating this critique might begin by substituting bourgeois publics with the role played by social movements. Social movements theory has also addressed the issue of participation through a critique of mass-society theory, calling attention to the shortcomings of its psychological analysis of the motives of collective action (Smelser, 1962:11). The concept of mass society was thoroughly revised by the two main paradigms of social movements theory. First, the resource mobilization paradigm argued that it is not possible to attribute collective mobilization to the existence of dissatisfaction because "there is always enough discontent in any society to supply the grassroots support for a movement" (McCarthy and Zald, 1977:1215). This directly challenged the mass-society theorists' assumption that collective mobilization was unleashed by psychological motives or the scarcity of material resources. Obershall called attention to a second problematic assumption of mass-society theory: its model of collective action formation. He noted that most mobilizations draw upon a network of preexisting community relationships or networks of existing voluntary associations. Thus, the second element of mass-society theory challenged by social movements theory was its practice of "reducing mobilization to a synonym for social disenfranchisement" (Melucci, 1996:291). Against this reduction, social movements theory showed that mobilization was more likely to occur where prior forms of social organization existed. Thus, collective action was not the reaction of disenfranchised and atomistic individuals to psychological stress but a rational act of establishing common identities or interests with other individuals.

Social movements theory also suggests a way for a theory of the public sphere to deal with the issue of identity within contemporary societies. It is precisely the impossibility of acknowledging difference through participation that is challenged by European social movements theorists. Melucci defines identity as "what people choose to be, the incalculable: they choose to define themselves in a certain way not only as a result of rational calculation, but primarily under affective bonds and based on the intuitive capacity of mutual recognition. Such a remarkable affective dimension is fundamentally 'non-rational' in character without yet being irrational. It is meaningful and provides actors with the capacity of making sense of their being together" (Melucci, 1996:66). Melucci dislodges identity from the terrain of irrationality and the concealment of difference, connecting it to the public presentation of difference. His approach thus allows the association of the public space with two dimensions inherent in democratic practice.

The first is the public expression of difference within contemporary societies. Contemporary societies are constituted not only by individuals seeking self-preservation but also by social actors who interact with, communicate with, and influence one another. Through communicative acts these actors build a space for mutual recognition and the acknowledgment of difference. Social movements are formed when social actors dispute the articulation of meaning within subsystems that seek to deny their difference: "Social actors enter in conflicts with systemic institutions to affirm an identity negated by them, or . . . to re-appropriate something which belongs to them" (Melucci, 1996:74). Thus, identity formation simultaneously involves the recognition of what is common and the attempt to show publicly what is different. Through the act of presenting their difference in public, social actors give an alternative response of social complexity: instead of aggregating difference through the formation of political majorities to be incorporated by the system of political representation, they side with the public presentation of an irreducible difference. The role of social movements is to publicly thematize identity difference by presenting it in public.

The second important dimension introduced by social movements is the association of the public sphere with the possibility of redefining the concept of politics. The public presentation of new identities is only the first step in the redefinition of the political. The crucial next step is to show that the definition of what is political is always contested and that contemporary societies utilize their public spheres precisely to broaden its definition. "The public space becomes the arena for the contested definition of what is political, that is, of what belongs to the polis. Its chief function is to bring into open discussion the issues raised by social movements—and . . . to enable society as a whole to assume its inner dilemmas . . . as its own, to transform them into politics" (Melucci, 1996:221). Alongside the problem of concealing difference lies another, expressive dimension of modern society, best represented by the public sphere, where social actors construct new identities by bringing them into public. By making difference a subject of public concern, the public sphere offsets the tendency to keep it private.

If social movements address the tendency of Habermas's concept of the public sphere to deny difference, they are unable to remedy the defensive nature of his conception of the public space. Habermas reconciles rationality and participation by proposing a separation among the public sphere, the state, and the market. This solution, as was pointed out above, allows him to avoid the Weberian or Schumpeterian dilemma of having to make the result of political participation rationally compatible with the logic of complex organizations. Yet, Habermas's separation of participation from the economic and administrative systems' internal logic has one consequence related to the role he assigns social movements. For Habermas, social movements can only perform the defensive role of preserving communicative structures:

> In this spectrum I will differentiate emancipatory potentials from potentials for resistance and withdrawal. After the American civil rights movement . . . only the feminist movement stands in the tradition of bourgeois socialist liberation movements. The struggle against patriarchal oppression and for the redemption of a promise that has long been anchored in the acknowledgement of universal foundations of morality and law gives feminism the impetus of an offensive movement, whereas the other movements have a more defensive character. The resistance and withdrawal movements aim at stemming formally organized domains of action for the sake of communicatively structured domains, and not at the conquering of new territory. (Habermas, 1984, 2:393)

Understanding social movements as defensive movements aimed to protect the communicative potentials of the lifeworld misses the problem of formal innovation and the public presentation of difference as means of further democratizing contemporary political systems. By limiting the role of social movements to preserving already existing communicative potentials, Habermas misses the point that these movements generate new solidarities, alter the associational structure of civil society and create a plurality of new public spaces while expanding and revitalizing spaces that are already institutionalized (J. L. Cohen, 1996:36).

The defensive character of social movements can, in my view, be overcome through an analysis of the structural duality of organizational structures, such as that suggested by the authors who recovered the concept of civil society (Arato, 1981; Keane, 1988a; 1988b; Cohen and Arato, 1992; Habermas, 1995). They proposed to analyze the bureaucratization of contemporary organizational structures in connection with the differentiation of public and bureaucratic forms of administration (Arato and Cohen, 1988). From this perspective, bureaucratization can be understood as a disjuncture between modernity's communicative potential and its available forms of organization. Many communicative potentials go unrealized because suitable organizational forms are not available. In addition, other communicative potentials are distorted by the attempt to implement them bureaucratically. If the origins of bureaucratization lie in this process, it is, however, possible to point out that all possible organizational forms are not given in advance and cannot be reduced to bureaucracy as it now exists. On the contrary, it is possible to maintain that "despite the potential for colonization in the contemporary situation . . . modernized cultural forms set in motion discursive practices and expectations that cannot be kept away entirely from everyday life through selective institutionalization. As associations are transformed into bureaucratic organizations, new egalitarian and democratic associational forms tend to emerge" (Arato and Cohen, 1988:50). In short, analyzing the processes of bureaucratization within a dual framework capable of pointing out new organizational potentials allows us to break with democratic elitism's one-dimensional analysis of bureaucratization.

The institutional duality of contemporary organizational structures opens up the possibility of new organizational forms as well as new institutional designs. New organizational forms can be generated by both social movements and voluntary associations. Both draw on the ability of the communicative infrastructure of contemporary societies to respond to the bureaucratization of previous forms of interest aggregation and issue articulation. Thus, the analysis of political parties and parliaments upon which democratic elitism based its conclusion that bureaucratization was inevitable need not be dismissed in order to point out the possibility of renewing the potential for democratic forms of collective organization. All that need be pointed out is that the available institutional forms do not exhaust the possibilities of social organization because they draw selectively on the limited organizational potentials of the nation-state and its hierarchical structure. Thus, it is possible to draw on an already existing potential in order to propose more democratic, less bureaucratic institutions.

Solving the problems of bureaucratization requires providing a solution for the democratic debate different from those proposed by elitists and advocates of participatory democracy (Pateman, 1970). A dual conception of politics assumes the feasibility of a parallel but not alternative framework to the traditional mechanisms of interest aggregation. In such parallel spaces of discussion, new themes, new identities, and moral issues can be dealt in ways that bypass the older forms of majority aggregation. The voluntary and democratic forms of action in this sphere renew the democratic potentials of the political system by facilitating discussion and decision within a local sphere of public participation that allows the aggregation of non-particularistic interests. By pointing out this new possibility, contemporary critical theory provides an alternative to the democratic elitist response to democracy. Instead of narrowing it to a procedure for resolving materially conflicted interests, critical theory points out the possibility of retrieving a parallel potential proper to associative life.

A local public sphere can become the primary place for discussing identities, forming solidarities, and discussing interests on a non-particularistic basis. Yet, the fact that such publics can develop an offensive capacity does not completely solve the problem of the inherently defensive nature of the public sphere unless we suppose that the organizational drives generated by voluntary associations are automatically transferred to the political system. If, however, we assume that these drives may or may not be transferred and that there are different institutional methods of transferring them, we can see that in order for a public sphere to become offensive it also needs to become deliberative.

FROM DISCURSIVE TO DELIBERATIVE PUBLICS

As we have seen, by providing an alternative framework for discussing participation, the concept of the public sphere is central to reconstructing a participatory conception of democracy. As table 2.1 shows, it provides a framework that overcomes the elite-masses dichotomy. Within a participatory and egalitarian public sphere, difference is acknowledged through the formation of collective identities based on the affirmation of cultural characteristics and through the act of publicizing issues that systemic actors would like to keep private. Through its discursive characteristics, the public sphere creates ways of generalizing social action, offering an alternative response to the problem of bureaucratizing collective participation. Introducing the concept of the public sphere allows us to point out that the bureaucratization of existing forms of collective action does not preclude the potential for new democratic designs. However, as table 2.1 shows, the concept of a public sphere falls short of providing an alternative framework for democracy because it fails to transform the retrieval of a public dimension into a framework for democratic practice.

TABLE 2.1
Conceptions of Democracy and Their Relation to
Participation at the Public Level

Classic Democratic Theory	Democratic Elitism	Public Sphere Theory
general will	multiple identities	public as a space for presenting difference
substantive reason	formal reason	public space as expression of formal reason
discursive public sphere	mass-society diagnosis	theory of social movements
generalizable interests	conflicts of interest leading to democracy	possibility of generalization of interests at the public level
participatory democracy	elitist democracy	defensive public space

There are two main reasons why it falls short of providing democratic theory with a non-elitist alternative: it limits the relationship between the public sphere and the political system to the transmission of influence; and it dramatically reduces public deliberation by limiting it to law-making. Following systems theory (Parsons, 1951; Luhmann, 1990), Habermas thematizes the relationship between the public sphere and the political system in terms of the transfer of influence. According to this view,

> within the boundaries of the public sphere or at least of a liberal public sphere, actors can acquire only influence, not political power. The influence of a public opinion generated more or less discursively in open controversies is certainly an empirical variable that can make a difference. But public influence is transformed into administrative power only after it passes through the filters of institutionalized procedures of democratic-opinion and will formation and enters through parliamentary debates into legitimate lawmaking. The informal flow of public opinion issues in beliefs that have been tested from the standpoint of the generalizability of interests. Not influence per se, but influence transformed into communicative power legitimates political decisions. (Habermas, 1995:371)

Habermas's position on the role of the public sphere within democratic political systems is clear: it is not to produce decisions or deliberation but through a symbolic form of communication he calls influence to demand that the consensus which emerges at the level of public opinion be reflected in administrative decisions. When power-holders choose not to incorporate this consensus, they face legitimation problems. This position fails to utilize the potential for democratic participation opened by his own theory, because the weight accorded to the results of public discussions is left to power-holders. Modern citizens do not find, within the Habermasian framework, a parallel forum for practicing democracy, nor do they find an answer to what they should do when the political authorities choose legitimation crisis over democratizing their political practices. Thus, Habermasian theory falls short of providing an alternative way of reconnecting reason and will because, regardless of the rationality of the results of public debate, it is left to power-holders to decide whether to incorporate them into policy (Bohman, 1996).

A second flaw in Habermas's thematization of the deliberative nature of the political public sphere lies in the way he binds deliberation and law-making. For Habermas, the connection between informal publics and political deliberation lies at the level of law-making:

> The principle of democracy thus does not answer the question whether and how political affairs in general can be handled discur-

sively; that is for a theory of argumentation to answer. On the prem-
ise that rational political opinion and will formation is at all possible, the principle of democracy only tells us how this can be institutionalized, namely through a sphere of rights that secures for each
person an equal participation in a process of legislation whose communicative presuppositions are guaranteed to begin with. (Habermas, 1995:110)

Habermas reduces the public sphere's deliberative aspect almost into a
fiction by connecting it to two devices that are not equally deliberative: a
process of public discussion that assigns equal rights to all participants
but does not establish a criterion for making discussion compatible with
deliberation; and a process of deliberative law-making in which the publicity and equality of decision-making depends ultimately on the law-
makers, since they are not bound by results of public deliberation. The
alternative provided by Habermas to bind reason and will falls short of
connecting the two. It only performs the heuristic role of showing the
rational characteristics of public participation.

A different response to the connection between the public sphere and
the process of political deliberation does succeed in binding public reasoning and deliberation (Cohen and Sabel, 1997; Bohman, 1996). This
perspective should not be regarded as contradictory to discursive consensus building; rather, it facilitates the formation of consensus on the policies to be implemented. According to this conception, "a legitimate political system should foster deliberation and, thus, increase the chances of
arriving at correct (or valid, fair or true) decisions" (Bohman, 1996:6).
Public debate is tied to a framework that "both facilitates public discussion among equal citizens by providing favorable conditions for expression, association and discussion, and ties the authorization to exercise
public power—and the exercise itself—to such a discussion by establishing a framework ensuring the responsiveness and the accountability of
political power to it" (Cohen and Sabel, 1997). Public debate and political deliberation should not be separated because both aim at not only
creating societal consensus but also establishing more accountability for
the exercise of power. Thus, a stronger mechanism than influence is required to connect the public sphere to the political system.

Joshua Cohen provides us with a different possibility for connecting
public debate and deliberation by stressing the institutional consequences
of deliberation. He argues that the members of a democratic polity or
public sphere should share "a commitment to coordinating their activities
within institutions that make deliberation possible" (1997:72). This
model provides a more effective way to bind deliberation and communi-

cation than Habermas's model does. In the latter, successful action coordination leads to consensus whereas unsuccessful action coordination disrupts communication, making deliberation impossible. Within a deliberative model, success and failure are different moments of the process of deliberation, in the first case because it is deliberation itself that provides the framework for a consensus agenda, in the second case because deliberation might also play a role in avoiding the disruption of communication.

The virtue of this concept of public deliberation is that it allows us to connect the three main elements of the public sphere (free expression and discussion, the formation of plural identities, and free association) with two further mechanisms that bind them with deliberation: public fora and accountability.

Public fora provide the public sphere model with one additional element it has been missing, namely the capacity to transform an existing consensus into public forms of deliberation. Cohen rightly assumes that democratic publics would prefer institutions that bind the results of their discussions with clear institutional outcomes. In addition, it is possible to argue that it is easier to achieve communicative success at the public level when discussion takes place in an institutionalized procedure about which there already exists a level of consensus.[8]

A second important element of the model I am proposing for deliberative publics is accountability. Democratic theorists repeatedly clashed on this issue because of its two-sided character: on the one hand, it is very difficult to defend system theory's account of administrative neutrality (Luhmann, 1990) because it smuggles the problem of access to deliberative fora into the technical requirement for deliberation (Melucci and Avritzer, 2000). Authors such as Bobbio and Luhmann defend the superiority of forms of decision-making based exclusively on the access of knowledgeable personnel to deliberative fora (Bobbio, 1987; Luhmann, 1990). Yet, they fail to address a second, related problem: by opting for expert fora, they subordinate public access to expertise. Both authors fail to show the compatibility of experts' access to decision-making with democratic legitimacy. Here seems to lie the tension between social movements and such fora, as has been argued by movements related to issues such as AIDS treatment (Gamson, 1989; Bohman, 1996) and the environment (Kaase, 1990), among others.

On the other hand, there seems to be an unresolved issue in the proposals, which do not take administrative complexity into account (Unger, 1998); here the Weberian critique of popular sovereignty has to be taken seriously. Extending the communicative model of the public sphere to the totality of society would imply extending the discursive mode of sociation to society as a whole. "This is impossible, for the simple reason that democratic procedure must be embedded in contexts it cannot itself regulate" (Habermas, 1995:305).

Conflating deliberative decision-making with public administration leads to precisely the issue the theory of public sphere presented in this chapter was intended to avoid, namely the association of participation with administrative rationality. Yet, only by giving public processes of communication and deliberation an institutional dimension can we transform public sphere theory from a theory of the possibility of participatory democracy into a truly democratic and deliberative theory. The two can be reconciled by proposing an intermediary form of democratic design capable of addressing both concerns.

I call this intermediate conception participatory publics, which involves four elements:

- First is the formation at the public level of mechanisms of face-to-face deliberation, free expression, and association. These mechanisms play the role of addressing specific elements in the dominant culture by making them problematic issues to be politically addressed.

- The second is the idea that social movements and voluntary associations address contentious issues by introducing at the public level alternative practices.

- Third is that they preserve a space for administrative complexity and, at the same time, challenge the exclusive access of technicians to decision-making fora. Participatory publics reserve themselves the prerogative to monitor the administrative implementation of their decisions.

- Fourth is that they bind their deliberations with the attempt to search for institutional formats capable of addressing at the institutional level the issues made contentious at the public level.

This democratic design would involve introducing a deliberative element at the public level while protecting the autonomy and internal complexity of the administrative realm. Such an attempt does not need to devise an alternative form of administrative rationality; it can assume the partiality of administrative rationality and its consequences for participatory democracy without proposing an alternative form of administration. Accountability connected with public deliberation can allow citizens to monitor administration and thereby avoid conflating administration and deliberation. Figure 2.1 compares the Habermasian model with the model proposed here.

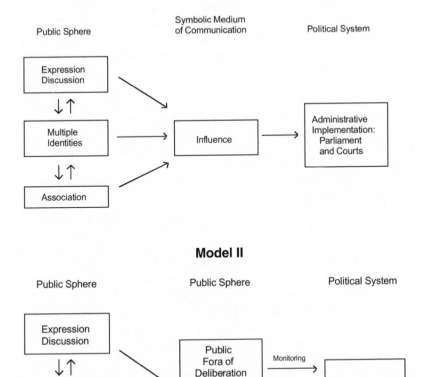

Fig. 2.1. Relationship between the Public Sphere and the
Political System, based on Habermas, *Between Facts and Norms.*

The model clarifies why democracy cannot abandon a public dimension. In Habermas's model, the process of public reasoning and deliberation to which democracy is linked precedes the bargaining and competition proper to the political realm. Instead, public discussion itself needs a deliberative instance. Only such a mechanism can transfer the results of public discussion to the democratic arena. In this sense, democratic elitism's solution to this problem, as shown in chapter 1, throws out the baby with the bath water when it precludes participation and rational discussion in order to make democracy feasible. A different solution to the problem of social complexity would be to replace the republican bias of alternative forms of administration, which have tended to disrupt social complexity, with two alternative institutions: public fora of deliberation and monitoring. The association between the two makes it possible to imagine, as figure 2.1 shows, a situation in which public fora incorporate a critique of administrative rationality into democratic practice without being seduced by the siren song of alternative forms of rational administration. Monitoring would complement decision-making, generating the institutions necessary to make clear to public administration the origins of its administrative power.

This model gives us a vantage point from which to analyze a second issue central to the aims of this book: introducing as a separate case societies in which the administrative structures of the modern state preceded the development of cultural practices that generate public spaces. I analyze the formation of Latin American societies from this perspective in the next chapter. This analysis allows me to point out why transition theory's assumptions concerning democratization lead to an internal contradiction: by reducing democratization to the restoration of political competition, it misses the dimension of public discussion and deliberation. This model, as was shown in chapter 1, cannot recognize the fact that restoring political competition does not entail full democratization. The next chapter presents a model of democratization based on the idea of participatory publics that deals with imbalances of power at the public level. This model seeks to reconcile the institutional problem with the cultural issue in order to give to democratization designs the capacity to strengthen emerging democratic values at the public level.

CHAPTER THREE

ℰℐ

Democracy and the Latin American Tradition

The analysis of democratization as the construction of a democratic public sphere implies the availability of the social practices needed to construct such a space. This might be considered both a political and theoretical issue. At the political level, it involves posing the problem of the relation between politics and different practices, pointing to the desirability of a renewal of traditional practices. At the theoretical level, a different yet connected issue arises: how should we conceive of the extension of democratic practices identified with a Western tradition in a region that has had its own version of this tradition (Diamond, Linz, and Lipset, 1989), or even a culture which, according to some authors, was formed as a reaction to Western modernity (Morse, 1989)? This problem is also connected to the elite-masses dichotomy insofar as Latin American elite culture has tended to consider itself connected to the West while charging the masses with "backwardness." What I have called dualist theories hoped to solve the problem of connecting Latin America to the West through modernization: elites would be the carriers of a process of modernization that would lead to the emulation of Western institutions. Democratic practices would be introduced, if not intentionally, then as the by-products of modernization. The aim of this chapter is to propose an alternative to this theory.

My point of departure is an issue that must be faced by any theory seeking to build democracy in a context where the local culture is ambivalent to democratic ideals, namely, the search for the elements within the democratic tradition that lend it a transcultural appeal. Such an appeal is rooted in the fact that if democracy is clearly a result of Western modernity, it is the Western cultural structure that has had the most general appeal.[1] Following John Dunn, one can consider democracy "the moral Esperanto of the present nation-state system; the language in which all nations are truly united, the public cant of the world" (Dunn, 1979:2). The democratic form of collective decision-making seems to be generalizable in a double sense: most power-holders claim to govern according to democratic rule, even those who do not concede that their aim is to move in this direction in the near future. However, acknowledging a generalizable element in democratic practices does not provide us with any clue as to the specific cultural combination that might make democracy attractive in non-Western or semi-Western environments.

Asserting the generalizability of democracy does not preclude posing two questions at the level of sociological and democratic theory. These questions constitute the axis around which we can reflect on the characteristics of political practice in countries whose cultures were not originally linked to the emergence of democracy.

The first question is essentially sociological and related to democracy as a societal form of organization and interaction between state and society. It is linked to the fact, noted by Eisenstadt (1973), that in order to construct a democratic political order outside the Western core one cannot, like earlier versions of modernization theory (Rostow, 1960), ignore the cultural specificity of these societies. On the contrary, democracy can only be constructed if it addresses the fusion of the Western tradition and the specific cultural traditions of non-Western societies. The first theoretical issue to be addressed in the process of constructing democracy is thus what is culture and which role does it play in democratization processes. Answering such a question implies analyzing which cultural practices in a specific setting might strengthen democracy and which might hinder its full realization. It is from this perspective that I approach issues such as hierarchical social relations in this chapter.

A second question central to building democracy outside the countries that were part of the first and second waves of democratization is related to democratizing societal practices and the institutional designs capable of strengthening such practices. Two problems have to be addressed in this regard. The first is the problem of democratic emulation. Authors in Latin America still approach the problem of democratization through the Huntingtonian matrix, which equates the construction of democracy with institutionalization. By identifying institutionalization with creating within Latin American countries the institutions present in the most successful contemporary democracies, these authors end up proposing the importation of institutions without evaluating how they fuse with local cultural traditions (Lamounier, 1992). The resulting fusion of traditions leads to institutions that often fail to strengthen democracy. A second institutional problem is the availability of local democratic practices and the inability of social actors to think about institutional designs capable of strengthening them. Here the problem of constructing democracy goes beyond the problematic established by Huntington and Dahl because it encompasses the evaluation of local democratic practices and broadens the problem of democratization to include the additional problem of devising institutional designs capable of transmitting democratic practices at the level of society to the political level. This is the approach I propose for analyzing the process of democratization in Latin America, specifically in Brazil. It requires the analysis of the cultural makeup of a specific country, the forms in which democracy is introduced at both the societal and the political level, and the specific character and availability of democratic practices.

This chapter has four parts. In the first, I analyze the best-known interpretations of the encounter between Western and Latin American civilization to show how modernization theories, the most familiar theoretical account of this encounter, systematically denied or responded naively to the issue of culture. This response rested on the hope that the introduction of Western economic structures (industrialization) would be sufficient to produce modern social actors who would in turn introduce democracy. In the second part, I show how dualism—the assumption of an opposition between modern and non-modern sectors that has characterized most theories of Latin American modernization—has been replaced by a theory of hybridization (García Canclini, 1995), which argues that the encounter between the modern and non-modern does not lead to untainted modernization but to a hybrid form typical of Latin American societies. Yet, contra Canclini, I show that with regard to democratization, hybridism becomes a deliberative handicap for recently democratized societies. It is from this perspective that I analyze the characteristics of the Latin American public sphere. In the third part, I introduce an alternative framework based on the importance of culture in relation to political structures as the central element of democratization. I argue that the rise of democracy in the West has to be deduced from a process of cultural rationalization. Yet, the first structures of Western modernity to appear in Latin America were market and state structures, which did not generate democratic practices. It is in relation to this framework that I approach, in the fourth part, the problem of institutional emulation and the relationship between the political institutions characteristic of democratic systems (parliament, the rule of law, political parties, elections) and the absence of a democratic culture at the societal level. This allows me to proceed from the societal level instead of the political level in order to analyze the recent processes of democratization of Latin America in the following chapter.

MODERNIZATION AND DUALISM: A REVISION OF THE ANALYSIS OF DEMOCRACY IN LATIN AMERICA

The understanding of democracy as a public space based on face-to-face interaction and the moral criticism of state action connects democracy to the historical formation of European societies and non-European societies and, thus, to the issue of culture and political culture. Social and political theory has analyzed culture as the way according to which ideas influence social action. This conception has its roots in Max Weber's focus on meaningful action, that is to say, on how individuals incorporate worldviews. For Weber, "culture shapes action by defining what people want and how they get it" (Swidler, 1995:25). Weber's conception of culture had a major impact on democratic theory through the assumption that worldviews—complex systems of ideas—might influence individuals' political attitudes.

Almond and Verba wrote the classic work on political culture in which the Weberian perspective on culture was transformed in a model for the analysis of political attitudes. The authors seek to further differentiate worldviews from political attitudes in order to propose a definition of political culture as the "attitudes towards the political system and its various parts and attitudes towards the role of the self in the system." (Almond and Verba, 1963:13). The political culture of a nation is a particular distribution of patterns of orientation toward political objects among members of the nation (Almond and Verba, 1963:15). The concept of culture and political culture employed by Almond and Verba has two main characteristics: it involves individual attitudes toward political objects, and it is the result of the internalization of available cultural patterns or worldviews. Almond and Verba's analysis has one major flaw: the understanding of culture as a category that belongs to the mind's interior. In contrast, recent cultural theory has pointed out that culture belongs to the realm of social practices (Swidler, 1995:28).

In this chapter culture will be understood as a collective and public category. Culture is collective in the sense that it involves sets of practices shared by a portion or the whole of society. Culture is public in the sense that it expresses itself in active relationships between groups, which take place at the public level (Melucci, 1996:70). It is through processes of interaction and communication that social actors create new values and new institutional patterns. I define political culture as the public struggle over the meaning of political practices that will determine new institutional behaviors in the polity. I will assume in this chapter that every society has a dominant political culture and that in every society there are attempts to challenge the dominant political culture through actions at the public level (Alvarez, Dagnino, and Escobar, 1998).

Latin American elites' itinerary in the twentieth century is a good demonstration of how culture influenced the approach to democracy. Throughout most of the twentieth century, Latin American elites tried to link nation building and modernity by sponsoring modernization as a gradual process of transformation of a backward into a modern social setting (Parsons, 1949; Parsons and Toby, 1977; Germani, 1971; Rostow, 1960; Eisenstadt, 1966; O'Donnell, 1973; Apter, 1965; Huntington, 1969; Inglehart, 1997), which means that they assumed that a structural change in the economic process would also produce a change in wordviews. The conception involved here was a structural and epiphenomenal conception according to which every modern society shares the same cultural patterns. Modernization theories proceeded from the simple assumption that the encounter between European and non-European civilizations leads the latter to assume the characteristics of the former. Modernization was thus seen as

> the process of change toward those types of social, economic and political systems that have developed in Western Europe and North America from the seventeenth to the nineteenth century and have then spread to other European countries and, in the twentieth century, to [the] South American, Asian and African continents. (Eisenstadt, 1966:1)

Modernization was understood as the reproduction of the economic, political, and social structures generated in the "Western core" at the beginning of modernity to countries outside the core. For modernization theorists, "industrial techniques and mentalities permeate most areas of human activity [in modern societies], while agriculture predominated and characterized most institutions of non-modern civilizations" (Germani, 1981:10). Thus, the framework proposed by modernization theorists was from the very beginning a dualist framework; it assumed a temporal process whose point of departure (t1) is a non-modern institutional structure and whose arrival point (t2) is the consolidation of modern institutions. Modernization takes place between (t1) and (t2). Industrialization is the process connecting the two temporalities and cultural change is the product of industrialization.

A second absolutely central point for theories of modernization, particularly in their first period in the 1950s, was the assumption that economic transformation leads to a follow-up effect capable of generating the other institutions characteristic of Western modernity. This assumption was based in classical sociological thought on the priority of the mode of production in relation to other social structures (Marx and Engels, 1848, 1871), or the linear nature of the rationalization of economic structures (Weber, 1978; Parsons and Toby, 1977). If this analysis has proven problematic in the case of the West, it is still more deeply flawed in relation to non-Western societies (Habermas, 1975). During the second wave of democratization, democracy in Latin America was considered a by-product of the economic modernization sponsored by national elites. The conception of the masses inherent in such an approach is exactly the same as that of the democratic elitist tradition: they are the subordinate elements in the process of modernization. However, once they become modern, they are deemed capable of being rational decision-makers (Leal, 1946). Thus, culture was completely missed as an independent variable in the production of democratic values.

Modernization theories rapidly moved in the direction of a second phase, which would have a deeper impact on the discussion of democracy. This phase was based on the discovery that "despite the development of various socio-demographic and structural indices of modernization, [such societies] did not develop within them a viable institutional structure which was able to deal with the problems generated by socio-demographic and structural changes, at least in the political field" (Eisenstadt, 1973:424). Eisenstadt's prognosis, shared by authors such as Guillermo O'Donnell, led to the development of a new strand of modernization studies based on two principles. First, instead of harmony between the modernization of Western and non-Western countries, there was a strain between the two processes, particularly at the economic level (Frank, 1970; Wallerstein, 1979; Cardoso and Faletto, 1979; Quijano, 1971). Second, instead of a linear process of modernization inside the nation-state, the same authors assumed an internal tension between what they called "pro-modernization" and "anti-modernization" forces. In the first group they included all the groups linked to industrialization and in the second, all the interests primarily linked to agriculture. The most important attempt to analyze this tension was dependency theory. For these authors, dependency has to be deduced directly from the economic encounter between developed and underdeveloped societies:

> The historical specificity of the situation of underdevelopment derives from the relation between "peripheral" and "central" societies. . . . The situation of underdevelopment came about when commercial capitalism and industrial capitalism expanded and linked to the world-market non-industrial economies that went on to occupy different positions in the overall structure of the capitalist system. (Cardoso and Faletto, 1979:16)

For Cardoso and Faletto, the central element determining the encounter between Western and non-Western cultures was the economic relation established between the center and the periphery. Yet, in contrast with the other versions of dependency theory, Cardoso and Faletto's version analyzes the overlap between economic factors and other social and political characteristics of Latin American countries. For them, a national economy achieves a certain degree of autonomy of decision vis-à-vis the international economic system when "a country breaks its ties with a given system of domination without incorporating itself totally into another" (18–19). Again, as in the case of modernization theory, it is possible to see the connection between dependency and elite theory. For Cardoso and Faletto the attempt to break with a dependent form of insertion into the world economy has to be made by economic and political elites. All other groups within a particular social formation should follow this originally elitist attempt. Thus, the problem of the cultural conditions for democracy is lacking in a strain of analysis that focused exclusively on the formation of a coalition group among the elites with the aim of creating a national production system.

Evaluating dependency theory and in particular its consequences for democratic theory in Latin America leads us to single out three elements, all of them highly problematic. The first is the strong economic framework and the way it determines certain societal features. Cardoso and Faletto analyze the formation of Latin American societies with regard to economic cycles. Different economic groups' understandings of themselves and their societies derives in part from the characteristics of these cycles. As Forment has pointed out, dependency theory discovers the formation of groups and political identities in economic dynamics. Thus, "a change in the world price of oil, copper, or sugar should produce a corresponding change in the collective interests and identities of groups" (Forment, 1991:44). In this way, instead of theorizing the specificity of Latin American societies, dependency theory produces an epiphenomenalist analysis of how certain characteristics could be overcome. Cardoso and Faletto were unable to break with the evolutionary framework of modernization theory, providing only an alternative explanation.

The second problem with Cardoso and Faletto's analysis is their denial of the importance of culture. The authors consider culture a superstructural variable and oppose it with a perspective that foresees political change capable of altering what they called "the ruling pact" (1979: 216). By reducing culture to the superstructure and treating it as epiphenomenal, their analysis ignores its reflexive potential and leads the authors to propose a sort of political voluntarism capable of remaking culture. Thus, in their analysis the authors fail to grasp the cultural elements capable of influencing both political continuity (Hagopian, 1992; Roeniger, 1989) and political change.

The third important flaw in Cardoso and Faletto's analysis arises from the fact that, despite their criticism of the dualism inherent in modernization theories, Cardoso and Faletto incorporate in their own theories another dualism expressed by the dichotomy inclusion/exclusion. Overcoming dependency should lead to the end of the dichotomy between inclusion and exclusion through social integration (1979; 204–5). Independent of our agreement with this substantive aim, it is important to point out that their theory operates within the same formal framework of other modernization theories: it assumes a temporal dimension in which Latin American societies begin with a dualistic social structure (t1) which, through economic transformations linked to industrialization, will be overcome (t2). Again, it is important to point out the similarity between this theory and elite theories of democracy. For Cardoso and Faletto, the road for building a democratic ruling pact was to forge a coalition among the elites capable of being autonomous vis-à-vis the international economic system. Such a coalition should be capable of integrating the masses in a subsequent time.

One searches in vain for a theory of democracy in Cardoso and Faletto's analysis of the encounter between European and Latin American civilizations. The authors miss all the analytical categories that could point out non-democratic political activities or a non-democratic political culture; they are dismissed because they are considered superstructural. Cardoso and Faletto argue that

> instead of insisting on the immutability of the cultural dimension and historical roots of corporativism . . . it is more important [to understand] . . . the essence of the contradiction between the interests of the people and the current style of development, between the state and the nation. In these relationships of opposition, if any cultural dimension exists and carries significance, it is . . . the capacity to rule. The effective battle is not between corporativism and the democratic tradition. It is between technocratic elitism and a vision of the formative process of a mass industrial society which can offer what is popular as specifically national and which succeeds in transforming the demands for a more developed economy and for a democratic society into a state that expresses the vitality of the truly popular forces (216)

This perspective was in tune with the major contemporary interpretations of the relation between culture and democracy (Almond and Verba, 1963; Barry, 1970). But, it prevented the authors from seeing in the encounter between Latin American and European societies the potential for constructing a democratic public space. Instead, the authors limit themselves to proposing a theory of the autonomous insertion of Latin American countries into the "capitalist world system," a project to be pursued by economic elites and whose success could eventually lead to democracy.

Thus, it is possible to conclude that, in its different versions, moderniza-tion theory has been unable to theorize the political implications of the encounter between the structures of political rationality proper to the West and Latin American societies. The specific characteristics of Latin American culture, such as the hierarchical relations between elites and masses and the lack of structures of mediation between individuals and the state, were all set aside in favor of a theory of economic moderniza-tion. The next sections of this chapter attempt to link this encounter to a theory of the adoption of democracy that breaks with the elite/masses dichotomy.

MODERNIZATION, TRADITION, AND THE BREAK WITH THE DUALIST TRADITION

Modernization theory in its two different versions vanished from the Latin American intellectual scene in the early 1980s.[2] Yet, it was only at the decade's end that a new theory of the encounter between Western and Latin American civilizations emerged, influenced by the new strand of cultural studies (Williams, 1981; Melucci, 1989, 1996; Geertz, 1973). This theory broke with the dualist approach of a division between tradi-tional and modern and proposed instead an alternative interpretation of Latin American societies based on what became known as "cultural hy-bridism." According to one of its major representatives, Mexican intellec-tual García Canclini:

> The conflict between tradition and modernity does not appear as the crushing of the traditionalists by the modernizers, nor as the direct and constant resistance of the popular sectors determined to make their traditions useful. The interaction is more sinuous and subtle: popular movements also are interested in modernizing and the hegemonic sectors in maintaining the traditional—or part of it—as a historical referent and contemporary symbolic resource."
> (1995:9)

García Canclini's account of how the traditional and the modern are intertwined in Latin American societies has no intention of transforming this pattern into a heuristic point of view or the standard for a normative critique of the continuity of traditional structures in Latin America, as modernization theorists did in the past. For Canclini, the cultural hybrid-ization of traditional and modern is only an empirical finding that allows us better to analyze Latin American societies. Three analytical elements allow us to perceive how this hybridization is expressed.

The first is the impossibility of integrating the whole population into the market, which leads to a conception of economic hybridization. This assumption can be considered both an empirical elaboration of a point made by both modernization and dependency theorists, as well as a cultural critique. Both theories assumed a historical-temporal crescendo through which the growth of the modern industrial sector would lead Latin American societies to overcome the existence of the traditional sector or the dichotomy between inclusion and exclusion (Germani, 1971; Cardoso and Faletto, 1979). Thus, at the end of the process of modernization or economic autonomization, there would be a common framework that would imply cultural homogeneity between Latin American and Western European and North American societies. For Canclini, the issue is no longer to propose a normative horizon for the full incorporation of the non-modern into the modern but to make the permanent existence of these dichotomies a constituent element for the analysis of the economy, politics, and culture of Latin America. At each level, these dichotomies lead to a specific combination of the modern and non-modern; modernization does not overcome but strengthens them.

The second analytical element proposed by García Canclini is linked to the interest of the members of the political system in incorporating non-modern elements in order to strengthen their legitimacy or hegemony. Once again, this observation elaborates on modernization theory's assumption of an automatic transition from a traditional to a modern political system. Authors such as Leal who studied the non-modern elements of Latin American societies assumed that phenomena such as clientelism and its secondary manifestations—nepotism, rigged ballots, disorganized public services—were related to the characteristics of an agrarian economy and therefore supposed that a modern social and economic structure would corrode their basis (Leal, 1946:140). In the case of dependency theory, we can point out that incorporating conflict into the dichotomy between modern and traditional was insufficient to free Cardoso and Faletto from the assumptions of political modernization. In their view, those who belonged to the modern economic sectors (industrialists, the middle and working classes) would automatically propose the adoption of an autonomous economic project whose corollary would be modern political practices. Canclini again breaks with this theoretical framework by transforming the normative critique of clientelistic politics into an empirical problem. Instead, he would have us acknowledge that non-modern practices are not left over from previous political periods or social structures but are articulated with modern forms of political behavior in most Latin American societies:

> The favor is as anti-modern as slavery but "more pleasant" and susceptible to being joined to liberalism because of its element of compromise and the fluid play of esteem and self-esteem to which

material interest is subjected. It is true that while European modernization is based on the autonomy of the person, the universality of the law, disinterested culture, objective remuneration and the work ethic, the favor practices personal dependency, the exception to the rule, interested culture and remuneration of personal services. . . We advance little if we accuse liberal ideas of being false. . . Liberal principles are not asked to describe reality but to give prestigious justifications for the adjudication exercised in the exchange of favors and for the "stable co-existence" that the latter permits. Referring to dependency as independence, caprice as utility, exception as universality, kinship as merit and privilege as equality might seem incongruous to someone who believes that liberal ideology has a cognitive value but not for those who are constantly living moments of "loaning and borrowing" (48–49)

For Canclini, the individualizing practices with which liberalism has identified itself have to be considered cognitive values unable to resist the process of cultural pluralization arising from the encounter between different cultures. Thus, there is no reason why one should claim that they are external to the local elements of a hybrid culture. On the contrary, we should revise our view of these elements in light of the empirical and pragmatic considerations proper to the trade in favors characteristic of Latin American societies. In this sense, the exchange of favors and modernity can, according to Canclini, be combined in an unproblematic way once we get rid of the culturally biased, value-laden background of liberalism.

Hybridism also tries to combine empirically modern and traditional elements in the cultural field. Canclini argues that modernization in Latin America has not been pursued against the so-called "popular cultures," as modernization theorists assumed; rather, there has been continuity between modern and non-modern forms of cultural production:

Even in rural areas, folklore today does not have the closed and stabled character of an archaic universe, since it is developed in the variable relations that traditions weave with urban life, migrations, tourism, secularization, and the symbolic option offered . . . by the electronic media. (155)

Once again, the author aims to divest modernization theory of its evolutionist and normative assumptions and replace them with an empirical analysis of how the economic interests of the producers of popular culture, an unequivocally modern interest, favor preserving non-modern cultures. It is precisely the association among economic modernity, political power, and cultural tradition that allows for the continuity of eminently

TABLE 3.1

*Explanatory Models of Latin American Societies and
Their Conceptions of Democracy*

	Form of Understanding Dualism	Understanding of Inclusion/Exclusion Dynamics	Conception of Democracy and Public Space
Modernization	result of insufficient advance of modernization	caused by insufficient economic modernization (lack of industrialization)	evolutionist: the public space as a cultural reproduction of Western political structures
Dependency	result of the form of insertion into the international economic system	caused by the heteronomous insertion into the international economy (lack of industrialization)	voluntaristic: the public space as a result of autonomous insertion in the international economic system
Hybridism	product of the sui generis combination of cultural tradition and modernity	caused by a peculiar combination of modern and traditional economic and political systems	hybrid: the public space as the result of the inevitable cultural articulation between traditional and modern

traditional activities on a modern basis. Table 3.1 systematizes the different conceptions between tradition and modernity discussed so far, pointing out how Canclini introduces a cultural element in his approach to Latin American society's dualism.

The thrust of the hybridist argument is clear: in Latin American societies, both the elites and the popular classes combine modern and traditional cultural elements, and the interpretation of these societies must take this into consideration. Canclini implicitly assumes a differentiation between the Latin American cases and the West because his idea of "socio-cultural hybrids" is envisioned to apply only to cultural encounters. In the case of Latin America, hybridization is linked to "the syncretic forms created by Spanish and Portuguese matrices mixing with indigenous representation" (241–42).

Canclini's approach does not solve two problems that are linked to the relationship between culture and democracy: it cannot indicate why there has not been cultural hybridism in the West, although there have been cultural encounters in the West too, because the West both passed through a process of modernization and had a popular culture.[3] In this sense, Canclini misses the opportunity to differentiate between different cases of hybridization—the Western case, in which at the end of a process of modernization, a modern and rationalized culture and political system became hegemonic vis-à-vis non-modern forms, and the Latin American case, in which modernization led to a long-term duality between different cultural patterns.

The second limitation of Canclini's approach is more central to the construction of a theory of democratization. It is related to the lack of any attempt by the author to make clear whether hybridization is a vice or a virtue—or whether it simply does not make sense to approach such a phenomenon through normative concepts. Evaluating the nature of the political practices generated through hybrid practices does not seem to be Canclini's main concern. However, there is one field in which he seems to point toward the growth of democratic practices, namely, the massive production of cultural goods: "[I]n modern democratic societies where there is no blood superiority or titles of nobility, consumption becomes a fundamental area for establishing and communicating differences" (16). This allows us to see where democratization takes place. For Canclini, processes of democratization are not connected to the emergence or pre-dominance of modern practices at the political level. On the contrary, democratization is the result of the expression of difference in cultural products, which can be either modern or non-modern. Thus, the hybrid nature of Latin American societies does not seem to contradict their democratization.

A more thorough analysis of hybridism as a conceptual tool to analyze the encounter between Latin American and Western societies reveals a fundamental heuristic problem related to the analytical levels on which the model is applied. On the one hand, the empirical model for the hybridization of the formal and informal economy or low and high art has completely different implications as we move to the political level, where hybridization between dependency and autonomy, universality and exceptionalism, and equality and privilege has strong anti-democratic consequences. In these cases we are speaking of a set of practices that bind elites and masses and pose problems for democratic institutions. These practices influence the operation of these institutions, obstructing their democratizing effects. Thus, the operation of democratic political institutions proper to the liberal democratic tradition is incapable of offsetting structures of power that have been partially overcome in the cultural tradition that gave birth to these institutions. We cannot reduce the problem to that of assimilating cultural standards because it generates an issue essential for democratic theory, namely, how a theory of the formation of Latin American societies should normatively address the problem of political domination and lack of equality at the public level.

Normatively situating a theory of the encounter of different cultures in relation to political domination is central to analyzing the specific political hybridism of Latin American societies. The hybridization of concepts such as individual autonomy, universality, and equality is less a problem for the cognitive orientation of social actors, as Canclini argues, than it is the result of their partial break with collective and hierarchical structures of social domination. Thus, the persistence of collective structures of domination cannot simply be an empirical problem. An empirical approach must be transformed into a framework for analyzing the specific alternative repertoires of collective action (Tilly, 1986, 1990). By approaching these repertoires as analogous to modern forms of overcoming domination, hybridism can be transformed from a cultural into a political theory.

A second problem for the hybridization framework is how to approach theoretically what has become known as the encounter between Latin American societies and "Western modernity." Canclini rightly rejects the idea first introduced by modernization theorists of a progressive substitution of modern for traditional practices. He points out that the Eurocentric background of this conception places European and North American political forms at the end of a teleological continuum and supposes that other societies should move toward them.[4] He shows that instead of this a priori progression, a combination between the formal and informal economy and between modern and archaic culture could develop. However, he discharges himself from the political obligation to discuss the effects of these combinations on the internal dialogues established between different political practices as well as from what desirable developments could arise from them. In this respect, Canclini's theory renounces the role of a theory of democratization. Such a theory might show the existence of two different political alternatives in late democratization societies with radically different implications for democracy: the first alternative is that the emergence of modern political institutions does not completely change political practices because, in late modernization societies, there is always the alternative of informal modes of political interaction based on hierarchical practices (O'Donnell, 1996). The second alternative is that cultural change will emerge at the public level and institutions that will propose changes in the dominant political pattern might become the dominant form of political interaction. Both alternatives have different implications for democratic theory because they point toward the need to differentiate the cases in which hybridization precludes the existence of deliberative equality from the cases in which new practices emerge at the public level.

In the next section, I return to the analysis of the encounter between European and Latin American traditions to show the consequences of the political phenomena it generated for a theory of democracy. I try to point out that an empirical theory of hybridization should not preclude the normative attempt to inquire into the productive dialogues that can emerge from the encounter between modern and non-modern political forms.

MODERNITY AND TRADITION, OR THE PARTICULAR AND THE GENERAL IN AN ENCOUNTER BETWEEN CIVILIZATIONS

My analysis of the encounter between the Latin American and Western traditions departs from problems discovered but left unresolved by modernization theory and hybridism. From modernization theory I take the diagnosis that the adoption of the economic, cultural, and political institutions proper to Western modernization has not been able to generate the democratic institutions it generated in the West in late modernizing countries (Eisenstadt, 1973; Apter, 1973). This essentially empirical diagnosis, however, has not led to a theory of the elements of the encounter between the two traditions responsible for that phenomenon. Hybridism differs from modernization theory in that its break with evolutionism allows it to perceive the reason why the dissemination of economic and political institutions outside the Western core has not led to similar results: for Canclini, the combination of the traditional and the modern leads to hybridization. Yet, by replacing a normative approach with an empirical one grounded on a skeptical attitude, he is unable to see that democratic theory must go beyond simply diagnosing the ineffectiveness of institutions in charge of guaranteeing individual autonomy and political liberty. My aim in this section is thus to reexamine the encounter between Western and Latin American traditions in search of the cultural roots of obstacles to the full flowering of democracy in Latin America.

Modernization theories ordinarily conflate cultural and institutional factors (Eisenstadt and Schluchter, 1998). Dissociating modernity from the emergence of Western rationalism, they conflate such processes as, on the one hand, differentiation, urbanization, increasing labor productivity, and the development of centralized political power and, on the other hand, the secularization of norms and values (Habermas, 1987). In this, they break with Weber's framework for the analysis of modernity, in which the emergence of modern structures of consciousness preceded the rationalization of economic structures. Weber differentiated between the two processes by pointing out the role of culture, in particular the rationalization of religious traditions, in the emergence of Western modernity (Weber, 1930; Schluchter, 1989).

Weber argued that every attempt to explain the specificity of modernity must "recognize the fundamental importance of the economic factor, above all take account of the economic conditions. But at the same time, the opposite correlation must not be left out of consideration. For although the development of economic rationalism is partly dependent on rational technique and law, it is at the same time determined by the ability and disposition of men to adopt types of practical conduct" (Weber, 1958:26). Thus, for Weber the phenomenon that laid the basis for modernization in the West linked culture to practical affairs: successive waves of ethical and moral generalization universalized the acknowledgment of the other as an equal (Schluchter, 1989; Habermas, 1984). Through these processes, universal religions linked rationalization to practical worldly action.

It is well known that Weber pursued this analysis in order to reveal a contradiction between economic and administrative rationalization, on the one hand, and its original cultural basis, on the other (Weber, 1930; Schluchter, 1989; Avritzer, 1996). This contradiction lies at the root of his diagnosis of a contradiction between modernity and bureaucratization. Yet, a second, equally important process can be deduced from this phenomenon, which is central for understanding the expansion of Western modernity and its encounter with non-Western traditions. This is related to the fact that, if Western modernity has its virtues—the possibility of morally and ethically legitimating economic and administrative rationalization—it spread through both the expansion of the market and the centralized administrative state and the diffusion of certain moral ideas. In its process of state formation, Latin America came into contact with modernity in some cases through the international market system (Wallerstein, 1979), in others through the construction of empires (Hobsbawm, 1987), and in others by establishing processes of internal dialogue that reflected the moral structure of modernity. Yet, in all cases, there is a differentia specifica between the constitution and the expansion of the West. In each case, the specific nature of the encounter determined the constitution of different political structures. These different combinations led to three main problems for establishing democratic institutions outside the centers of modernity.

The first is related to an ambiguity of the democratic form. If we understand democracy as the continuation of ethical rationalization on a secular basis, we should note that different traditions within and outside modernity do not equally favor the idea of human equality; some are ambiguous or reject the values upon which democracy is founded. The central element of the Iberian tradition,[5] which most influenced the formation of Latin American societies, is "the acceptance of a hierarchical, diversified and functionally compartmented social order" (Morse, 1964:124). Thus, the development of Latin American societies always involved different combinations of traditions, in particular different combinations of universalism with the specific particularisms formed in the region prior to its encounter with the main Western tradition. However, if Latin American societies had their differentia specifica, they also took the liberal tradition as a constitutive reference. Thus, at the time of independence, not a single Latin American country claimed an alternative tradition. The attempt to claim liberalism as a doctrine of economic and political emancipation in turn threw Iberianism into question.[6] In this sense, from the very moment of their formation, Latin American societies had to face the tension between their liberal normative horizon and the impossibility of applying liberalism to their existing structures. This should have implied a need to discuss the tension between culture and institutions.

A second aspect of the combination of traditions in Latin America was the uncritical transfer of institutions, or "institutional emulation." This practice had two, equally troubled sources. First, the very idea of transferring modern institutions is itself problematic, as the retrieval of the distinction between cultural and societal rationalization allows us to see. Attitudes toward this process are predetermined by a process of cultural rationalization that precedes the effort to build institutions. Thus, while it is possible to emulate institutions, it is not possible to emulate their meaning in a modern polity. Tocqueville pointed this out in a somewhat metaphysical way when he analyzed the Mexican attempt to adopt a constitution similar to that of the United States:

> The Mexicans were desirous of establishing a federal system, and they took the Federal Constitution of their neighbors, the Anglo-Americans, as their model and copied it entirely. But although they had borrowed the letter of the law, they could not carry over the spirit that gives it life. . . . To the present day Mexico is alternately the victim of anarchy and the slave of military despotism. (Tocqueville, 1966:167).

Véliz (1981) describes a similar process in all Latin American countries: all adopted liberal constitutions and federalism after independence and, after less than two decades, all were back to centralized and personalistic systems of power. Thus, the second problem for adopting democracy in light of Latin American traditions involves not only the tension between culture and institutions, but also the fact that institutional designs do not take this tension into account.

The third problem arising from the encounter between local and Western traditions concerns popular culture. To understand the role played by popular culture in the assimilation or rejection of the democratic tradition, it is necessary to bear in mind a second way in which the formation of a national identity in Latin America inverted the European model. In Western Europe the cultural unification of the national state took place in opposition to existing popular cultures (Burke, 1978). In Latin America, this process took on a very different temporality: national unification and the recovery of the popular culture were simultaneous, leading to the association of national identity and popular culture. This simultaneity had two consequences central to the encounter between European modernity and the Latin American tradition. First, national elites did not reject popular culture. On the contrary, in most countries, popular culture became the main element of the national culture. Thus, popular culture in the region was not the leftover of an extinct cultural form, as it was in most European countries in the nineteenth century (Burke, 1978) but the result of a political articulation by the elites who aimed to preserve cultural and political autonomy in the face of integration into the world economic system (Barbero, 1987). A second consideration for the political status of popular culture was the fusion of the romantic notion of the people—folk—with the Marxian idea of class, generating the concept of popular classes (Weffort, 1979; Laclau, 1978). In this form, the conception of the people assimilated the romantic notion of purity (Herder), transforming the people into a unified, homogeneous entity that preceded the process of internationalization (Pasquali, 1962; Schiller, 1969; Mattelart, 1986). This conception prevented the principle of autonomy from being extended from the cultural to the political realm. It is beyond the aims of this chapter to consider the consequences of this process for our understanding of culture.[7] Our concern is to evaluate the impact of this conception of popular culture on the construction of democracy. In this regard its main effect seems to have been to emphasize local and societal particularities in the process of nation building.

Thus, we can now point out the combination of two obstacles for democracy in the process of Latin American nation building: the transfer of administrative structures of rationality already available in Western societies was associated with the valorization of a non-differentiated and homogeneous popular culture. The universalization of structures, which could have led to the production of a democratic repertoire, did not take place for both internal and external reasons. Our conclusions are thus quite similar to those of hybridist analysis: the encounter between the Western and Latin American traditions led to a combination of modern and non-modern, and Western and non-Western, elements. Yet, unlike the hybridist school, our attempt to supplement this empirical analysis with a normative one leads us to observe that this combination led to three phenomena, all of them very pernicious to the construction and consolidation of democracy.

First, in Latin America the differentiation between private and public took on a completely different form than it did in the West (Habermas, 1989, 1992; Benhabib, 1992; Thompson, 1995; Melucci, 1996); one could even say that it failed altogether. Due to its specific form of colonization, the early modern differentiation between the household economy and the private did not take place in Latin America until the nineteenth century. In the context of nation building, this resulted in a disproportionately large private sphere and the always open possibility of extending personal relations to the political realm. Franco (1974) shows how in postcolonial Brazil the public activities of free men took place in the private space of the haciendas. Guerra demonstrates a similar phenomenon in Mexico, where the large haciendas "constituted more important centers than the small villages. For those who inhabited their centers as well as for those who inhabited their peripheries . . . they represented the centers for the exercise of worship, festivals, etc" (Guerra, 1988, 1:134). As the Brazilian anthropologist Roberto Damatta points out, this historical phenomenon had deep political consequences. It led to the establishment of what he calls a relational form of citizenship, in which personal relations between individuals are a counterpoint to the universal precepts of equality and citizenship. For Damatta, in the Brazilian social world what is expected in every situation of conflict or dispute is a ritual of acknowledgment that humanizes and personalizes formal relations, helping everyone involved to establish some sort of hierarchy. Citizenship, the universal and abstract subjection to law, is contrasted against more familiar, personalized social relations (Damatta, 1985:68). In this sense, the subject of citizenship should be understood through this relational form of differentiated social spheres:

> In Brazil, liberalism is a matter of the world of economics—metaphorically, the universe of the street—while the ideology and values of favor and patronage in general function in the universe represented by the metaphor of the home. Not only does each set of values carry a different weight, but they move in very different spheres. (274)

The phenomenon pointed out by Damatta, despite the author's analytical shortcomings, is an excellent point of departure for understanding the relation between culture and institutions within democratic theory.[8] The introduction of supposedly universalizing institutions has to be approached in relation to the specific culture in which they are inserted and analyzed in relation to the specific outcomes of this combination. In Latin America, democratic institutions and particularistic cultural traditions are intertwined in different kinds of political hybridization, which, contra Canclini and Damatta, pose serious problems of deliberative inequality within the public sphere.

A second potential cultural obstacle to democracy in Latin American societies is the way their specific traditions of association developed. In both the colonial and the postcolonial periods, there was no tradition of plural and democratic associations. In the case of Brazil, the only forms of association during the colonial period derived from religious traditions (Boxer, 1962:319; C. Boschi, 1986). The most important characteristics of religious associations such as the Misericordias or the third order fraternities were their racial homogeneity, religious intolerance, and concomitant inability to represent social pluralization. The first plural forms of association to emerge in Latin America were the Masonic lodges founded in Peru in 1755, in Mexico in 1785 (Guerra, 1988), and in Brazil in 1815 (Mello Moraes, 1982). Yet the Masonic lodges evolved in such a way as to become compatible with Catholicism and, in Brazil, even with the monarchy. A weak tradition of independent associations in Latin America emerged, at best, in the late nineteenth century, already influenced by the development of mutual aid societies and even by the socialist movement (Hahner, 1986; Baily, 1982; Conniff, 1975). Thus, it is possible to point out the lack of collective forms of association or their late emergence as a second characteristic of the Latin American process of societal formation.

A third phenomenon to have in mind when analyzing the nature of the public space in Latin America is the development of a tradition of undifferentiated social mobilization at the moment when social movements started to emerge around modern issues. These movements appropriated the idea of the popular, which led them not to follow the logic of structural and social differentiation already taking place in countries such as Argentina, Brazil, and Mexico. On the contrary, the repertoire of collective action remained undifferentiated, leading to the association of the ideas of class and people through the unlikely entwinement of the Marxian and romantic traditions. In this sense, one can argue for a three-sided explanation for the difficulties of implementing democracy and constructing an egalitarian public space in Latin America, resting on the conjunction of three interrelated factors: (1) commercial and administrative elements, unable in themselves to generate democracy, were transferred from the West; (2) these elements intertwined with the broad privatization and lack of association that prevailed during the process of nation formation; and (3) these traditions were not easily overcome during the process of modernization because national elites opted for a cultural struggle whose main focus of opposition against the outside was a popular and supposedly untainted culture, which was itself not democratic. Three key elements were thus in play in the formation of Latin American societies: the outside, elite culture, and popular culture. Table 3.2 summarizes the institutional and cultural factors that obstructed the constitution of a democratic public sphere in Latin America. In the following remarks, I show the drawbacks of this model for the formation of a democratic public sphere.

The Political Consequences of Hybridism and the Democratization of the Public Space

The above analysis of the encounter between Western and Latin American cultural traditions explains how the hegemonic political culture avail-

TABLE 3.2
Consequences of Hybridism at the Public Level

Cultural Element	Institutional Element	Hybrid Form
broad private sphere	separation between private and culture	penetration of the public by the private
homogeneous and non-plural forms of association	rights of association	non-plural sphere of associations
homogeneous forms of collective mobilization	rights of communication	undifferentiated popular mobilizations

able in Latin America today was formed. As we have seen, the Iberian tradition and the institutions it created in Latin America failed to generate an alternative set of political institutions in spite of its early rejection of liberalism and political equality. The specificity of Latin American cultural formation led to hybrid structures, which had a serious effect on the organization of three institutions proper to democracy: the relations between private and public; public forms of association; and the nature of popular mobilization. Each of these structures obeys a double logic—a constitutional normative logic that opens room for democracy and alternative and informal practices that make what could have been a democratic public space into a hybrid structure. Yet, contra Canclini, the presence of these structures in Latin American public life should not only be diagnosed empirically but also normatively criticized to figure out how to overcome the cycles of authoritarianism and populism through the construction of a vigorous democratic public space. Such a normative critique must be based on an understanding of the obstacles hybridism has created for the construction of democracy in Latin America and its implication in the process of the formation of a democratic public space.

Political hybridism, the hegemonic political culture formed in Latin America, has promoted two major tendencies within the region's democratic moments: instrumentality in relation to political institutions and deliberative inequality at the public level. An instrumental relation to democracy was central to Latin American political culture throughout the process of nation building, and has been assimilated in different ways by the elites and the masses. Among the elites it is reflected in the open possibility, as we saw in chapter 1, of challenging the results of elections ex post facto. It has persisted as an extra-normative element of political life, one strengthened by the democratic elitist assumption that democracy need not be normatively grounded in order to survive.[9] The masses expressed this instrumentality by subordinating democracy to the furthering of popular interests by seeking national economic autonomy. Thus democratic elitism and Marxism, the two most influential traditions in Latin America in the 1950s and 1960s, had complementary views on the normative assumptions of democracy; each in its own way considered

TABLE 3.3
Democratic and Hybrid Forms of Public Space

Democratic Public Space	Hybrid Public Space
rights of free expression and communication	penetration of the private into the public
pluralization of identities	non-plural popular identities
free assembly and communication	private claims mechanisms rather than collective association

democracy instrumentally. Only with the constitution of a common public sphere could such a conception be shattered.

A second, equally serious problem for democracy in Latin America has been the prevailing deliberative inequality caused by political hybridization. The principle of deliberative inclusion is central to the idea of public reasoning: the members of a deliberative forum must have equal opportunity to deliberate (Joshua Cohen, 1997:73–74). Political hybridization affects the capacity of individuals to express themselves freely by introducing private elements into public discussion; it precludes the formation of plural identities by establishing a contradiction between the popular identity and pluralism; and it leads to weak and non-plural forms of association by privileging personal and relational mechanisms for making claims, such as the favor. Thus, as Table 3.3 shows, political hybridization weakens the three central elements for establishing an equal process of political deliberation.

We can thus attribute Latin America's failure to build a democratic public sphere during its process of nation building to its political hybridization. It is beyond the aims of this work to point out how the advent of authoritarianism in the Southern Cone of Latin America was facilitated by these elements. Yet, we can note the absence of forces capable of occupying the public sphere throughout the breakdown of Latin American democratic structures during the 1960s and early 1970s—largely due to the impossibility of dissociating politics from particularism. In the next chapter I examine the development of a democratic public sphere in Latin American societies as a reaction to political hybridization. I will depart from the assumption that important changes in terms of cultural practices emerged in most Latin American countries and were expressed by different types of social movements. I will show how during the so-called political liberalization of the authoritarian regimes of the 1970s and 1980s some of the central elements of the hegemonic cultural tradition were challenged by social actors at the public level. My aim will be to show how transformations at the societal level led to a new idea of public space, the first element in the process of the constitution of participatory publics.

CHAPTER FOUR

༄

The Transformation of the Latin American Public Space

We have seen that the process of nation building in Latin America involved the importation and emulation of Western political institutions. The encounter between these institutions and local cultural traditions led to a process of hybridization through which institutions proper to the Western democratic tradition did not produce the effect they produced in their original cultural setting. I traced this duality to three interconnected facts: the transfer of institutions that privileged their administrative side at the expense of their cultural side; the political behavior of elites, who were willing to pursue non-democratic strategies within democratic political settings; and an idea of popular culture that homogenized forms of collective action. The political consequence of this specific reception of democratic practice in Latin America was a tradition of instrumentality in relation to democracy, that is to say, a practice by both elites and social actors who regarded political rules from a particular standpoint: the results of elections could be challenged ex post facto; the rules constituting the normative infrastructure of democracy could be bypassed to one's advantage. At the same time, a second important phenomenon completely annulled the possibility of a democratic public space—the predominance of deliberative inequality at the public level. The conflation of private and public made it impossible to retrieve a generalizing element in political life. The particularization of the public promoted clientelistic interest representation, accentuating the deliberative inequality already prevalent at the public level with a hierarchical understanding of political representation. As a result, the normative consensus upon which democracy is based was broken or never truly established. The breakdown of democracy remained an ever-present possibility during the second wave of democratization in Latin America.

The failure to consolidate the second wave of democratization in Latin America was inescapable by the mid-1970s. Whereas most countries in the region held democratic elections at one point in the 1950s, only two continued to do so by 1974 (Huntington, 1991). The breakdown of the fragile rules of the democratic political game made political instrumentality more pervasive. The new authoritarian regimes that emerged in Brazil, Argentina, and Chile (O'Donnell, 1973; Collier, 1979)—as well as the authoritarian inflection of post-1968 Mexico—led to a deeper conceptual and practical disregard for civil rights, communication, and political rights. Human rights violations became widespread in the Southern Cone countries. The new Latin American authoritarian regimes also abandoned the ideal and practice of communication rights and tried to impose a definitive break with the concept of electoral competition.[1] It was precisely during this period, however, at the height of the break with the democracy, that two important transformations started to occur: one in the understanding of the moral infrastructure that precedes political competition, and the other in the occupation of the public sphere. In Brazil, Argentina, and Mexico, the self-understandings of social actors and the role of the public sphere changed fundamentally during the so-called process of liberalization, a moment in which authoritarian power-holders retained almost total control of the political scene.

This chapter proceeds in two parts. In the first, I discuss the processes leading to the transformation of the Latin American public sphere during the liberalization in Brazil, Argentina, and Mexico. I show that the assault on democracy led social actors to reevaluate the meaning of central elements of local traditions of collective action. This reinterpretation contested the privatization of the public arena, the homogenization of collective action, and the lack of independent associations. I then analyze how three new traditions emerged in Latin American countries as a result of such a process of reevaluation: a tradition of occupation of the public sphere to voice political demands; a tradition of collective mobilization around pluralistic demands and plural identities; and a new tradition of formation of voluntary associations organizationally autonomous from the state. Each of these new traditions represented a reevaluation of the meaning of the democratic public sphere that took place during the authoritarian period, making room for the emergence of democratic movements at the public level.

In the second part, I analyze the emergence of three social movements that became very influential in Latin America in the 1970s and 1980s: human rights movements in Brazil and Argentina; urban social movements in Brazil and Mexico; and movements and campaigns for monitoring political society in Brazil and Mexico. Each of these movements raised an issue that was later incorporated into the public understanding of politics. Human rights movements exposed the lack of a moral foundation for political competition. They represented a claim to reestablish the right to life and physical integrity as prior to and outside the boundaries of political competition. Urban social movements and neighborhood associations raised the issue of organizational autonomy from the state and equality underlying claims for negotiable political goods. They sought to break the link between the material deprivation of the poor and the instrumentalization of politics by changing how material benefits were claimed: instead of concessions provided by political mediators, benefits would become rights attached to citizenship. Movements for political monitoring tried to reestablish the generalizing dimension of politics by creating a realm outside the political system from which political practices could be judged or criticized independently of political competition. Two dimensions were crucial in this process: campaigns to force political society to follow generalizable rules; and monitoring as a means of enforcing accountability without intervening in the administrative realm. I argue that morality and organizational autonomy were the new themes around which a new conception of public space was articulated in Latin America.

The central purpose of this chapter is to show that during liberalization there was a significant renewal of political practices at the public level. In the chapter's concluding remarks I take issue with both the critiques of this renewal as well as transition theory's conception of a provisional occupation of the public sphere in order to show that they both miss the extent of political innovation that has taken place at the public level in Latin America. Yet, my central contention is that these innovations have not been incorporated or led to a significant renewal at the political level, resulting in a fundamental tension between actors who occupy the public sphere and actors in charge of representation and political administration. This tension is addressed in the remaining chapters.

LIBERALIZATION AND THE TRANSFORMATION OF THE LATIN AMERICAN PUBLIC SPHERE

The transformation of the Latin American public sphere was linked to the beginnings of liberalization in Brazil, Argentina, and Mexico. Liberalization was the first moment of the transition to democracy (O'Donnell and Schmitter, 1986:6–8)[2] and was marked by two contradictory facts: on the one hand, there was an effective curb on human rights violations and illegal acts by the authoritarian regimes; on the other, rules for political competition were uncertain and there was no consensus about electoral laws. The period of liberalization saw an increase in political activity, but also the possibility that the authoritarian regimes still had control over access to political power. Thus, instead of the institutionalization of the rule of law, the central element of liberalization was the restraint of the authoritarian power-holders. Restraint took two primary forms. At the level of civil rights, gross human rights violations were curbed by controlling the paralegal apparatus of repression without introducing meaningful legislation which would allow the prosecution of such violations and other political crimes. At the level of political competition, liberalization in most Southern Cone countries and in Mexico involved some form of electoral competition between the authoritarian power-holders and the democratic opposition.[3] At least in Brazil and Chile, these controlled forms of competition created the opportunity to remove the authoritarian power-holders from power. However, this may not have been their most important characteristic.

During liberalization, the former democratic opposition and new social actors took advantage of the lower level of repression to initiate radical changes in their forms of public action, leading to two major innovations. The first was a revision of so-called state-centered politics. Popular sectors in Latin America had focused their political activities in the 1950s and 1960s on searching for a form of economic development independent from the international economic system (see chapter 3). The central variable in this approach was state control, and its failure to strengthen society was one of the reasons authoritarianism could so easily seize political control. The first important revision made by the Latin American democratic opposition during liberalization was to shift politics from the state to the societal level. In the words of Brazilian social scientist Francisco Weffort, if society did not exist it had to be invented—and, indeed, it has been. The second important innovation was the retrieval of the moral dimension of politics. Throughout the 1950s and 1960s in Latin America, the moral dimension of politics was subordinated to a substantive conception of political emancipation, typically expressed by the opposition between formal and substantive democracy. The exclusion of morality from politics was thoroughly compatible with a non-normative understanding of political competition. The overall consequence of the amoralization of politics was the loss of any generalizing dimension within the act of making politics. Thus, losers in elections would call the military to intervene, social actors would easily join political conspiracies and there were no defenders of the rules of the political game. The Latin American authoritarian regimes took advantage of this when they abolished many civil guarantees after seizing power. Indeed, the only institutions that kept their commitment to moral values during the authoritarian period were the family (Weffort, 1989; Jelin, 1994) and the Church (Bruneau, 1974). Because their commitment to morality was pre-political, they became the center of weak structures of social defense and, later, the founders of human rights movements. Thus, the second important revision made by the democratic opposition during liberalization was the acknowledgment of the need to introduce a moral dimension in order to reconstitute a pacified space for the exercise of politics.

These two structural changes in the understanding of political discourse brought about a change in how the public space was understood. The role of the public expression of political ideas was transformed, as was the meaning of a public and democratic identity. Last but not least, social movements and voluntary associations became the standard ways of organizing and occupying the public sphere. Allow me to develop each of these dimensions.

Expression

In their effort to redefine their political roles, social actors reconceived the aims of politics as the process of liberalization of former authoritarian regimes began in Brazil in the mid-1970s, in Argentina in the early 1980s, and in Mexico in the late 1980s.[4] The first important sign of their new understanding of the aims of political action was a change in the form of occupying the public space. A different political language emerged at the public level, which would later constitute a common ground for social movements and voluntary associations. Doimo describes the elements of this new self-understanding of social actors: they saw themselves as independent subjects, as proponents of grassroots forms of discussion and participation, and as claimants of human and social rights (Doimo, 1995:124). She shows how this transformation led to a change in the expression of social demands. Social actors occupied the public sphere by expressing their aims to one another. The number of publications on issues of concern for the poor, such as transportation, health care, and housing, skyrocketed during the Brazilian liberalization, as figure 4.1 shows.

The growing number of documents, publications, and other forms of communication utilized by social actors reveals two important trends. First, it indicates an effort to develop a common language unlike the populist discourse of the previous democratic period. In contrast to the earlier populist language, the focus of the new language was on the capacity of society to be the place for the plural organization of claims and demands. Second, the occupant of the public sphere was no longer a homogeneous and dispossessed mass (see chapter 3) but an autonomous actor capable

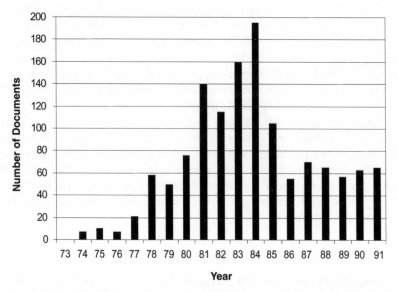

Fig. 4.1. Number of Documents on Social Movements in Brazil (1973–1991), reprinted, by permission, from Doimo, *A Vez a Voz do Popular*.

of deciding his or her claims and the means of presenting them. Ramirez shows how the attempt to establish an autonomous form of occupying the public sphere grew in other Latin American countries, such as Mexico. In the late 1980s, social actors in Mexico had broken the control of the party-state—the PRI—over neighborhood organizations. They also challenged the government's monopoly over representation on the boards of several associations, such as parents' associations (Ramirez, 1990:243). Thus, the liberalization of political spaces by authoritarian regimes in Brazil and Mexico enabled social actors to challenge monopolies over expression and representation at the public level. The central element of this process was establishing horizontal forms of communication between social actors as part of an attempt to create new forms of public expression, such as new publications in Brazil, new types of public demonstrations across Latin America, and the creation of a public sphere in an antagonistic position against the state. State claims to truth were publicly disputed by the Argentinean and Brazilian human rights movements and the Mexican civic movements against electoral fraud. State claims and policies regarding the material conditions of the poor were publicly challenged and alternatives were presented. In all these cases, the source of this new form of politics adopted by social movements was a transformation in how claims were expressed at the public level.

Identity

Social actors in Latin America during liberalization constructed a new kind of collective identity based on two innovations, one formal and one substantive.[5] The formal innovation was a challenge to the traditional popular identity. Throughout Latin America, social actors resisted the idea of belonging to a homogeneous, undifferentiated popular sector and started to understand themselves as belonging to a pluralistic social space. Social actors reacted to the earlier external attribution of their identity and started to evaluate the meaning of their primary and secondary ties. This led to a different form of politicizing the social, one in which issues that had been contained at the private level started to be brought into public. The adoption of the slogan "the personal is political" implied breaking with the idea of an identity constructed on a single level, the economic (Laclau, 1985:30). This was related to a reinterpretation of the meaning of constructing a public identity. Again, this challenged a deterministic and teleological view of the public space centered on a single actor and a single conflict. Instead, different actors occupied the Latin American public sphere, seeking the acknowledgment of their particular pleas as citizens, a demand only formally equivalent to those of other actors.

> Popular mobilizations are no longer based on a model of a total society or on the crystallization in terms of the equivalence of a single conflict which divides the totality of the social into two camps, but on a plurality of concrete demands leading to a proliferation of political spaces. (Laclau, 1985:41)

The new element that emerged during liberalization was social actors' reevaluation of their form of public action. Public identities in Latin America during the 1950s and 1960s were rational in scope, teleological in their historical perspective, and functional in their understanding of the level at which an identity should be constructed. During the Latin American liberalization, all three elements, which together formed a substantive conception of politics, were displaced by more plural and democratic identities. First of all, identities started to be conceived as local rather than functional. Second, they were oriented to the present instead of the future. And finally, rationality ceased to be identified with a project of homogeneous action and was instead linked to a conception of politics in which the plurality of social action would be a permanent feature of collective action. Social action was based on raising issues such as improving living conditions or creating forms of solidarity to forge a tighter social network, or searching for a form of political autonomy that would put an end to the instrumentalization of material claims by political intermediaries. Improving poor neighborhoods, strengthening the identity of city dwellers, and constructing the democratic citizen were all important elements of this new identity. The pluralization of actors and demands is the important issue. Social actors claimed different social services or resources, established different relations with political mediators, related in different ways to culture, and adopted different models for organizing their actions. Thus, the second way in which the public space was reconceived in Latin America during liberalization lay in the challenge of a plural and democratic identity to the older, homogeneous, and teleological one.

Association

Social actors in the Latin American liberalization challenged the role traditionally played by political mediators (Leal, 1946; Uricochea, 1984; Hagopian, 1996) and the determination of politics by the state. The alternative to both these long-standing practices was an increase in association. A new associative drive arose in Brazil, whose culture traditionally had low levels of associative activity. In Mexico, actors began to challenge the existing forms of politicization and the party domination of existing associations.[6] In both cases, the new associative drive involved two interconnected processes: a quantitative increase in the number of voluntary associations, and the emergence of new types of associations. The increase in the number of voluntary associations was especially remarkable in Brazil, as table 4.1 shows.

Particularly notable was the proliferation of Brazilian neighborhood associations, which expanded by 10 percent in the 1970s and by 90 percent in the 1980s, illustrating a new approach to demands for material improvements. The number of associations concerned with health and education issues also increased sharply in Brazil, indicating a change in the form of claims for social services. Thematic and/or post-materialist associations, practically nonexistent in both countries before liberalization, constituted a completely new way of occupying the public space.

TABLE 4.1
Number of Associations Created in the Major Brazilian Cities 1940–1990

	1941–1950	1951–1960	1961–1970	1971–1980	1981–1990
São Paulo	288	464	996	1871	2553
Rio de Janeiro	188	743	1093	1233	2498
Belo Horizonte	120	204	459	584	1597

Source: W. Santos, 1993; Avritzer, 2000

TABLE 4.2
*Composition of the Univérse of Existing Voluntary Associations in
São Paulo and Belo Horizonte*

Type of Association	Belo Horizonte (%)	São Paulo (%)
Neighborhood	9.7	27.4
Religious	20.3	—
Professional	9.3	6.6
Educational	7.5	12.2
Improvement of health conditions	1.1	2.9
Recreational	20.1	—
Environmental	0.2	2.0
Feminine	0.7	7.2
Human rights	0.1	2.5
Ethnic	0.1	2.9
Self-help	10.1	—
Defense of specific causes	3.9	6.3
Cultural	5.2	10.4
Academic	6.5	2.6
Personal philosophy	2.1	—
Entrepreneurial	1.4	8.0
Not classified	1.7	9

Source: Avritzer, 2000

Voluntary association in Brazil during the 1970s and 1980s grew due to the way they expressed a demand for organizational autonomy from the state, due to their role as societal institutions for the claiming of public goods from the local administration, and due to their role of expression of new cognitive values such as the defense of the environment, ethnic minorities, and human rights. The composition of voluntary associations in Brazil by the end of the 1980s is shown in table 4.2.[7]

Voluntary associations continued to be organized during the 1980s in Brazil and the share of those associations in charge of representing interests and post-material cognitive values increased vis-à-vis the traditional forms of voluntary associations (recreational and religious based, which used to predominate in most Brazilian cities). Some forms of voluntary associations that were not very strong before the mid-1970s increased in number and influence, for example, neighborhood organizations: in Belo Horizonte, their number increased from 71 to 534. The increases in São Paulo and Rio de Janeiro were also very impressive: among the total number of neighborhood associations in the two cities, 97.6 percent and 90.7 percent were created after 1970, respectively, as were 68 percent of those in Porto Alegre. Other types of associations were also completely new in all three cities: 92.5 percent of the associations of health professionals in São Paulo were created after 1970; 76.2 percent of the lawyers associations in Rio de Janeiro were also created after 1970 (Santos, 1993). In Belo Horizonte, all associations dealing with environmental, human rights, and ethnic issues (29 associations) were created in this period.

These transformations at the levels of expression, identity formation, and association in Brazil, Argentina, and Mexico represented a break with the Latin American tradition of heteronomous forms of interest representation and mass mobilization and the rise of a more autonomous, democratic, and horizontal public sphere. The transformations also implied a change in the relationship between public and private. The culture of the favor and clientelistic political intermediation started to give way to more autonomous forms of social organization. This does not mean that all kinds of clientelistic political intermediation were abolished or that all action in the public space became democratic.[8] It does mean, however, that there was a significant effort to change the pattern of heteronomous associations in Brazil, Mexico, and Argentina and that this effort had a demonstration effect on other movements and in less central regions in the three countries. In addition, autonomous action became perceived as feasible, and many social movements started to establish fields of conflict in relation to the state. They emerged within spaces that had previously been considered private and raised issues that had been hitherto regarded as extra-political.

Social Movements and the Transformation in the Forms of Occupying the Public Sphere

The process of liberalization in Brazil, Mexico, and Argentina led to the emergence of new social movements in all three countries. These movements represented both an internal and external reaction to authoritarianism. The internal reaction was evident in the self-criticism of the left and the democratic forces, who sought to understand the reasons for their defeat and for the reemergence of authoritarianism in Latin America (Coutinho, 1982; Barros, 1986; Mainwaring and Viola, 1985; Sader, 1989). The external reaction was linked to the features of the authoritarian regimes and the constitution of a field of conflict in relation to human rights issues, material demands, and the traditional forms of political mediation (Melucci, 1985, 1996).[9] Authoritarianism in Latin America generated three broad fields of conflict by radicalizing the existing traditions (see chapter 3) of excluding moral considerations from politics, taking advantage of material needs in order to build clientelistic networks of political support, and expanding the role of political mediators at the expense of societal autonomy. At each of these levels, new types of social movements emerged. Conflicts over the moral nature of politics led to the emergence of human rights movements; conflicts over how the claims of city dwellers were addressed gave rise to urban social movements; and conflicts around the actions of political mediators led to monitoring movements and campaigns against political society.

Human Rights Movements in Argentina and Brazil

Among what could be called Latin America's new social movements, human rights movements represented perhaps the most radical break with the region's political tradition. Human rights movements emerged in Brazil in the first phase of liberalization and in Argentina at the very beginning of the country's authoritarian period and even before.[10] There had been earlier human rights organizations especially in Argentina, such as the Liga Argentina Por Los Derechos Del Hombre, created in 1937 (Jelin, 1994:39). Yet, it is possible to argue that human rights groups represented a form of new social movement in at least two senses. First, they presented human rights as a non-negotiable cognitive value, which is to say in the same way that the claims of social movements in Europe and the United States are considered non-negotiable (J. L. Cohen, 1985; Melucci, 1980, 1985; Offe, 1985). The novelty of the movement was the non-negotiable nature of its demand for the protection of the right to life (Mainwaring and Viola, 1985:30) and the constitution of a moral sphere outside the bounds of political competition. Second, they made these claims in public. In both Brazil and Argentina, human rights organizations utilized the elements of expression proper to the creation of a public sphere in order to make their claims visible: they united their constituencies and addressed the public through political acts such as demonstrations, the publication of reports, and public challenges to government statements.

Human rights movements emerged as defensive organizations in both Argentina and Brazil. The Argentinean Assemblea Permanente por los Derechos Humanos preceded the authoritarian regime and was created in 1975, when kidnapping and political assassination were on the rise (Jelin, 1994). Families of the victims of human rights violations began to organize after the emergence of authoritarianism. The Madres was formed by a group of mothers who met in the corridors of the state bureaucracy searching for information about their sons and daughters. In April 1977, fourteen of them started to meet weekly in front of the government palace, displaying photos of their missing relatives (Brysk, 1994). In Brazil, the emergence of human rights movements coincided with the beginning of liberalization as the relatives of political prisoners and exiles demanded their return or release from prison through a general amnesty. In both Brazil and Argentina, human rights organizations were founded and protected within non-political or pre-political spaces such as the Brazilian Catholic Church (Casanova, 1994). As the names of the Madres, Abuelas, or Brazil's Feminine Committee for General Amnesty indicate, they were defensive movements constructed from basic kinship ties and expressing the most fundamental form of family solidarity: the defense of a relative's right to live. Human rights movements occupied the pre-political space in both Brazil and Argentina because the instrumental politics of the previous democratic period in both countries left no generalizing structures for them to use, even where the right to life was involved. These actors—the victims' families—were the only ones whose bonds of solidarity did not depend on their political convictions. The only other available space, depending on the country, was within religious institutions.[11] Catholic organizations in Brazil and Jewish institutions in Argentina offered their protective umbrella to human rights activists because they were the only institutions whose commitment to life and bodily security was non-political. Human rights movements arose from the initiative of both the families of those directly affected by human rights violations and the efforts of religious institutions to establish forms of socialization and collective action for such families. The road for the reconstruction of the moral foundations of politics thus ran from the retrieval of the familial and religious bases of solidarity to the reconstitution of solidarity at the societal level (Weffort, 1989). These organizations were active during liberalization in publicizing the acts of the authoritarian regimes, disputing the information provided by the regimes about the fates of political prisoners and raising non-negotiable claims at the public level.

The Argentinean human rights movements, which comprised several different organizations with plural foci,[12] made two main public demands: during the authoritarian period it demanded the *aparición con vida of the desaparecidos* (the living return of the disappeared); and, after the disclosure that many political prisoners had been assassinated, it demanded justice and the punishment of those responsible. These claims created a field of conflict with the authoritarian regime and later (as I show in chapter 5) with democratic regimes over the notions of truth and justice. Several episodes between 1976 and 1983 were part of a public struggle over the nature of the actions of the Argentinean state. Between 1976 and 1978 the regime simply denied all charges of human rights violations (Brysk, 1994:57). Silence was also the official attitude of other organizations, such as the Catholic Church and the press. Thus, the first field of conflict between human rights groups and the state in Argentina was around the issue of truth. Human rights groups insisted that there were missing people whom state authorities should account for. In 1979, after several charges of human rights violations were made in international fora, a group of lawyers and legal scholars was invited by the Organization of American States (OAS) to compose an inquiry commission. The very existence of this commission indicated the success of human rights groups in transforming the fate of the *desaparecidos* from a private into a public, international issue. The commission concluded in its final report that thousands of citizens had been killed, confirming the human rights groups' claims (Leis, 1989:20) that the state had violated the right to life of thousands of citizens. This led to a second stage for the human rights movement: the acceptance by Argentinean society as a whole of the legitimacy of its claims, creating a field of conflict over the state's responsibility for the missing citizens.

Argentina's human rights groups faced the task of extending the concern for human rights and the moral foundations of politics from their activists to society as a whole. Although not all Argentinean human rights associations were formed by the families of the victims, many were, and in their first stages they faced a sort of you-and-us societal divide (Leis, 1989). After 1981, human rights movements in Argentina won the general support of Argentinean society, expressed in the willingness of the common citizen to join activities whose main aim was to publicize the illegal acts and the untruthfulness of the dictatorship. The Madres de Plaza de Mayo called for the first public demonstration in support of their claims on the fourth anniversary of their inauguration in 1981: 2,000 people attended despite a police ban on the demonstration (Leis, 1989). Yet, it was only after the Malvinas War that public demonstrations in support of human rights associations' claim of *aparición con vida* started to include established political groups and other societal segments such as trade unions. In June 1983, 50,000 people marched in the streets to show their rejection of the authoritarian regime's account of the fate of missing political activists (Leis, 1989:29–30). On October 5, 1983, 200,000 people signed a petition calling for *aparición con vida*. The road along which the private call for *aparición con vida* (Jelin, 1994) became a general societal claim was a long one along which human rights social movements turned a private plea for solidarity into a public demand for truth and accountability. This transformed the human rights movement from a defensive movement at the level of the lifeworld, defending the right to life, into a movement that established a field of conflict with an authoritarian state on the moral dimension of politics, the content of policies, and the public accountability of government officials. Once it became clear that the *desaparecidos* would not return, the focus of the human rights movement changed: the new democratic Argentinean political society should reject the old regime's account of human rights violations.

As they withdrew from the political scene, Argentina's authoritarian power-holders issued what they called a final document on the war against subversion and terrorism. It supposedly gave an account of what happened and issued self-amnesty for participants in human rights violations. The human rights movements occupied the public sphere to challenge both acts. Again, the question of truth, even if retroactive, became contentious and the center of the attempt to reconnect morality and politics. Public campaigns by different human rights groups placed a past and a future question on the political agenda, each connected to the institutions of the emerging democratic society. How could the new consensus on the reality of human rights violations, mainly a moral consensus, be reconciled with the two central characteristics of politics—pragmatism and the aggregation of majorities? A tension started to develop that has never been resolved: the new societal consensus on the relation between morality and politics involved a truth claim in relation to the past and a moral claim in relation to the future, but it could not establish itself as the organizing principle for the new democratic society.

Brazil's human rights movements followed a very different pattern from those in Argentina, largely because of the greater instrumentalization of civil rights in the Brazilian tradition.[13] Human rights violations have tended to be more widespread in Brazil because of the hybridization between a constitutional tradition and privatistic, hierarchical social relations throughout the nation-building period (W. Santos, 1977; 1979). Civil rights were in principle guaranteed since the enactment of the first constitution in 1824. However, the constitution virtually ignored slavery and did not bother to make it compatible with its legal framework. After the abolition of slavery, there was an influx of former slaves to the major cities and the institutionalization of a tradition of a poor population living at the borders of the law, controlled by the unlawful use of violence (Fausto, 1983). Extra-legal means have been part of the repertoire of the Brazilian police ever since: detention without legal mandate; violation of the physical integrity of detainees; and the use of sheer brutality within the penitentiary system (Pinheiro, 1984:33). Thus, unlike the Argentinean case, human rights violations were part of the everyday administrative practices of the police since the formation of the Brazilian state.

Authoritarianism in Brazil led to an increase in the scope of human rights violations and abolished the divide between those whose civil rights were acknowledged and respected by the state and those whose rights were not respected. Thus, in unleashing the police for political purposes the authoritarian regime did no more than connect the political with the civil police, in effect transferring certain administrative practices from one level to another. In addition, the regime ensured that the courts would not respond to habeas corpus claims—or, when they did, that the state could safely deny being in the possession of the corpus.

Human rights movements in Brazil were created at the beginning of liberalization by making public the networks of social solidarity that emerged in response to civil rights violations. Three main institutions were developed to broaden human rights networks beyond the families of the political prisoners and the Catholic Church: the Brazilian Committee for General Amnesty, the Justice and Peace Commission of the São Paulo Archdiocese, and the Human Rights Commission of the Brazilian Bar Association. All three associations represented either at the personal or political level a reinterpretation of the moral dimension of political action. For the families participating in the Amnesty Committee, struggling for human rights meant reinterpreting their condition as citizens with innate human rights. It implied perceiving the dual or hybrid nature of the enforcement of rights in the country. Even for the Brazilian Bar Association, joining the struggle for human rights represented the renewal of a tradition of supporting rights without making their violation a political issue. Human rights associations in Brazil publicly demanded guarantees for the physical integrity of political prisoners, the reestablishment of habeas corpus, and a general amnesty for political prisoners. These issues were pursued by publicizing human rights violations and by establishing a field of conflict with the authoritarian regime on the truth of its claims and the legality of its actions.[14] General amnesty became a public campaign in Brazil in the late 1970s. Massive demonstrations in all the major cities led the authoritarian regime to broaden its initial offer of a limited amnesty. The amnesty movement's massive occupation of the public sphere led to the effective recovery of the right of free expression. In its attempt to institutionalize the liberalization process, the government introduced civil guarantees that have effectively curbed human rights violations against political detainees.

After the amnesty was won, another issue immediately became the focus of human rights activism: the broad human rights violations against the urban poor. Already in the final moments of the Brazilian transition in 1983, when the democratic opposition won elections for state governors, the problem emerged in the state of São Paulo: a number of killings by the São Paulo police showed clear signs of being executions. People without criminal records were killed as they supposedly resisted the military police. The control of police violence would need to be tackled by a democratic political society if it wanted to avoid a return to the status quo ex-ante. This problem involved an unavoidable political dimension:

how could changes at the public level, which broke with a tradition of ambiguity in relation to civil rights, be connected with a political tradition that had institutionalized the possibility of human rights violations?

Human rights movements in Brazil and Argentina embody the first development that I will analyze in this chapter's concluding remarks: there have been meaningful transformations in the local traditions of political instrumentalization and heteronomous social action. These movements have been able to reintroduce a moral component to public collective action, illustrating a process of cultural change that can lead to a transformation in how social actors constitute a public sphere. They introduced non-negotiable cognitive claims, which can build the foundation for a consensual moral infrastructure for political competition. However, a problem remains: how can the new practices and identities developed at the societal level make their way to the political level, especially where they do not overlap with the aggregative dimension of political society? I address this problem in the next chapter. Before doing so, however, I analyze two types of social movements to emerge during the Latin American liberalization, namely, urban social movements and movements for monitoring political society.

Urban Social Movements in Brazil and Mexico

Social movements seeking to improve the material infrastructure of the urban poor emerged in the largest Latin American cities in the mid-1970s. In some cases, such as Brazilian cities, they coincided with the process of liberalization; elsewhere, they began as issue-oriented movements, as in Mexico City, where the earthquake of 1985 changed the nature of urban politics (Dias-Barriga, 1996). The important novelty of these movements was the establishment of a new field of conflict in relation to how material goods were distributed by the state. Until the mid-1970s in Brazil and the early 1980s in Mexico, the prevailing models had been corporatist and populist, based on political mediators and heteronomous forms of action. Material claims were made through mediators, who brought them into the state (Gay, 1994). This form of mediation between the urban poor and the political system began to unravel as both authoritarian regimes attempted to accelerate their countries' modernization. In a few years cities such as São Paulo, Rio de Janeiro, and Mexico City gained millions of new inhabitants from the countryside through the operation of impersonal economic processes. Determining where they would settle and what kind of access they would have to services and basic urban infrastructure quickly became contentious. In both Brazil and Mexico, the decision to locate the urban poor on the outskirts of the big cities and settle the growing middle class in renewed central areas became a source of administrative and political conflicts. Even where some of the urban poor accepted resettlement, new conflicts emerged because most of the areas they were sent to were poorly served by transportation systems and public sanitation barely existed; many places were not even connected to water mains or power lines. Thus, living in a big city was associated with the experience of being excluded from most of the rights and services provided by the administrative state. The relation of the poor to clientelistic political mediators started to change at this time because of the mediators' political bias or the ineffectiveness of their administrative interventions. In his study of neighborhood associations in Rio de Janeiro, Gay shows that clientelistic political mediators refused to act when slum dwellers in Vidigal faced the prospect of relocation (Gay, 1994:73). Ramirez (1990) shows a similar process following the response of the Mexican government to the 1985 earthquake. With the support of political mediators, the government planned to relocate the poor affected by the earthquake to the outskirts of Mexico City. The population facing relocation responded by creating autonomous associations, even where the population accepted relocation.

These urban social movements renewed political practices at the urban level in Brazil and Mexico in three different senses. In the first place, they changed how material claims were presented, most important by moving to independent forms of association. In Brazil there was a huge increase in the number of neighborhood associations. In Rio de Janeiro, 166 neighborhood associations were created between 1979 and 1981, more than the total number of associations created in the entire previous democratic period (R. Boschi, 1987). In the city of São Paulo between 1977 and 1987, 470 new neighborhood associations were registered by one of the city's eight notaries (Avritzer, 2000). In Belo Horizonte, 387 of the city's 534 neighborhood associations were created between 1970 and 1980 (Avritzer, 2000). In a survey of members of community associations in Belo Horizonte, 60.6 percent of the respondents claimed that they would stop participating in their associations if they established links with political parties (Avritzer, 2000). Thus, it is possible to point to a trend away from clientelistic political mediation toward autonomous forms of organization.

A similar phenomenon developed in Mexico. Urban social movements seeking tenure over urban land or urban services and resources emerged after the mid-1970s, successfully organizing themselves around a national coordinating committee in 1981. These movements challenged traditional forms of political mediation in two ways: they challenged the political incorporation of social movement leaders by not accepting the usual connection between receiving material benefits and party incorporation (Ramirez, 1990:237); and they challenged the decision-making capacity of those with access to administrative planning. After the 1985 earthquake, a new field of conflict developed between the technocratic decision to remove the poor from central Mexico City and the urban social movements' decision to struggle against relocation (Dias-Barriga, 1996). This conflict led the movements to contest the prevailing urban decision-making processes, in particular its exclusion of the initiatives of urban actors. The political culture changed as the leadership of urban movements started to act independently from the guidelines set up by the party-state (Olvera, 1995). The first important change introduced by urban social movements was thus their challenge to the role of political mediators.

The second important transformation was at the level of political practice. Urban social movements changed local politics and the negotiation over the distribution of public goods by introducing autonomous forms of action for social actors. At the level of discourse, the idea of material improvement as a concession to be made by the state was replaced by a claim for citizenship rights. In Brazil, movements for better transportation, health care, infrastructure, and housing articulated their demands as right claims. Banck and Doimo pointed out the growing awareness of urban citizens that material needs entailed rights (1988:126). This discursive change was followed by a change in political practice. Escobar and Alvarez (1992), Gay (1994), Doimo (1995), and Alvarez, Dagnino, and Escobar (1998) note three components of the self-understanding of the new urban social actors: these movements present material claims directly at the public level; they mobilize grassroots forms of support to exert pressure on administrative agencies; and they acknowledge the plurality of their constituencies. Urban movements broke with the idea of one single identity, for instance by recognizing that they had not only poor constituencies but also middle-class constituencies (R. Boschi, 1987; Tarres, 1992).

Finally, Latin American social movements also began to present alternative policies and establish monitoring bodies. Both institutional innovations had important democratic consequences because they challenged two central elements of the prevailing administrative culture: the exclusive access of technocrats to decision-making fora and the assumption of administrative neutrality. Ramirez shows how, in the events following the 1985 earthquake, Mexico City's social actors presented alternative solutions to the housing problem:

> The government's initial reconstruction plans were based on relocation—removing the quake's victims from their inner-city neighborhoods to the periphery of the metropolitan area. This attempt not only denied popular values and traditions but also impinged on le-

gal rights. . . . But the government was forced to change most of [its] plans. . . . The earthquake victims stayed in their neighborhoods and the reconstruction proceeded according to their own plans. (Ramirez, 1990:240)

Observing the movement to improve health and sanitary conditions in São Paulo, Jacobi describes how it developed monitoring capacities vis-à-vis the policies of the city administration. The population of São Paulo grew by more than 60 percent between 1970 and 1980, but the number of health centers increased by less than 5 percent. In the context of precarious health and sanitary conditions, urban social movements organized themselves to demand that these services be improved. Aware of the social planners' tendency to invest in buildings without allocating money for personnel, the health care movements insisted on monitoring bodies; an alteration in an existing law led to the creation of a council for monitoring health policies. In the first election for monitors, 8,146 people participated, electing twelve delegates (Jacobi, 1986:159). Monitoring councils were extended to other neighborhoods in São Paulo and to other cities in Brazil. The movement to improve health conditions was successful in linking health care policies with monitoring by citizens. The Mexican and Brazilian examples illustrate two central features of the new form of occupying the public sphere in Latin America. Urban social movements not only broke with the existing tradition of heteronomous action, they also became sources of policy innovation and formal political innovation through their capacity to propose new political and administrative bodies. Yet, as Brazil moved toward democratization and as negotiations for controlled elections advanced in Mexico, a different problem emerged: how could the innovative potential of urban social movements be sustained when the reactivation of political society meant rebuilding clientelistic networks (Auyero, 1997; Avritzer, 1995; Cammack, 1990; Mainwaring, 1990)? I return to this issue at the end of this chapter, where I consider how the potential introduced by social movements might be extended to the political sphere.

Monitoring Movements in Mexico and Political Campaigns in Brazil

A third important innovation in Brazil and Mexico was the occupation of the public space to demand changes in the practices of political society. Again, these major changes coincided with liberalization and were intimately connected with the restoration of political competition. Mexico and Brazil were similar insofar as both authoritarian regimes tried to sponsor limited political competition. In Brazil, some contestation at the political level had always been allowed, although control over central decision-making was never at stake (Cruz and Martins, 1983). The regime introduced electoral competition at the local and state levels but imposed severe limitations on who could compete (Kinzo, 1988; Avritzer, 1995). The result was a mixed form of authoritarianism that deepened the hybrid characteristics of an already hybrid political system, in particular clientelism and lack of accountability. In Mexico, a similar process was built into the political system at the moment of its institutionalization during the Cardenas period (Olvera, 1995). Mexico has always had presidential elections, but two controls over the formation of political will were built into the political system: the monopoly of political representation through a fusion of party and state (Camin, 1990); and a comprehensive system of fraud built into the electoral process itself. Political liberalization in Brazil (1974–1984) and Mexico (1988–2000) gave rise to public challenges to the hybrid characteristics of the political system because political competition could not bring about real democratization. In Brazil, this challenge took the form of a huge public campaign to restore direct presidential elections, that is, to abolish the mechanism established by the authoritarian regime to make electoral competition feasible. In Mexico, it led to the constitution of a monitoring body capable of publicly challenging the mechanisms of fraud within the political system.[15]

In the Brazilian campaign for direct presidential elections, the occupation of the public sphere led to the completion of the transition or at least to the withdrawal of authoritarian power-holders from the political scene. This campaign involved coordinated action by members of the political opposition and social actors. After a constitutional amendment was proposed in Congress, there was a massive occupation of the public space by social movements, social actors, and members of political society, coordinated with broad forms of public monitoring. Pressure was applied on political society by the independent press and by the social movements themselves. Lists of the parliamentarians in favor of and against direct presidential election were published by the press or posted in the streets, leading many members of the regime's party rapidly to change their position. The reconnection between a hybrid political system and a renewed public sphere did not take place automatically, as transition theories tend to assume, but through an offensive political process, which in the end was only partially successful. Although direct presidential elections were not restored, the *diretas* campaign led to the implosion of political support for the regime in Congress (Mainwaring, 1986). The question that remained, however, was whether the partial reconnection of new political practices that emerged in the public space and political society would constitute a new standard for the relations between state and society. The aftermath of the campaign answered this question in the negative, as broad negotiations within political society between the opposition and the supporters of the authoritarian regime led to a high degree of continuity at the political level between authoritarianism and the newly emerging Brazilian democracy.[16]

In Mexico, the point of departure for both liberalization and the creation of monitoring bodies was massive fraud in the 1988 election. Though several cases of electoral fraud at the state level took place before 1988, the outrageous nature of the 1988 electoral fraud with the interruption of the process of ballot counting as electoral results showed opposition candidate Cuauhtemoc Cardenas taking the lead, and the resumption of ballot counting with later results surprisingly showing the PRI candidate regaining the lead, changed public opinion's conception of the electoral system. The fraud made clear to the public and social movements that, despite the formal political competition, the party-state was not ready to relinquish political power. Thus, the massive fraud of 1988 was a two-sided phenomenon: although the regime succeeded in remaining in power, it signaled to the opposition the need for free and fair elections to reestablish democracy (Aguayo, 1996). Following the acknowledgment of the importance of fair elections, several civic organizations began to monitor local and state elections. In December 1993, seven NGOs with different origins, backgrounds, memberships, and aims—the Mexican Academy by Human Rights; the National Accord for Democracy; the Council for Democracy; the Convergence of Civil Organizations for Democracy; the Arturo Rosenblueth Foundation; the Higher Institute for Democratic Culture; and the Citizens' Movement for Democracy—started to meet with the aim of promoting free elections (Aguayo, 1996; 160). They initiated a project of comprehensive observation, which involved taking polls, advocating electoral reform, and inquiring into cases of vote buying and coercion. On the day of the 1994 presidential election, Alianza Cívica was present at 10,000 polling stations. More than 18,000 Mexican citizens participated in monitoring activities. Alianza Cívica has continued its work monitoring state elections and has been a key player in many subsequent electoral reforms.

Alianza Cívica exhibits two characteristics of new social movements. First, it is based on a non-negotiable cognitive value, namely political fairness. It breaks with the Latin American tradition of subordinating normative concerns to strategic or substantive interests by defending the non-negotiable principle of political fairness at the societal level. One innovation thus consists in its renewal of the moral foundations of political competition and trying to expand them to the political level.

While this might make Alianza Cívica an exclusively defensive movement, its second major innovation lies in its attempt to develop a non-administrative, societal form of decision-making. Since the 1994 election,

Alianza Cívica has advanced the proposal of a citizens' control institution in charge of the process of electoral organization. In spite of many clashes between Alianza Cívica and the political parties, particularly the PRI, on the issue of the autonomy of the IFE, a form of electoral fraud control finally emerged in Mexico in the mid-1990s placed at the societal level. (I will discuss the emergence and transformation of the IFE in chapter 6). In this sense, as we have seen in Brazil, it is clear that the process of renewal at the societal level has not been transferred to the political system. It only has been able to establish a new framework of acceptable practices within a hybrid political system that continues to include non-democratic practices and establishes a tension between the public and the political levels. Again, the question that remains is how to make the innovations at the societal level operative at the political level in a democratized setting.

POLITICAL INNOVATION AND DEMOCRATIZATION: AN ANALYSIS OF THE LATIN AMERICAN PUBLIC SPHERE

The liberalization of authoritarian regimes prompted a reevaluation of Latin America's long tradition of political instrumentalization and hybridization. The novel ways in which new and old social actors occupied the public sphere reflected an internal evaluation of their previous political practices and beliefs (Dagnino, 1998). We have seen how this process led to three innovations in the occupation of the public sphere. First, the movements tried to introduce moral limits to political competition, leading to a new field of conflict around the non-negotiable nature of rights, in particular human rights. Second, they brought about changes in how material demands were expressed, leading to new conflicts over how to deal with these demands at the political level. In these conflicts, material claims came to be understood either as ways of constituting cultural identities (Alvarez, Dagnino, and Escobar, 1998) or as social rights. Third, social movements and voluntary organizations developed forms of campaigning and monitoring that represented formal innovations vis-à-vis the tradition of popular mobilization inherited from the previous democratic period. Thus, a central development during liberalization in Brazil, Argentina, and Mexico was a renewal in the constitution of the public sphere.

The apparent innovation of the social movements that emerged during democratization in Latin American was subject to three types of critique: one political-institutional, one historical, and a third material. The political-institutional critique challenged the existence of a renewed drive for social autonomy on the part of social movements. Foweraker argues that "although popular social movements may aspire to autonomy, they must seek to survive in the real world of institutional politics" (Foweraker and Craig, 1990:44). This argument gives shape to a widespread misconception concerning the nature of the innovations introduced by Latin American social movements, which understands the drive for autonomy as excluding any attempt to make moral or material demands at the political/institutional level.[17] Yet, a central aspect of political renewal in Latin America was precisely the effort to present claims institutionally without being dragged into the old corporatist, clientelist structure. Thus, autonomy—as an innovation in the constitution of the public sphere—did not entail the refusal to act strategically or to present claims (Munck, 1990), but a change in social actors' understanding of how to connect themselves to the political realm. Latin American social movements introduced two principal innovations in this regard: movement leaders refused to be incorporated into the state structure in exchange for the acceptance of their demands; and they did not renounce independent forms of association and public presentation of demands in exchange for the acknowledgment of their demands. In this sense, they innovated precisely in establishing a new type of relationship with the state, a project fully compatible with the drive for organizational autonomy from the state.

The historical critique argued that the actors who participated in renewal during the liberalization period were not as new as the literature has claimed. Knight reviews different mobilizations in Mexico's history to point out that a long national tradition of protest has been "maintained by myth, legend, and symbols passed down . . . from generation to generation" (Knight, 1990:88). Assies similarly remarks that in Brazil "neighborhood associations had existed before 1964 . . . with the establishment of the urban social movement literature a phenomenon that had existed for some time acquired a new name and a new significance" (Assies, 1994:83). In both cases, a historical argument is presented as empirical evidence against societal renewal, yet these authors miss two important dimensions. First of all, the fact that a movement or an association existed for a long period of time does not prove that there has not been renewal. Thus, in the case of Argentina, the fact that human rights associations had existed in the country since the 1930s does not prove that the human rights movements of the 1970s and 1980s did not lead to a significant process of renewal. On the contrary, the form of mobilization at the public level and the creation of a field of conflict with the political system concerning the morality of political action were in fact innovations introduced by human rights movements. The fact that they were associated with the proliferation of human rights groups made these groups more important, but the point here is that one should look to the significance of the facts rather than the mere presence or absence of certain empirical elements. The same holds true for neighborhood associations in Brazil: the issue is how they asserted their autonomy and how they transformed material demands rather than whether a handful of such groups already existed in the late 1950s.

The third critique challenged the idea of renewal by pointing to the nature of the demands presented in public. Authors such as Azevedo and Prates (1991) argue that the novelty of new social movements lies in their post-material values but that this element was lacking in countries like Brazil. For them, movements such as urban social movements were not new because they were organized around material claims. Again, the authors miss the link between materiality and innovation. New social movements in the West also presented material claims linked to identity, as was the case with the feminist movement. Thus, the novelty of a social movement lies not only in the post-material nature of its claims but also in how social actors understand their claims. The decisive fact in the case of Latin American urban social movements was the way they linked collective action to a new language for expressing material claims and a new form of discussion and organization. Thus, it is possible to argue that Latin America saw a significant renewal in the form of occupying the public space, one that led to a new understanding of the nature of the public sphere and its relationship to political institutions.

The response to the three critiques brings us back to the discussion on collective action during the processes of transition. Transition theory approached liberalization with tools provided by the democratic elitist tradition. Two analytical arguments are presented to explain the high level of societal activity during this period. The first, advanced by O'Donnell and Schmitter, is based on rational choice theory and related to the decreasing cost of political participation. According to O'Donnell and Schmitter, the reduction of the level of political repression allows new forms of collective action and the emergence of new political identities (1986:48–49)

This understanding of the relationship between liberalization and participation combines a democratic elitist line of explanation with a rational choice interpretation of the motives for collective action. The moment liberalization begins, collective action increases due to the lower cost of political participation, whereas in the moment of redemocratization, collective action decreases because its costs and benefits have to be weighed against other forms of political representation. A second explanation for the increase in public participation during the liberalization period is the substitution approach. For authors such as Stepan (1988), public participation during the process of liberalization was motivated by the unavailability of the instruments of political competition and representation. Thus, collective action increases when political society is outlawed and decreases when political representation is restored, an analysis which would in the first place require that Latin American political parties indeed be instances of political participation, which, with the exception of Chile, has not been the case.

From this vantage point, the central feature of liberalization was the provisional nature of the ways in which social actors occupied the public sphere; once democratization took place, political society would automatically replace civil society. Transition theory explained the social actors' occupation of the public sphere by the fact that the cost of action was lower for social actors than for political actors. Once the costs of action became equal for everyone, the occupation of the public sphere would give way to political society. Thus, transition theory analyzed action in the public sphere through the elite-masses dichotomy: the masses had to occupy the public sphere because elites were prevented from doing so, but once the costs of elite action fell, they would resume their traditional place in politics by restoring normal political competition. In this sense, social forms of occupying the public sphere should be seen as provisional. However, the central fact of the Argentinean, Brazilian, and Mexican transitions is that the ways of occupying the public sphere developed by voluntary associations and social movements became permanent forms of collective action. Human rights movements did not leave the public space in Argentina or Brazil, nor did groups claiming material goods or monitoring political procedures in Brazil and Mexico. Not only did the issues not leave the public space, but the ways of promoting them remained essentially the same, as I show in chapter 5. Thus, the ostensibly provisional nature of these forms of public action has been refuted by political developments after democratization. These forms of action remained essentially the same because their new ways of raising foundational moral claims, presenting material demands, and criticizing prevailing political practices represented a reevaluation of the political tradition and could therefore not be reduced to the fight against authoritarianism. They also expressed opposition to a hybrid political system that found its worst expression in authoritarianism, but was not limited to it.

The problem the new Latin American democracies have still not solved is how to redesign democracy to strengthen the demands for renewal against the tradition of hybridization. In the next chapter, I argue that two frameworks are available for understanding the relationship between the public sphere and the political system. The first, which I have been criticizing throughout this study, is that of transition theory, which either ignores these changes (in O'Donnell and Schmitter's version) or accepts them without problematizing the transfer of their potential from the public to the political level (Linz and Stepan, 1996). The second framework is provided by Habermasian social theory, which locates innovation at the societal level, but also fails to problematize the transference of these potentials to the political system. In the next chapter, I analyze the relationship between the public and the political level in each of the three cases examined in this chapter—human rights, material demands, and public campaigns—to show that only a stronger version of a public sphere theory, one that relinquishes some deliberative capacities to the public level, can preserve the innovative potentials hitherto insulated from the political system. It is to this process that I will link a conception of full democratization.

CHAPTER FIVE

ℰℛ

Democratization in Latin America
The Conflict between Public Practices
and the Logic of Political Society

The formation of a democratic public sphere in Latin America during the transition from authoritarianism to democracy posed a problem for the new democracies: how to connect the newly emerged public sphere with the recently reempowered political society. This represented a problem both for those who argued that the organization of social actors during the authoritarian period was facilitated by the outlawing of political society (O'Donnell and Schmitter, 1986; Oxhorn, 1995) as well as those who saw the emergence of a democratic public space as the result of a long-term change in social actors' self-understanding (Weffort, 1989; Avritzer, 1994, 1995; Olvera, 1995, 1997; Peruzzotti, 1993, 1997; Costa, 1994, 1997; Jelin, 1994; Alvarez, Dagnino, and Escobar, 1998). In the first case, the existence of organized actors within an active public sphere constitutes a problem because it "unnecessarily" broadens the political agenda, introducing elements that might contradict electoral competition or pose unnecessary strains on political society. Some authors have argued that even demands for human rights or the rule of law would cause such a strain.[1] For those who saw the emergence of a new organized public space as a fundamental break with a previous societal tradition, the fact that the public sphere organized itself during the transition to democracy constituted a problem because the relation between the actors who occupied the public sphere and the reconstituted public arena would have to be considered a new issue to be tackled by social actors.

Within theories of democracy and democratization, the problem of the relationship between organized actors at the public level and political society received two solutions, neither of which was able to cope with this tension. The first was provided by Linz and Stepan within the framework of what they called "arenas of democratization": "[I]f a functioning state exists, five other interconnected and mutually reinforcing conditions must also exist and be crafted for a democracy to be consolidated: . . . a free and lively civil society . . . , a relatively autonomous and valued political society . . . , the rule of law . . . , a state bureaucracy . . . , and an institutionalized economic society" (1996:7). Linz and Stepan argue that even if democratization occurs in more than one arena, political society, and thus the restoration of electoral competition, should be primary (8). Yet, even if the authors' terms are assumed to be correct, the priority of political society is problematic, especially where social actors at the public level played a central role in overthrowing authoritarianism. Oddly enough, the "arenas of democratization" perspective argues for a complete harmony between the actors of civil society and political society: "[P]olitical society, informed, pressured and periodically renewed by civil society[,] must somehow achieve a workable agreement on the myriad of ways in which democratic power will be crafted and exercised" (10).

Linz and Stepan's conception of a workable agreement on the ways political power must be exercised corresponds to what Przeworski coined recently as political accountability, a situation in which rulers are periodically elected and might or might not be sanctioned by citizens for their acts. Przeworski reinforces the democratic elitist aspect of democracy by emphasizing citizens' inability to give instructions to governments between elections. According to this perspective, citizens and elites are connected through processes of accountability during the electoral moment. "Governments are 'accountable' if citizens can discern representative from unrepresentative government and can sanction them appropriately, retaining in office those incumbents that perform well and ousting from office those that do not. An accountable mechanism is, thus, a map from the outcomes of actions . . . of public officials to sanction by citizens. Elections are a 'contingent renewal' accountability mechanism, where the sanctions are to extend or not to extend the government's tenure" (Przeworski and Stokes 1999:10).

Przeworski's concept of accountability and Linz and Stepan's understanding of a workable agreement between civil and political society during democratic consolidation show a common weakness. Both perspectives assume, in a rather naive way, that processes of accountability will work, that is, that political society will be effectively held accountable or that the connections between civil and political society will lead to a workable agreement. However, processes of transition to democracy involve different ways of reconstituting political society, different ways of restoring the rule of law, and different relations between the actors that emerged at the public level and the political system. The very idea of arenas of democratization shows that the pace of democratization within each of these arenas will be different. Thus, for instance, restoring the rule of law is, perhaps surprisingly, easier in the countries in which the legal system did not have any autonomy during the authoritarian period (Chile and Argentina) than in countries that passed through a semi-legal form of authoritarianism and experienced greater legal continuity between authoritarianism and democracy (Brazil and Mexico). This is so because in the cases in which authoritarianism changed the structure of the rule of law, it is almost impossible to enforce retroactively the rule of law in relation to the period previous to democratization. Linz and Stepan's argument assumes a reverse way of conceiving the relationship between social actors at the public level and political society: in cases where social actors played a large role in democratization and political society was outlawed for most of the authoritarian period, there is a problem reconnecting the two dimensions. Thus, instead of allowing democratization theory to integrate the different arenas, Linz and Stepan's approach, by giving priority to political society, makes the relationship among civil society, the political system, and the rule of law a political desiderata unable to tackle the tension between the different arenas of democratization. In fact, the implementation of political accountability in such a situation is often more difficult than these authors assume, as I will show in this chapter.

The second approach to the relation between the public space and the political system is provided by Habermasian democratic theory. Habermas also supposes that there is a distinction between the public and political society. Within a democratic system, he argues, "binding decisions to be legitimate must be steered by communicative flows that start at the periphery and press through the sluices of democratic and constitutional procedures situated at the entrance of the parliamentary complex and the courts" (1995:356). Unlike Linz and Stepan, Habermas assumes that there is a tension between communicative debate at the public level and the administrative practices of the modern state. Thus, to legitimate its decisions, modern administration must seek to connect itself with a process of communication that starts at the periphery of the political system and might or might not make its way into the political system.[2] Accordingly, instead of working with the concept of accountability, Habermas's analysis works with the idea of legitimation problems (Habermas, 1975, 1984). Yet, there is connection between political accountability and the Habermasian concept of flows of communication between the public and political society. This connection arises from Habermas's functionalist conception of the operation of the political and administrative subsystems. By assuming that "interaction mediated by legitimized power is systemically rather than socially integrated." (McCarthy, 1991:166),

Habermas too easily assumes the operation of both political and administrative accountability. Both are conceived as the result of automatic exchanges between the public space and the political system. Yet the problem in recently democratized societies is precisely to make these exchanges operational. Thus, Habermas's theory tells more about how an ideal democracy should work than about what democratic social actors should do if they wish to broaden the limits of the democratic system in which they live. In this sense, the theory presented in *Between Facts and Norms* offers little as a theory of democratization.

My method in this chapter is the reverse of that adopted by Linz and Stepan, Przeworski, and Habermas. Instead of departing from the likelihood that the practices that emerged at the public level will be integrated by political society (parties, parliament, and the state administration), and hence that political accountability is a necessary consequence of democratization, I assume that the relation between public social actors and the reconstituted political society has to be derived directly from the logic of the transition itself and the specific means by which political society was reconstituted. I analyze how Brazilian, Argentinean, and Mexican political society reacted to social actors' demands on issues such as respecting human rights, introducing structures of political accountability, and respecting the autonomy of the societal realm. I analyze such issues according to the following criteria: (1) the nature of the transition and the way it allowed pockets of authoritarian and non-democratic practices to survive; (2) the majoritarian or minoritarian nature of the demands made by social movements and the way they reverberated at the political level; and (3) the level of integration within the political system between the actors who were part of the reinterpretation of practices that occurred during democratization and the actors who became the leaders of the opposition and crafted the transitional pacts.

Brazil, Argentina, and Mexico followed very different paths of democratization. Argentina's transition, like that of Greece, was a classical case of transition by collapse caused by defeat in war (Stepan, 1986). The defeat led to a rapid deterioration of the authoritarian regime's capacity to rule and to its disorganized withdrawal from the political scene. Argentina's defeat in the Malvinas War led to the resignation of the military president General Galtieri. General Leopoldo Bignoni then led the military on an eighteen-month disorganized return to the barracks, after which the transition to democracy was completed (Zalaquett, 1996a:21).

In Brazil, the authoritarian regime conducted a process of transition lasting eleven years (1974–1985). The authoritarian regime lost control of the transition only after it was defeated in state elections in 1982 and after the political success of a massive campaign for direct presidential elections (Avritzer, 1995). Nevertheless, the withdrawal of the Brazilian authoritarian regime from the political scene was organized. Moreover, the regime had a civilian branch, which continued to be politically viable in spite of its huge defeat in the first congressional elections after the completion of the transition.[3]

Mexico, in contrast, has seen an endless, non-pacted transition with almost permanent renegotiation of the rules for electoral competition. The long duration of the Mexican transition was related to two facts: the impossibility of a pact between the two main opposition contenders; and the fact that the PRI stayed in the middle of the political spectrum, flanked on the left and right by the two opposition parties. Thus, the only chance of partially completing the Mexican transition would be a victory of one of the opposition parties in a non-pacted election, as happened in the case of Fox victory in 2000.

The difference among the three transitions as far as political society is concerned is that there was much greater continuity between the authoritarian regime and political society in Brazil and Mexico than in Argentina. In Argentina, authoritarian power-holders left the political scene immediately after their defeat in war and the completion of the transition; in Brazil there has been more continuity between authoritarianism and democracy with political society reflecting this continuity. It is too early to evaluate the Mexican transition, but it is already clear that it will present the largest degree of political continuity for two reasons: first, because the PRI has been a strong social force, particularly in the countryside; and second, because the aftermath of Fox's victory already shows that the non-pacted elements of the Mexican transition will influence its process of democratization and will not preclude the possibility of recomposition of the PRI.

This chapter has four parts. In the first three I develop a model for understanding the relation between the claims made by social actors at the public level and the decisions taken by political society on three major issues: human rights policies, the distribution of material resources at the local level, and the establishment of rules of political accountability and civil autonomy. I will assume that all these issues represent a good measure of the operation of mechanisms of administrative and political accountability in the new democracies. I will show through an analysis of human rights policies in Brazil and Argentina, of clientelism in Brazil, and of the introduction of standards of political accountability in Mexico that there has been a gap between the attempt to move to a democratic system and the actions of political society in each case. Based on this analysis, in the concluding section I propose an alternative to Linz and Stepan's, Przeworski's, and Habermas's models of political society's relationship with the public sphere in the new democracies. I will argue that political and administrative accountability involves a long and short cycle and that, in Latin America, the continuous interruption of the long cycle by political and administrative conflicts requires what I call the creation of deliberative spheres with the presence of social actors.

HUMAN RIGHTS IN BRAZIL AND ARGENTINA

The different paths of transition as well as the different ways in which political society was reconstituted led, as table 5.1 shows, to different relations between social actors and political society regarding human rights. In Brazil, human rights organizations were formed during the first phase of the transition (1974–79) as a reaction to human rights violations. This was when the Truth and Justice Commission of São Paulo's archdiocese and the Brazilian Committee for Amnesty were formed. The claim for amnesty became an important public issue as the authoritarian regime tried to create a competitive electoral environment. Some former political leaders were in exile and a system of full electoral competition required their return. Thus, in Brazil amnesty was the result both of the authoritarian regime's attempt to avoid persecution for its human rights violations and of demands made by social actors (Zalaquett, 1996). In this sense, it indicated the authoritarian regime's control over the process of transition and at the same time the success of social movements' pressure at the public level. Precisely because of the success of the amnesty, human rights issues were left off the democratization agenda in Brazil.

In contrast, human rights were at the center of negotiations during the Argentinean transition. In spite of their public nature and international support, very few of the demands for truth and justice made by Argentinean human rights movements in the first phase of the authoritarian

TABLE 5.1
Influence of the Transition on the Relation between the Public and Political Society

	Nature of the Transition	Form of Reconstitution of Society	Type of Amnesty	Influence of Human Rights Movement on Political Society	Result
Argentina	collapse	reevaluation of conception + continuity of actors	self-amnesty as part of the retreat of authoritarian power-holders from politics	high	human rights policies were part of political society program
Brazil	long-term process of negotiation	continuity with previous political society	amnesty partially met the demands of social actors	low	political society ignored human right issues

period (1976–82) were granted by the regime. In addition, the process of settling accounts with the past, which took place during the eighteen-month transition, was completely one-sided and ad hoc. On April 28, 1983, the regime responded to the demand for truth by saying that all the missing were dead. On September 22 of that year, it issued an amnesty for all criminal offenses committed for political motives—a blatant act of unilateral self-amnesty (Zalaquett, 1996a:22). Thus, in contrast to the Brazilian case, in Argentina the human rights issue became central to the process of democratization and created a strong connection between social actors' demands at the public level and the newly reconstituted political society. I will briefly analyze each of these cases and later compare how the tension between the public and the political emerged in each case.

The Human Rights Issue in the New Argentinean Democracy: The Tension between Morality and Force

The new Argentinean democracy is a good example of the tension between the commitment of members of political society to reconnect morality and politics and the obstacles to such a reconnection within the country's political tradition. The election of Raul Alfonsín as president in 1983 represented the best possible political choice for pursuing what Linz and Stepan call a "workable agreement" between social actors and political society. Alfonsín had been an early activist for the human rights cause, making for a perfect match between the concerns of human rights movements and the reorganization of political society. In addition, the collapse of the old regime entailed a low degree of continuity between authoritarianism and democracy. In his opening speech to law-makers, Alfonsín stressed such a change of course by proclaiming the intention of his government to "resume [the state] tradition as defender of the rule of law and civil liberties" (Brysk, 1994:64). In December of the same year, Alfonsín sent two decrees to Congress, one declaring the necessity of prosecuting leaders of the armed opposition and the other aimed at bringing to trial the nine officers who formed the three military juntas. In February 1984, Law 23.049 was enacted, whereby "all crimes committed by members of the security forces in the context of anti-subversive operations should be tried by the Supreme Council of the Armed Forces. It also provided for an appeal to the civilian Federal Courts of Appeal" (Zalaquett, 1996a:23).

The Alfonsín government's decision to try the commanders of the military juntas and crimes committed by the security forces reinforced the logic established by human rights movements at the beginning of the transition. The discussion of the former regime's human rights violations thus assumed a public nature. Two important public activities took place during the inauguration of the new Argentinean democracy: the establishment of Conadep (the National Commission on the Disappearance of Persons) and the trial of the junta's generals.

Conadep was established as a commission of notables in charge of investigating human rights violations during the authoritarian period. The commission was made up of five members of human rights organizations and members of the two houses of Congress. It worked over a nine-month period, during which it was able to document 9,000 unresolved disappearances and identify 340 clandestine detention centers (Brysk, 1994:70). The commission publicized its findings in a book called *Nunca Mas* and also a television series. *Nunca Mas* became the best-selling book in the history of Argentina and more than one million people watched the television series. Thus, the first important dimension of the attempt to integrate human rights movements' actions with the state's attempt to deal with the human rights violations proved to be very successful: public awareness of human rights violations increased, and as it increased the problem of how to carry out justice became more acute.

The second important public way of dealing with the past in Argentina was the trial of those responsible for human rights violations. At this point the tension between social actors and political society started to surface. The Alfonsín government favored a limited trial that would bring the former leaders of the armed forces to some form of justice. However, the executive's lack of control over both public opinion and the judiciary—which is normal in a democracy—transformed the trials into a much more important issue than the government had expected or wanted. The trials began in April 1985 in the civil courts after the military court had argued that "it could not judge the alleged crimes because the order issued in the war against subversion was unobjectionable" (Brysk, 1994:76). The public impact of the trials in the civil court far exceeded the government's expectations. Witnesses' accounts of how they were abducted and mothers' accounts of how they searched in vain for their sons and daughters had a huge impact on Argentinean society (Leis, 1989:43). The sentence condemning five of the nine defenders and opening the way for implicating many more created a sharp divide between the public and the political sphere. On the one hand, it showed that within political society the courts were less subject to the pressure of the military than were the political parties and parliament. On the other hand, the latter started sharply to separate themselves from both public opinion and the courts, as subsequent events revealed.

During the 1987 Holy Week a group of military officers seized a barrack in an area called Campo de Mayo and demanded the end of the trials. Social actors' reaction was immediate: "[B]etween 100,000 and 200,000 people gathered at *Plaza de Mayo* and provincial capitals. After a few days of back and forth negotiations it became clear that no one within the armed forces would be willing to repress this small group of officials. . . . That was when the population using its private means of transportation occupied the gates of the barracks" (Leis, 1989:49). At the same time that the population occupied the access to the barracks, the Alfonsín government took the opposite stand, deciding to negotiate with the rebels. A few weeks after the end of the rebellion, the Alfonsín government proposed the "due obedience" law, which made the military chiefs of the junta solely responsible for state terrorism. All other military officials and soldiers were excused on the grounds that they had only followed orders from above. The obedience law represented the government's change of will in its attempt to replace force by morality in settling accounts with the past.

A close analysis of the way the new Argentinean government dealt with the human rights issue shows that even in cases in which human rights becomes a central component of public discourse, its internalization by political society can be problematic. In the Argentinean case, two types of tension between public opinion and political society emerged. The first tension appeared between force and morality as the basis of political action. Contra authors who assume the compatibility of social practices and the management of political power, the Argentinean case shows that the problem of connecting the two dimensions can be complicated in situations where the means of violence are not fully controlled by the state. Autonomous pockets of power continued to exist after the end of authoritarianism and political society's response to this was at best ambiguous. Political society was responsive to social actors' demands to reconnect morality and the exercise of political power, but it did not have enough power to impose this conception on all sectors of the polity. Thus, a gap emerged between, on the one hand, the growing consensus on the necessity of enforcing the rule of law that emerged from the public activities of Conadep and the trials of the junta and, on the other hand, the impossibility of carrying out this consensus at the political level. Although no one can criticize a state that backs down from its promise to carry out justice under the threat of force, the Uruguayan case shows that such a retreat is more legitimate when it involves mechanisms of public deliberation.[4]

The second tension was between the legal system and the rest of political society. The Argentinean case also illustrates the different dynamics that can emerge between the public sphere and political institutions. The fact that human rights movements mobilized public opinion made it easier for the judicial system to make legality the sole consideration for bringing former human rights violators to justice. Again, the Argentinean case poses problems for both Linz and Stepan's theory of a workable agreement as well as Habermas's conception of a flow of communication because it shows that the connection between the public and political society can vary according to the institutions involved. Political parties are, in this case, driven by a majoritarian logic whereas the judiciary follows a more legalistic logic.[5] Yet even in cases such as the Argentinean one, in which the legal system was willing to stick to its logic, it is possible to argue that political accountability is blocked by the political system, as has been the case with Menen's amnesty of human rights violators. Thus, the problem faced by the new Latin American democracies regarding political accountability is that the electoral process does not guarantee citizen control over the political process. On the contrary, incidents such as the Campo de Mayo episode show that the political system is not always strong enough to assert its own logic and that the public may be obliged to act in order to detain non-democratic actors. Thus, the full cycle in which elections play the role of a contingent renewal mechanism never reaches its end. In its place we see the interruption of the political accountability process by the irruption of social actors at the public level. However, while social actors can limit the uses and abuses of power, they cannot impose sanctions at either the political or legal level.

Human Rights in the New Brazilian Democracy: The Tension between Legality and Administrative Continuity

The Brazilian case, although very different from the Argentinean, is also a good indication of the tension involved in the new Latin American democracies between a new consensus at the public level, in particular among human rights associations, and the pragmatic decisions taken by members of political society. Brazil's point of departure differed from Argentina's (see table 5.1) in three respects. First, the Brazilian authoritarian state did not sponsor the proliferation of decentralized apparatuses of political repression. On the contrary, very early in the *abertura* it decided to curb the unauthorized actions of the repressive apparatus, keeping the number of dead and missing much lower than in Argentina. During twenty-one years of authoritarianism in Brazil, 240 people were "killed in action" and around 150 disappeared. The lower number of missing and dead as well as a previous tradition of police violence accepted by the Brazilian left made the trial of human rights violators a low priority on the democratization agenda. Second, Amnesty in Brazil involved the effective liberation of political prisoners and the return of political activists from exile. In this respect, it met the demands of the opposition. There was therefore no political group in Brazil proposing to annul the amnesty in spite of the fact that it failed to address the responsibility of members of the state apparatus in human rights violations. In Brazil this issue was effectively tabled.[6] Third, Brazil's transition was very different from Argentina's as far as the form of reconstitution of political society was concerned. Congress was not outlawed and there was always an opposition party. Congressional elections were never interrupted in Brazil despite the huge restrictions on free political organization until 1980 (Avritzer, 1998). As a result of the semi-legal form of Brazilian authoritarianism (Linz, 1973), there were fewer restrictions on political organization during the authoritarian period but also more continuity in administrative practices once democratization took place. These three factors together help explain the human rights policies of the new Brazilian democracy.

The new democracy's human rights policies were characterized by a sharp divide between an idealistic acceptance of human rights principles on the one hand, and administrative practices and political decisions completely contradicting the ostensible policies on the other. Between 1985 and 1990, the Brazilian government submitted the International Agreement on Civil and Political Rights for congressional ratification, signed the International Convention on Torture, and even accepted the presence of monitoring missions inside its territory (Pinheiro, 1996a:20). During the Constituent Assembly of 1987–88, a very broad definition of civil rights was adopted, allowing federal intervention in cases of human rights violations (17). Thus, at the legal level, Brazil's political society, like Argentina's, accepted the integration of human rights within the newly emerging normativity. However, as in Argentina, the new normativity collided with surviving pockets of authoritarian culture. In Brazil, these pockets were related not to the past but to the present—the violations of the human rights of the rural and urban poor by military police. Already during the Constituent Assembly, a tension emerged between the intention to follow human rights precepts and a decision not to change the administrative and judicial structure of the military police. The military police was already known to commit human rights violations. The ability to curb such human rights violations was limited during the authoritarian period by the existence of special military tribunals—introduced by the semi-legal authoritarian device of a law decree in 1969—with the prerogative to judge crimes committed by the military police. This structure was retained and incorporated into the new democratic regime by article 124 of the Constitution of 1988 (Human Rights Watch, 1997:21). Thus, from the very beginning there was ambiguity within Brazilian political society between the normativity it wanted to abide by and the administrative structure it wanted to keep, a structure responsible for human rights violations.

Human rights violations in the new Brazilian democracy were against two groups: the urban poor and landless peasants.

Violence against Landless Peasants

Conflict over the tenure of rural land is common in Brazil, a country with one of the highest concentrations of land ownership in the world. The Constituent Assembly allowed agrarian reform only in the so-called non-productive lands, despite the fact that 65.6 percent of the country's fertile land belongs to only 1.9 percent of landowners (Dimenstein, 1996). A movement of landless peasants for agrarian reform has been strong in Brazil since the late 1970s and early 1980s, when the first massive occupation of land took place in Ronda Alta. The Movement of Landless Peasants (MST) took to occupying non-productive land which, according to the 1988 Constitution, should have become available for agrarian reform. In so doing, it created two broad fields of tension in the new democracy. The first relates to the application of the law. The tenure of rural land in Brazil is usually legally controversial. Many land-tenure certificates are falsifications of tenures belonging to the state itself, as in the case of the Pontal do Paranapanema in the state of São Paulo. Nevertheless, the government fails to enforce the law in such cases. The second field of tension is among the military police, the judicial system, and the landless peasants. Many conflicts arise during occupations of unproductive lands and the military police is often called in to force the peasants to withdraw from occupied land or to liberate blocked roads. Such conflicts frequently result in mass killings of peasants.

In April 1996, in a place called Eldorado dos Carajás, nineteen people were killed by the military police of the state of Pará in an attempt to liberate a blocked road. The military police argued that the killings were the result of a conflict in which it was attacked. However, evidence soon emerged of executions of landless peasants; landowners even suggested off the record that the killings had been commissioned. Because it was up to the military police to conduct the investigation, it was deeply flawed, revealing a lack of administrative accountability. It was not possible to determine individual authorship of the murders because routine administrative procedures, such as gun registration and timely gunpowder examiniation, had not been performed.

The justice system had no alternative but to propose collective responsibility, despite its contradiction with the rule of law. In the Eldorado dos Carajás case, even after the jury was transferred to outside the conflict area, the officers involved in the operation were all acquitted. The main reason for acquittal was administrative flaws in the process (FSP, August 30, 1999). Public opinion strongly disapproved of the government's handling of the case, in which the lack of minimal structures of administrative accountability became evident. Public opinion also condemned the legal system's handling of the case. However, the disapproval of the government's handling of human rights cases remained an isolated episode that did not influence electoral outcomes. The possibility that Congress would change the law on the special forum for military police charged with civil crimes only slightly increased.

Violence against the Urban Poor

In large Brazilian cities it is up to the military police to respond to crimes. The military police has special "shock units" whose task is to make what is called in Brazil "ostensive policing." In the periphery of large Brazilian cities, ostensive policing leads to a high rate of "killings in action." A São Paulo journalist investigated 4,179 cases of citizens killed by São Paulo's military police and found a pattern of police killing suspects, including those who gave themselves up, those who resisted arrest, and those who tried to flee (Barcelos, 1992; Dimenstein, 1996:86). Human Rights Watch described how punishing human rights violators is systematically evaded by the military courts: "[T]he military justice system is administered in such a way as to make the convictions of policemen for violent crimes almost impossible. Crimes committed by the military police are investigated by the members [of the] military police who, not surprisingly, almost always determine that homicides were the result of shootouts" (Human Rights Watch, 1997:22).

Attempts to address the pattern of human rights violations in democratic Brazil show two large areas of tension between public opinion and political society.[7] The first is between political society's willingness to support human rights formally and its unwillingness to support the legal and administrative changes needed to enforce them. In this regard, it is instructive to analyze the inability of the Brazilian Congress to approve a law that would move the trials of military officers from military to civilian courts. Such a law was first proposed by former prosecutor and São Paulo MP Hélio Bicudo. It lay abandoned in Congress for many years until it became Bill 899 in 1995 and was approved by the lower house in 1996 in the aftermath of the Eldorado dos Carajás massacre. Law 9.299 received a last-minute amendment in the Senate, which limited the jurisdiction of civilian courts to common crimes committed by the military police while preserving the military courts' jurisdiction in two key areas: informing the legal processes and trying violations of physical integrity (FSP, September 20, 1996). Thus, the Brazilian case, like the Argentinean one, illustrates the survival of pockets of authoritarianism within a democratic order and the ambiguity of political society to such pockets. In Brazil, this ambiguity is more problematic because political society is not threatened by force. Nevertheless, most of its members are not willing to defend the human rights of the poor; in some cases, they share the beliefs of human rights violators.

The second source of tension concerns the punishment of human rights violators. Especially when public opinion is engaged, the courts in Brazil and in Argentina show more willingness to take human rights abuses seriously than political society or local administration. Yet in Brazil, unlike Argentina, the courts lean more toward indemnifying the victims than punishing the abusers, and sometimes their decisions might even help human rights abusers evade justice.[8]

The Brazilian case illustrates the problem of enforcing human rights in new democracies where there is a large measure of continuity within political society during the process of transition. The murder of landless peasants shows the difficulties in establishing a connection between the public's support for human rights and the actions of the legal system. Again, as in the Argentinean case, instead of a connection between public opinion and political society there is a tension caused by the fact that a public consensus does not become the standard of political behavior. This tension cannot be solved through an automatic connection between the public and the political. Thus, the issue of political and legal accountability returns to the forefront of our discussion. Political and administrative accountability cannot be established in these cases because of the lack of institutions and political will to enforce the existing human rights laws. The result is again a crisis in which social actors' (in this case landless peasants') occupation of the public space only serves to point out the absence of the public control and sanction that are characteristic of the democratic system. Again, it is clear why the concept of accountability cannot explain this dimension of the new democracies. The electoral agenda is broad and plural. Human rights beliefs might inform the general functioning political institutions, but unless they become a central issue, as in the Argentinean case, it is very unlikely that they will become a pressing political issue. Thus, political accountability in Przeworski's sense is unable to connect the public and the political in the case of human rights issues (Przeworski and Stokes, 1999). In addition, continuities from the old regime create a tension between political society and public opinion because new beliefs about the importance of human rights, which emerged during the transition, start to compete at the level of political society with a strictly majoritarian logic, which refuses to bring human rights to the forefront of the political agenda. The level of mobilization of public opinion is central in this respect, as the Argentinean case shows when it is compared with the Brazilian: it was precisely because human rights reached the top of the Argentinean political agenda that courts could enforce human rights and political society could try to reconnect itself with the rule of law. In Brazil, there has been no support in

Congress for a law that would condemn human rights abusers in the present and curb future violations.

The gap between public opinion and political society around human rights again poses problems for both Linz and Stepan's concept of a workable agreement and Habermas's idea of a flow of communication. The high level of tension between the two dimensions in the Brazilian and Argentinean cases requires an alternative explanation of their relationship in new democracies. In the concluding remarks of this chapter I will show how conflicts like the ones discussed here lead to the interruption of the accountability cycle, a cycle that assumes citizens periodically distinguish between representative and unrepresentative governments by either restoring power-holders to or removing them from administrative positions. The cases I have presented in this chapter show a different dynamic in the new Latin American democracies. According to this new dynamic, the accountability cycle does not come to a close because the government's lack of control of human rights issues leads to public mobilizations against the political system. The result is a crisis that leads to the interruption of the cycle and to the notion that public opinion lacks the instruments to control and sanction its power-holders. The interruption of the accountability cycle is precisely the point that demands an alternative theorization of the relationship between the public and the political system. In the next parts of this chapter, I will characterize the same process in two other areas: the role of political mediators in negotiating the delivery of material goods (Brazil); and the inability of the existing laws to make public officials accountable to citizens (Mexico). I will then point out the analytical implications of the three cases.

RECLIENTELIZATION IN BRAZIL

Brazil is a case in which political society strengthened clientelism as a direct result of the return to a competitive electoral system. In Brazil, the logic of political competition led to renewed clientelism due to the unwillingness of democratically elected presidents to negotiate their policies in Congress. Elected presidents in the new Brazilian democracy have resisted restoring Congress's role as a mediator in the decision-making process. Thus, clientelism is strengthened as a way of dissociating the restoration of congressional prerogatives from the executive's desire to keep tight control over the decision-making process. As a result, material concessions to MPs and their electoral bases are exchanged for their support of the executive's agenda. The drawback of this policy is that it reduces the autonomy of social actors in negotiations over material goods and strengthens the role of political mediators—a role that, as I showed in chapter 4, was weakened by the creation of autonomous forms of claiming material goods. Allow me to explain in detail why reclientelization in Brazil poses a problem for theorizing the relationship between the public and political society.

In Brazil, redemocratization resulted from both the erosion of support for the authoritarian regime in Congress and the articulation of an independent opposition at the societal level. In the Brazilian case, the social movements and voluntary associations that emerged at the public level did not make a significant effort to connect themselves with political society, nor did political society made an effort to integrate social actors or to become responsive to their demands. An attempt to find an institutional solution for this tension between renewal at the public level and continuity at the political level was made during the authoritarian period. Through two constitutional amendments in 1977 and 1982, an institutional reform changed the balance between modern and traditional constituencies in the Brazilian Congress. It granted a minimum of eight MPs to every state and imposed ceilings on the heavily populated states.[9] Thus, less modern and more rural states would be proportionally overrepresented relative to the modern parts of Brazil, where the opposition to authoritarianism was stronger. Through this move, the authoritarian regime established a contradictory logic between public actors and their practices and political society. On the one hand, the move to voluntary forms of association and to the rejection of political mediators increased between the 1970s and the 1990s (see chapter 4); on the other hand, the political power of clientelist politicians also increased.

The second factor tending to strengthen clientelism in post-authoritarian Brazil concerned the relationship between the executive and Congress. Since the early stages of modernization, this relationship was marked by a tension between the need of a very active executive to have safe majorities in Congress and the politicians' demand to use the state apparatus to deliver the concessions of pork-barrel politics. The result was a contradiction between the administrative standards required for economic development and the administrative inefficiency characteristic of clientelist policies. A cycle of authoritarian periods, in which the executive branch isolated itself from Congress, and democratic periods, in which the executive maintained its prerogatives by clientelistic means, has been part of Brazilian politics at least since the Vargas period (Cammack, 1990; Avritzer, 1998). Thus, as democratization took place in 1985, the new Brazilian democracy faced two options concerning state-society relations: it could restore the balance between citizenship and the distribution of social resources and political power, moving in the direction of what Linz and Stepan call a workable agreement with social actors; or it could increasingly rely on clientelistic mechanisms, if it chose to retain them.

Brazilian political society, represented by its four civilian presidents, opted for the second course.

Clientelism in the new Brazilian democracy is a system operating between Congress and the executive. At the executive level, the Ministry of Planning is responsible for distributing federal resources to local administrations. In the first year of the Sarney government—Brazil's first civilian government after authoritarianism—a network of exchanging material resources for political support was put in place. The Ministry of Planning, the central institution of the developmental state, was transformed into a mechanism for organizing patrimonial exchanges. A new minister was picked for his background as a negotiator of government concessions (Dimenstein, 1988). Throughout 1987 he transformed the Ministry of Planning into an agency devoted to getting support for the president in the Constituent Assembly. In order to do so, he set up a system for distributing resources on political grounds. At the congressional level, each year MPs propose amendments to the federal budget; the approval of these amendments, as well as the release of the funds, depends on the support the MPs are willing to give to the executive's proposals in Congress. Since resources have to be distributed on a political basis, there is little control over how these resources are employed. Dimenstein (1988) reports cases of institutions linked to MPs without an office receiving government funding. A considerable part of the resources received by institutions like this go to finance electoral campaigns or to build patrimonial networks of support. This system has allowed for a disconnection between political society and public opinion in central issues of the post-authoritarian period, such as extending the mandate of the first civilian president, key votes during the Constituent Assembly on issues such as agrarian reform, and the reelection amendment of current President Fernando Henrique Cardoso. The system has been maintained by all democratically elected presidents. Allow me to explain its operation and the conflicts it generated between political society and social actors at the public level in each of the presidential mandates.

During the Sarney government (1985–90), when clientelism was adapted to a democratically elected Congress with full prerogatives, planing agencies and welfare institutions linked to the federal government were transformed into institutions whose resources were spent according to political criteria. The relationship between citizenship and the application of federal government resources was abolished. In a survey of the resources distributed by the Ministry of Housing in 1987, Mainwaring found that the state of São Paulo, with almost one-fourth of the population of Brazil, did not receive any funding and Rio de Janeiro received only 8 million cruzados, whereas the state of Amazonas, with 1 percent of Brazil's population, received 520 million (Mainwaring, 1990). Two criteria became crucial in the distribution of central government resources: the construction of political support at the local level and the fulfillment of demands from poor and rich clienteles. The networks of patrimonial political support in post-authoritarian Brazil are built from the center to the bottom through a system that rewards and punishes mayors of small and midsize cities who depend on federal government resources. Their loyalty to governors—or, in the case of governors hostile to the Sarney government, their direct loyalty to the president—becomes a sine qua non condition for receiving government resources. At the same time, once a local or state government receives the federal government's support, it provides jobs for its constituencies or projects to be allocated to their wealthy clients. In some states of the northeast, during the Sarney government, as much as 35 percent of the workforce were employed in public administration (Mainwaring, 1991). This system became so pervasive that it destroyed the efficiency those agencies had attained in previous periods. At the state and local levels, the overemployment of under-qualified personnel increased the weight of payrolls on the total budget without, most of the time, providing better services to the population. Wealthy clients become the financiers of very expensive electoral campaigns, which made them the favorite bidders for public works. The latter were overpriced, a generalized system of kickbacks was established, and political campaigns became more expensive as the practice generalized.

The clientelist system introduced by the Sarney government posed problems for the relationship between public actors and political society and blocked the establishment of political accountability. Patrimonialism proved a useful strategy for winning elections and building majorities in Congress. Yet it could not connect itself to modern forms of control and accountability due to the reaction of organized sectors of society to particularistic political practices. The use of patrimonialism leads to a large number of suspicious deals between government and MPs which have their center in the Ministry of Planning, leading under the Sarney, Collor, and Cardoso governments to the interruption of the long cycle of political accountability through the emergence of political scandals.

The publication of a list of congressmen who lobbied for special resources and the amount involved in each case was the first big scandal involving a president in post-authoritarian Brazil. A Parliamentary Inquiry Commission (CPI) was set up to investigate the acts of the minister. After a few weeks of investigation it came very close to holding the president responsible. His own state received 16.5 percent of the total resources dispersed by the Ministry of Planning. Most of which were misused and involved generalized corruption. Sarney survived the condemnations, which would have led to his impeachment by negotiating votes in Congress. The first congressional hearings to investigate a president in post-authoritarian Brazil showed the limits of workable agreements between the public and the political system. On the one hand, the use of clientelism is instrumental to winning elections. On the other hand, the practices introduced by clientelism, once they are revealed, acquire an explosive dimension that short-circuits the mechanisms of political accountability, leading to the presumption on the part of public opinion that the available legal controls over public authorities will prevail. However, these mechanisms do not always prevail, and even when they do, the Brazilian experience shows that clientelism continues after the trial and removal of certain officials due to its connection with the internal logic of electoral campaigns and the building of majorities in Congress.

The mandate of Brazil's second civilian president, Fernando Collor de Mello (1990–1992), was a decisive experience concerning the difficulties of establishing a workable agreement between actors at the public level and political society. Collor de Mello belonged to the traditional oligarchy of a very poor state in Brazil's northeast. Members of his family and his wife's family together held seventy-five political jobs in their state, including the governorship, three federal congress seats, two state assembly seats, and dozens of top echelon jobs (*Veja*, September 4, 1991). The president campaigned against traditional political oligarchies but could never prove his independence from them. As president, Collor de Mello inherited from the Sarney government the federal mechanisms of patrimonial politics. Collor de Mello not only kept most of these mechanisms intact but personalized their use. He generalized the already broad system of kickbacks and monopolized it in the hands of his former campaign treasurer. In so doing, he further particularized the state and contributed to the reduction of his capacity to compensate the poorer clients who voted for him. The state lost not only the capacity to perform any administrative role but also the ability to generate minimal standards of social cohesion. Due to its incapacity to generate a universal political relation with its constituencies, the Collor government had to appeal to the particularistic forms available, such as releasing public funds to MPs' electoral districts and accepting the political nomination of administrative personnel in state agencies and public banks in exchange for support in Congress. In exchange for their nominations, these nominees released public funds to MPs' districts. The drawback of the whole system is that it goes around the existing mechanisms of administrative control, fostering administrative wrongdoings.

The influence-peddling system set up by Collor de Mello collapsed when the president's brother gave an interview to a weekly magazine stating that the president was the chief organizer of the influence-peddling system (*Veja*, May 27, 1992). The Collor government initially denied this. A CPI was formed, similar to that which had investigated the previous government. The government expected the same result; as the president's chief of staff stated clearly: "[T]his commission will lead nowhere." However, contrary to the president's expectations, the C.P.I. acquired real power because it expressed the new conception of public action held by social actors who had been active since the mid-1970s. Millions of people went to the Brazilian streets asking for the removal of the president. Such an act reestablished a partial connection between actions in the public space and actions at the level of political society. The CPI's report concluded that "the President received unlawful economic advantages which were in conflict with the rule of law and incompatible with the exercise of the presidency" (FSP, September 25, 1992). Ninety percent of Congress approved the impeachment of the president one month later. Collor de Mello's removal shows again how the conflict between actors at the public level and political society ignites a mechanism that can short-circuit the process of political accountability. This mechanism blocks the completion of the cycle described by Przeworski, in which elections operate as a contingent accountability mechanism. What takes place instead is an interruption of the process of representation with the substitution of the members of political society holding administrative positions.

Collor de Mello's impeachment was not enough to bring a halt to the system of exchange of material goods for political support. This system continues to operate during the Cardoso government (1994–2002), which institutionalized it by pre-setting the amount of resources to be distributed in a clientelistic way. Each MP is allowed to propose up to twenty amendments every year to the federal budget. In 1996, a local election year, US$600 million were set aside for the patrimonial budget, leaving on average roughly one to $1.5 million in amendments for each MP (FSP, 1996). Most MPs opted in 1996 to divide the resources under their control. Thus, for a public works project budgeted at US$2 or 3 million, an MP could present an amendment allocating US$200,000, which means its forecasted conclusion could be fifteen or more years away. In June 1996, 2,214 public works projects involving more than US$15 billion were not expected to be completed because the necessary resources were not budgeted. There is no requirement that an MP who originally proposed a project continue to ask for resources for its completion.

Reclientelization in Brazil poses a double problem for connecting the public sphere to political society. At the level of representation, it severs the connection between political will and political representation because it interferes with public debate during the law-making process, replacing it with the exchange of material goods. At the level of local public spheres, clientelism disempowers local associations and publics by cen-

TABLE 5.2
Characteristics of the Brazilian Transition

Nature of the Process of Transition	Relationship between Authoritarianism and Political Society	Form of Reconstitution of Political Society	Influence of Social Actors and the Democratic Opposition on Political Society	Result
long-term process of negotiation	semi-legal authoritarianism with congressional elections	through changes of the political rules	low	reclientelization as an attempt to maintain executive prerogatives

tralizing resources and thereby transferring deliberative capacity from these publics to the executive. In both cases, it creates a tension between the public and the political system precisely regarding deliberation: political society as a deliberative body renounces its deliberative capacity in exchange for material resources. In addition, clientelism reverses the mechanisms intrinsic to the logic of accountability because political mediators threaten citizens with the withdrawal of public services if they do not get the expected vote in exchange for concessions. In this sense, it reverses the logic of control proper to mechanisms of political accountability (Fox, 2000), as table 5.2 shows.

In the concluding remarks of this chapter, I will reflect more generally on the problem of the relationship between the public sphere and political society in light of this case.

THE CONFLICT BETWEEN THE RULES OF PUBLICITY AND THE LOGIC OF MAJORITARIAN POLITICS IN MEXICO

Mexico's transition was different from both Argentina's and Brazil's. Mexico was a case of a long-term and stable authoritarian regime centered on three poles: corporatist forms of social control that only began to shake up after the 1985 earthquake (Olvera, 1995); a state-party monopoly on appointing public officials that endured from 1929 to 1983, when the regime for the first time acknowledged defeat in local elections and let the opposition assume office in twenty-five cities (Blum, 1997:33); and, last but not least, a dichotomy between the law and the regimes' political practices. On the one hand, unlike in Argentina and Brazil, the authoritarian regime in Mexico never outlawed elections. On the contrary, there has been no interruption in the structure of electoral competition at any level from 1929 onwards. On the other hand, the fact that the opposition never won elections between 1929 and 1983 points to the possibility of electoral hegemony based on continuous fraud. The growth of political support for the National Action Party (PAN) in the northern parts of the country during the 1980s and the growth of the PRD in the federal district increased concerns about electoral fraud. As I showed in chapter 4, political rights and clean elections became a field of conflict between the authoritarian regime and the opposition. This conflict primarily involved two areas. First, negotiations to change the electoral law became stronger as the opposition acquired the capacity to win general elections (1988) or local elections, as was the case in San Luis de Potosi and Guanajuato in the early 1990s. The second area of conflict was in electoral monitoring, especially the autonomy of monitoring institutions. These institutions reduced the leeway of the authoritarian regime and challenged its central feature, the predictability of presidential succession.

In this section, I will discuss the logic of the Mexican transition to democracy and how it created a tension between established legality and the organization of social actors at the public level. In the first case, I will show how Alianza Cívica challenged the existing structures of political and legal accountability by appealing in a political campaign to existing legal mechanisms such as petition rights and *derecho de amparo* (writs of security) to receive information about the office of the president. The fact that the government could afford not to rely on existing law created a legitimacy problem and revealed the tension between laws guaranteeing political accountability and a political practice that does not take the law into account. The second case also concerns the tension between the law and actual practice. Its differs from the first case, however, in that it does not involve making the government itself accountable, but rather shows the attempt to control societal forms of organization that demand political accountability. Both cases point to the heart of the contradiction of the Mexican political system before its full democratization (which might or might not take place with the election of President Fox in July 2000). The tension emerges from the contradiction among the letter of the law, the structures of political and legal accountability that it prescribes, and prevailing political practices.

The first case of conflict between social actors in the public space and political society took place during a campaign called "Adopt an Official" (*adote un funcionario*). The campaign was based on a proposal made by the Mexican Academy for Human Rights to take advantage of the existing laws in order to monitor public officials.[10] The campaign was based on articles 6 and 8 of the Mexican Constitution, particularly article 8, which establishes the conditions under which petition rights can be exercised. According to the Mexican Constitution, "all officials and public emplyoyees should respect petition rights, if the former are exercised in a written and respectful way" (Constitucion Politica, 2000). Alianza Cívica launched the *adote un funcionario* campaign toward the end of 1994 to test the limits of the law and to make its enforcement binding on public officials. The first dimension of the campaign was educational: citizens were informed about how to exercise petition rights through the explanation of the law. Members of Alianza Cívica were informed about the nature of the law and advised to write petitions to officials based on a standard form, which included seven points: the name of the authority on whose activities information was being sought; the name of the citizen seeking the information; his or her address; the clear expression of the information being sought; the reasons why such information was being requested; the place and date of the petition; and its official whereabouts (Alianza Cívica, 1995a). Thus, as in the Brazilian case, the campaign was directed at the elementary bases of political accountability.

The first public official "adopted" by the campaign in the beginning of 1995 was the Mexican president himself. Given that almost 25 percent of the presidential budget was labeled as a secret fund (*partida secreta*), two members of Alianza Cívica exercised their petition rights in March 1995 (Olvera, 2002) by asking the president to make public the following information: "a complete diagram indicating all the president's offices and advisors . . . an explanation of the spending of funds which by law have been designated to the nation's president . . . information about the amount of public funds received by the president and his monthly income. . . ." (Alianza, Cívica, 1995b).

Almost a year passed during which time no response from the Mexican president was forthcoming. Under these conditions, Alianza Cívica's leadership decided to utilize another legal instrument in the Mexican constitution, the so-called *juicio de amparo* (writ of security), an instrument that in the Mexican legal tradition allows a citizen who had his or her rights violated to appeal to a federal judge (Olvera, 2002). Again, the campaign *adote un funcionario* had an educative dimension. Alianza Cívica distributed to all its local offices a document explaining what the *juicio de amparo* was and in which situations it could be exercised. In its written document to a federal judge, Alianza Cívica's leadership made the following allegation: "[T]he action which is the subject of this petition is the unjustified failure on the part of the responsible authority to respond to our written petition. . . . As Mexican citizens exercising our rights to petition and information, we direct this demand to the president of Mexico, Dr. Ernesto Zedillo Ponce De Leon. . . . We are identifying his failure to respond as an action in violation of our rights" (Alianza Cívica, 1996a). Alianza Cívica asked the federal judge to decide on the merits of its claims and to take action in order that the responsible officer, in this case the president, answer the earlier petition. Again, what was at stake in that case was the capacity of written law—in particular, existing legal structures for political accountability—to be binding on officials exercising political power. Unexpectedly, the judge ruled in favor of Alianza Cívica, with the president's lawyers interposing several requests for revision, showing their intention to go around the law and not present the required information (Olvera, 2002).

At a press conference in June 1996, Alianza Cívica raised the issue of the lack of public knowledge of the president's income and his use of discretionary budget power. According to Alianza Cívica, "the lack of information on year end compensations or stipends that raise monthly salaries, led to a great deal of ambiguity with respect to the president's total income" (Alianza Cívica, 1996b). Available information on the presidential budget showed that the Mexican presidency had a secret, discretionary fund of $86 million. In addition, the so-called line 00023 of the federal budget, aimed at protecting public servants' salaries, absorbed roughly $2 billion. Thus, Alianza Cívica publicized the information it had and asked for a public form of accountability on the employment of such resources. The next day, the office of the president issued a public announcement denying the facts disclosed by Alianza Cívica. According to the briefing, the president's salary had been reduced 52 percent in that year due to the devaluation of the peso and budget cuts proposed by the president. To this day, despite the favorable judgment of the writ of security at the lower court levels, it is still not known whether the presidential announcement contained the right data. In June 1997 the presidency gained its appeal and had the judge who first ruled on providing the required information revoke her decision. This case shows the limit of legal instruments for political accountability in situations in which there is a tension between the existing laws and actual practices. At the end of the *adote un funcionario* episode, the mechanisms of political accountability proved themselves useless. The only result of Alianza Cívica's political campaign was to show the basic ambiguity between the existing law and its enforcement. The cycle of political accountability did not take place because the law intended to trigger accountability mechanisms did not manage to intervene effectively. Given the legal continuity involved in the electoral form of completion of the transition with Fox's election in July 2000, it is not clear that this will change significantly.

A second case, involving the creation of National Political Association (APN) legal status and the subsequent denial of this status to Alianza Cívica, also illustrates the dilemmas of legal institutionalization in Mexico. Since the victory of the PRI's candidate in the 1994 election, negotiations took place involving the government, the parties, and the civic movements with a view to reforming the electoral law. (I will fully approach the Chapultepec negotiations in the next chapter). The negotiations made sense according to the logic of both the Mexican authoritarian regime and its transition. Due to its tradition of incorporating social claims, the regime was willing in many situations to trigger negotiations concerning electoral laws. This was the case in the 1996 electoral law in which, among several novelties, the regime acknowledged a new definition of APNs, and the creation of a new status for civic associations. Article 33 of Electoral Code on Institutions and Electoral Rules (COFIPE) defined APNs as "citizenship associations whose role is to help the development of democratic life and political culture as well as the development of a better informed public opinion." This new definition was considered an innovation in relation to the old regulation, under which APNs were considered proto-parties or parties that could not get their registration. The introduction of a broader conception of APN was thus considered an attempt to integrate several civic associations into public life. The law required several procedures for a civic group to become an APN, among them the presentation of a petition with 7,000 signatures and the existence of organized branches in ten states in the country.

Alianza Cívica opened a discussion to register itself as an APN by the end of 1996. This move was contested both inside and outside the association. Inside Alianza Cívica, some of its members feared its transformation into a political group, since the law opened space for APNs to nominate candidates for electoral offices. Alianza Cívica rejected this possibility but decided to file for registration as an APN, keeping a pluralistic, open, and non-partisan profile. In the action plan it filed for registration as an APN, it described itself as having five aims: the organization of citizens' groups to exercise their political rights; electoral polls; electoral observation; the monitoring of public employees; and the defense of citizens' petition rights. According to the plan, in order to accomplish these aims, Alianza Cívica should refrain from nominating its own political candidates; that is, Alianza Cívica was at the same time seeking to become an APN and keeping its non-partisan character. In order to make this distinction clear, Alianza Cívica proposed an organizational principle: no member of Alianza Cívica as a voluntary association would be obliged to join Alianza Cívica as an APN (Alianza Cívica, 1997a). Yet even within the organization there was disagreement over becoming an APN. Alianza Cívica branches in the states of Jalisco and Sonora did not accept the move, many of them fearing that its independence to monitor elections might be compromised by becoming an APN.

Alianza Cívica's application for APN status was accepted with restrictions by the IFE. Its application was approved, provided that the group agreed to revoke its program of electoral monitoring, giving it two choices: it could renounce the aim of monitoring elections or become ineligible for public funding and tax exemptions (McConnell, 1998:5). In their resolution, the general councilors of the IFE[11] made the following remarks: "[T]he action plan of the association filing for acknowledgement as an APN includes among its activities electoral observation, which according to the electoral code on institutions and electoral proceedings (COFIPE) is an activity not supposed to be performed by parties or political organizations" (IFE, 1997). Thus, the conflict between Alianza Cívica and the IFE concerned the exclusive prerogative of state institutions to monitor elections. Instead of acknowledging the autonomy of social sectors to decide on their own organizations, the recently constituted IFE followed a long tradition of state intervention into the activities of civic associations.

Alianza Cívica appealed the IFE's ruling, filing a document in which it made the following claims: (1) that it maintained a differentiation between its constitution as an APN and its constitution as a voluntary association; (2) that the law and its interpretation by the IFE general council violated the autonomy of the voluntary associations; and (3) that electoral observation was a right of Mexican citizens and could not be legally restrained. Thus, Alianza Cívica's argument was that the law was being used to curb a legitimate citizens' activity. The application to reconsider the ruling was not accepted by the IFE in spite of the fact that around forty different types of voluntary associations were acknowledged by the IFE's general council as APNs, showing that the distinction between a political party and a national political organization was a fact, and that the acknowledgment of Alianza Cívica was a political issue. In a document issued February 22, 1997, Alianza Cívica decided not to change its constitution and remain a voluntary association committed to electoral observation.

These two cases are good examples of how the law can be utilized by the state to disconnect the public from the political system. This can be explained by the semi-democratic nature of the Mexican political regime prior to the 2000 elections, in which elections and the functioning of the legal system reflected the PRI's unwillingness to relinquish power. However, it also poses a problem for understanding the role of law in "new democracies," because other Latin American democracies share the semi-legal nature of the Mexican regime and were prevented by institutional continuities from overcoming this instrumentalization of the law after democratization. The consequence of the instrumentalization of the law is that the available instruments for the exercise of accountability cannot be utilized by the citizens, establishing a perverse dynamic between the public and the political system. In Mexico, a semi-legal authoritarian regime until July 2000, due to the non-enforcement of the instruments of political accountability, elections could not play the role of distinguishing between representative and unrepresentative government. On the contrary, at the end of each electoral cycle there has always been doubt about whether the new government reflects the citizens' will. This has led the

PRI government to propose many changes in the electoral rules, trying at the same time to keep control of the electoral process. What is not clear even as the Mexican transition seems to come to completion with the electoral removal of the PRI candidate is whether the parallel structure of legal and societal control will survive the PRI's electoral defeat. If it does, elections and political accountability will not, as in the Brazilian and the Argentinean cases, be linked. In this chapter's concluding remarks I will analyze the issue of accountability in terms of the non-overlap of the public and political dimensions, showing the limits of the analytical frameworks based on legal structures of accountability in the new Latin American democracies.

Political Society, Accountability, and Deliberation

Redemocratization in Argentina, Brazil, and Mexico accentuated the conflict among the timing, values, and beliefs involved in public forms of action and the internal logic of restoring political competition. New democratic identities and democratic and autonomous forms of association and expression were introduced in all three countries as a result of a change in social actors' understanding of the moral foundations of politics and their autonomy vis-à-vis the state and political society. Yet no institutional devices exist to mediate the relationship between actors and practices at the public and political levels. I approached this issue in this chapter from both an empirical and analytical standpoint. I chose four empirical examples, one in Argentina, two in Brazil, and one in Mexico, to show that central elements of democratic practice—such as ensuring the rule of law, respecting human rights, pursuing a monopoly over the means of coercion, respecting the principle of citizenship in the distribution of social resources, and accepting legal forms of social control—become sources of political tension in the new Latin American democracies. At the same time, political actors had no difficulty establishing continuities with the pockets of authoritarianism that persisted in all three countries for basically two reasons: first, because of the strong legal and administrative continuity between authoritarianism and democracy due to the semi-legal nature of authoritarianism, particularly in Brazil and Mexico; and second, because of the strong continuity in actors and practices in such important institutions as the army, the police, the judiciary, and the political system.

I utilized these four empirical examples to analyze theories of democracy and democratization that acknowledge a distinction between the public and political realms in order to find out how they conceived this relation. I singled out two theories, Linz and Stepan's idea of a workable agreement and Habermas's conception of a flow of communication, as a

TABLE 5.3

Pattern of Relations between Public Social Actors and Political Society

	Claims of Social Actors	Position of Political Society	Main Determinant of Political Society's Position
Human rights in Argentina	truth and punishment of human rights abuses in the past	truth and selective justice	use of force by surviving pockets of authoritarianism
Human rights in Brazil	punishment of human rights abuses in the present	partial political support in contradiction with administrative actions	political influence by pockets of authoritarianism
Distribution of social resources in Brazil	autonomy and participation in the distribution of resources	distribution of resources through clientelistic mechanisms	necessity of political majorities in Congress overcomes demand for autonomy
Political accountability and social autonomy in Mexico	control of public officers and social autonomy	for PRI rejection of both claims; for PRD and PAN, prudent distance	demarcation between public actors' claims and internal negotiations of political actors with the regime on electoral competition

guide to approaching the issue. From the two approaches I deduced a conception of political accountability. Table 5.3 shows how the relationship between the public and political society evolved in the four cases.

An attempt to apply either Linz and Stepan's or Habermas's theory to post-democratization settings faces the problem of how to cope with pockets of authoritarianism and their capacity to establish links with political actors and influence the political culture. Thus, neither a "workable agreement" between the public and political system nor a direct flow of communication can be established for two reasons. First, the practices that could constitute the background of an agreement between social actors and the political system are still disputed by social actors and members of political society. This assertion does not assume that there is a societal consensus on all the practices required for the existence of democracy. Rather, it means that a significant process of renewal has taken place at the social level and that the adoption of different types of institutional designs could strengthen or weaken democratic practices.[12] However, table 5.3 shows that there is a contradiction between the requirements inherent in the competitive logic of political society and the claims made by a democratic public sphere, a contradiction related to the fact that in post-democratization settings it is possible to build majorities by non-public means.

The second reason has to do with the instrumentalization of legal institutions. Linz and Stepan and Habermas make a common assumption about the role of the legal system. For Linz and Stepan, a workable agreement between the actors of civil society and political society requires that "all significant actors—especially the democratic government and the state—must respect and uphold the rule of law" (1996:10). Habermas goes further, establishing a direct connection between the deliberative dimension of democracy and the rule of law: "[T]he democratic principle states that only those statutes may claim legitimacy that can meet with the assent of all citizens in a discursive process of legislation that in turn has been legally constituted" (1995:110). Thus, both theories operate on the assumption that the law acts as an automatic transmission belt between the consensus achieved at the public level and a deliberative process at the political level. Yet in the new Latin American democracies, the operation of the legal system is part of the problem for connecting the two dimensions.

The conflict between actors at the public level and practices at the level of political society poses a very difficult problem for establishing structures of political accountability precisely because accountability presupposes the existence of a connection or flow of communication between the public and the political. If we take, again, Przeworski's definition of accountability as citizens' capacity to use the electoral process "to retain in office those incumbents that perform well and ousting from office those that do not," we can note that the problem involved in establishing structures of political accountability in the new Latin American democracies is that the cycle of accountability cannot come to a close. In our four examples, none led to such a close. In the Argentinean conflict over making human rights violators responsible for their acts, the political system had to reverse the results achieved by the public trials. In the Brazilian case of human rights abuse by the military police, no condemnations were made. In both cases, there is no cycle of either administrative or political accountability because there is a founding ambiguity in the legal structure and in the political actors. This fosters the feeling in public opinion that the differentiation between representative and unrepresentative government cannot be made because political actors act autonomously of the electoral process. Thus, the political legitimation provided by the completion of the long cycle of political accountability never takes place; instead, there is a permanent crisis of legitimacy. In the Brazilian case of reclientelization, again the long cycle of accountability does not come to a close because the incumbents' mandates are either interrupted by impeachment, as in the case of Collor de Mello, or, even worse, suspicions of corruption are not investigated and impunity prevails. Again, the distinction between representative and unrepresentative government does not take place, leaving the citizens with the impression that their electoral choice is between two different forms of unrepresentative government. In the fourth case (Mexico), the structure responsible for providing citizens with structures of accountability showed its inability to do so, and again the long cycle of political accountability never takes place because the existing law is unable to regulate the interaction between citizens and their political representatives. In all four cases, instead of mechanisms of accountability, we see a crisis caused by the tension between public demands for accountability and the inability of the political system to satisfy these claims.

In a recent text, Guillermo O'Donnell triggered a discussion on the problems of establishing mechanisms of accountability by pointing out the lack of mechanisms for horizontal accountability in the new Latin American democracies. O'Donnell distinguishes between the electoral mechanisms described by Przeworski, which he calls mechanisms for vertical accountability, and what he calls mechanisms for horizontal accountability. According to O'Donnell, the new Latin American democracies suffer from the lack of horizontal mechanisms, described as the existence of

> state agencies that are authorized and willing to oversee, control, redress, and if need be sanction unlawful actions by other state agencies. The former agencies must have not only legal authority but also sufficient de facto autonomy vis-à-vis the latter. What I am talking about of course, is nothing new and goes under the familiar heading of separation of powers and checks and balances. It includes the executive, legislative and judicial branches, but in contemporary polyarchies also extends to various oversight agencies, ombudsmen, accounting offices, fiscalias and the like. (1998:119)

O'Donnell attributes the absence of these instruments to the absence of two traditions, liberalism and republicanism.[13] It is possible to see in this approach, as in those more fully criticized in chapter 1, the presence of an elite perspective in which the analysis of the shortcomings of democracy is related only to elite practices. Another problem with O'Donnell's framework is that he conflates under the same heading two different processes: citizens' control over their representatives and the separation of power between branches of government, a mechanism that in some cases makes government accountable but has been devised to limit intra-branch abuses of power. Often, this latter mechanism has a completely internal modus operandi, as when the mechanisms for evaluating the actions of public employees remain non-public (even impeachment processes have non-public dimensions). In such cases, they are not linked to structures of accountability.

A different, not incompatible line of analysis emerged recently in Latin America, proposing to add a third dimension to discussions of accountability: the societal dimension. Peruzzotti and Smulovitz (2002)[14] define societal accountability as "a non-electoral, yet vertical, mechanism of control that rests on actions of multiple arrays of associations, movements, or the media aimed at exposing governmental wrongdoing." The authors bring a new dimension to the accountability debate, but their theory faces one major problem: it appears that the sanctioning of wrongdoing lies beyond the power of public actors who pursue accountability. In order to work, societal mechanisms of accountability require the action of either administrative or political control mechanisms. I would prefer to call them societal mechanisms for calling for accountability, mechanisms that involve actions at the public level, as I described in this chapter.[15] However, the problem with these mechanisms is that they call for accountability but do not produce it, precisely because they have to break with the modus operandi and the long cycles of both administrative and political institutions. Societal calls for accountability mean that neither the normal cycle of the representative system nor the legal cycle of administrative agencies can operate as usual. It is precisely at this level that conflict between public actors and the political system emerges in the new Latin American democracies.

Brazil, Argentina, and Mexico show that the legal connections between the public and the political system are more complex and require an alternative theory. In regard to the connection between the public and the political, such a theory proposes to substitute accountability for the public forms of deliberation I proposed in chapter 2. This points to the importance of two issues at the center of our analytical discussion. The first is strengthening deliberative capacities at the public level at the expense of elite-based structures. The empirical cases in this chapter have shown that the majoritarian logic of political society strengthens the pockets of authoritarianism that survived democratization. Some of these pockets, such as parallel violence in Brazil and Argentina, were only strengthened due to the overrepresentation that insertion into political society gives to such values and forms of behavior. Thus, privileging deliberative fora or deliberative mechanisms that are clearly related to the new emerging public space could allow new actors (members of neighborhood associations and human rights activists), new values (societal autonomy), and new forms of political behavior (monitoring) to make their way into mainstream political behavior.

There is also a second, institutional issue, directly connected to the previous discussion of elites. Contra both Linz and Stepan's and

Habermas's formulations, the institutional problem in new democracies cannot be reduced to connecting renovation at the public level with traditional forms of representation and deliberation (that is, parties, parliament, and courts). The institutional problem has to be understood in different terms, namely, as how to design institutions that can strengthen innovations which emerged at the public level while, weakening the continuities of traditional political culture at the level of the political system. The link between a new public space and deliberation has to be strengthened in three senses: in its capacity to encourage reflection on participation; in its capacity to strengthen democratic values; and in its capacity to increase the occasions in which deliberation takes place (Joshua Cohen, 1998). In the next chapter I will use two examples of participatory deliberation to show how these analytical conclusions can be made effective. I will analyze them in the participatory budgeting introduced in some Brazilian cities and in the formation and *ciudadanización* ("citizen control") of the new electoral institution in Mexico, the IFE.

CHAPTER SIX

❧

Participatory Publics in Brazil and Mexico
The Compatibility of Public Deliberation
and Complex Administration

Our analysis of the relationship between the public and political dimensions of the new Latin American democracies has revealed two dilemmas arising from the failure to transfer new political practices, which emerged in the public culture, to the political level. I showed the empirical nature of this dilemma in chapter 5 in order to point out that the current attempt to construct and consolidate democracy based on competition among elites for administrative positions is bound to fail. The reasons why this attempt is problematic were explored in chapter 3; they include ambiguities in elite political practices regarding the rules of the political game, the failure to cultivate a moral consensus prior to political competition, and difficulties in adopting impartial rules for distributing public goods in a region where poverty still represents a danger to the consolidation of democracy. Translated in terms of both moral legitimacy and efficiency, the ambiguities in the political practices of Latin American elites generate democratic instability because they fail to generate a moral consensus on the desirability of democracy and subvert its capacity to deliver public goods.

I also showed in chapter 5 that the conflict between social actors at the public level and political society hinders the generation of structures of political accountability. In order for these structures to work it is necessary that citizens feel comfortable within a long political cycle formed by elections in which they distinguish representative from unrepresentative government, rewarding the former and punishing the latter. I have shown that in the context of the new Latin American democracies this cycle is incessantly interrupted by public actions demanding the removal of power-holders, the end of corruption, the punishment of human rights violators, or the nullification of electoral results. In such a situation the public and the political cannot be connected. The novelty of the recent democratization in Latin America lies in the possibility of introducing changes from outside the elite culture. I showed in chapter 4 how the demands to introduce a moral component prior to political competition and to acknowledge the organizational autonomy of social actors vis-à-vis the state emerged at the public level throughout the struggle against authoritarianism. The dilemma of the new Latin American democracies is how to transfer the new elements within the public culture to the political level in situations in which communication between the public sphere and political society seems to be blocked.

In chapters 2 and 3, I presented a model of the relations between the public and the political system as an alternative to the transition to democracy approach, which focuses on restoring competition among elites. The alternative model I proposed, which I call participatory publics, is based on four elements:

- First, participatory publics operate at the public level through the formation of mechanisms of face-to-face deliberation, free expression, and association. These mechanisms are meant to address specific elements in the dominant culture by identifying problematic issues and placing them on the political agenda.
- Second, social movements and voluntary associations address contentious issues by introducing alternative practices at the public level, such as non-clientelistic forms of claiming public goods or practices that are compatible with human rights.
- Third, participatory publics preserve a space for administrative complexity while challenging the exclusive access of technicians to decision-making fora. They strike this balance by reserving the right to monitor the implementation of their decisions.
- Fourth, the deliberations of these publics are bound up with the search for institutional forms capable of addressing the issues raised at the public level.

This model of participatory publics is based on two ideas: that innovation in a democratic culture emerges at the public level; and that democratic practices cannot be based only on informal publics. I thus propose to assign a stronger deliberative capacity to the public itself. This could be part of an institutional design capable of strengthening positive and democratic elements within the public culture through the participation of social actors in deliberation and decision-making. Participatory publics can also address specific problems in elite culture, demonstrating the virtues of institutional designs that are more resistant to practices such as hierarchical inequality and clientelism. An additional positive role of these publics would be to provide a democratic and participatory response to the problem of administrative complexity, which has led to a strong consensus on elite rule and has not been satisfactorily addressed by different proposals for participatory democracy (Pateman, 1970). By separating deliberative issues from technical ones and by monitoring political society and administration, deliberative publics could better respond to the apparent tension between democracy and complexity. A model based on these elements could lead to an alternative bridge between the public and the political system in democratizing polities.

In this chapter I analyze two recent experiments in Brazil and Mexico that fulfill in different ways the outlined model of participatory publics. The first has been introduced in some Brazilian cities, notably Porto Alegre (since 1989) and Belo Horizonte (since 1993). The initiative is called participatory budgeting, and it involves the constitution of deliberative fora for allocating municipal budget resources. I argue that participatory budgeting (PB) in a context of democratization offers an alternative means of connecting the participatory culture that emerged at the public level during democratization to political decision-making over the distribution of public goods. The second experiment is the organization of an electoral institution in Mexico, the IFE, based on citizen participation. I will show that the Mexican model of integrating citizens into the structure of election organization, leading to the *ciudadanización* of the IFE, similarly transfers positive potentials that emerged at the public level to a participatory institutional design, allowing the incorporation of new practices of public deliberation at the institutional level.

In this chapter, I will describe participatory budgeting in Brazil and the organization of the IFE in Mexico. I will show how new elements in the public culture of each country were transferred from the civic to the public level. New elements of the Brazilian public culture that emerged during democratization were preserved in the practices of voluntary associations, which later proposed and engaged in participatory budgeting in Porto Alegre and Belo Horizonte. And in Mexico, Alianza Cívica's actors were incorporated into the organization of the electoral process. I show how it is possible to bridge public participation with complex administration at the local level, while also exploring the specificities of each of the experiments. My contention is that once the problem of complexity is contemplated by participatory designs that create incentives for incorporating new practices at the institutional level, a new connection between the public and the political can be established. Such new designs simultaneously incorporate new cultural elements at the institutional level, creating incentives for new practices and disincentives for old practices, and renovate the stock of democratic practices available at the political level. Thus, they offset the return to oligarchic practices within political society that is currently taking place in the new Latin American democracies.

Participatory Publics in Brazil and Mexico: Understanding the Public and Deliberative Logic of the New Institutions

Brazil and Mexico offer two very different experiences of the transfer of positive potentials from the public to the political level. Yet the cases have an important commonality: emergent social actors who expressed cultural changes—in relation to the distribution of material goods and social services by the state in Brazil, in relation to the struggle against electoral fraud in Mexico—were able to participate in new institutions. In the Brazilian case, a movement of neighborhood associations became strong by the late-1970s in Rio de Janeiro, São Paulo, Porto Alegre, and Belo Horizonte. The number of neighborhood associations increased dramatically in all these cities. Participatory budgeting should be seen as a way of incorporating this new cultural drive into institutionalized processes of deliberation.

In Mexico, a large civic movement against electoral fraud arose somewhat later, in the 1990s. After the fraud in the 1991 elections in San Luis de Potosi, a movement organized by the chief victim of the fraud, Dr. Nava, led to the creation of the Movimento Ciudadano por la Democracia. Also in the 1990s, a group of Mexican intellectuals who had been dealing with human rights transformed their NGO, the Academia Mexicana de Derechos Humanos, into an institution for the struggle for political rights. These two institutions, representing different actors, converged with five others in 1994 to create Alianza Cívica, devoted to election monitoring. On election day 1994, more than 18,000 people participated in monitoring activities. Throughout 1995 and 1996, despite the victory of the PRI candidate in the 1994 election, negotiations took place in Castillo de Chapultepec to renegotiate the Mexican electoral system. The IFE *ciudadanizado* incorporated these positive elements, which emerged in the fight against fraud, at the institutional level. Allow me to describe the functioning and main deliberative mechanisms of each of these institutions.

Participatory budgeting (PB) is a local policy that includes social actors, neighborhood association members, and common citizens in a process of negotiation and deliberation. It takes place in two stages: a participatory stage, in which participation is direct, and a representative stage, in which participation occurs through elected delegates and/or councilors. It now operates in more than one hundred cities in Brazil, among them Porto Alegre, the city in which the practice was introduced, and Belo Horizonte, the third largest city in Brazil.

The Porto Alegre and Belo Horizonte PBs operate in similar ways. In Porto Alegre it involves two rounds of regional assemblies, one round of intermediary meetings, and the operation of a councilors' body called the PB Council. Together, these make up an annual cycle. The cycle begins every year in April when the first round of district assemblies takes place and ends in September when the city budget is delivered to the city council. In Belo Horizonte it involves two rounds of regional assemblies, a forum of priorities, and the election of a year-round monitoring body called *Comissão* de Fiscalização do Orçamento (Comforças). I will describe the functioning of the PB in detail to show how it incorporates positive energies that emerged in social movements and voluntary associations.

In its first stage in Porto Alegre and Belo Horizonte, PB involves the organization of a round of regional assemblies. In Porto Alegre, the population attends an assembly in each of the regions. Every first-round regional assembly is attended by the mayor, and a short account-settling process begins with a description of the implementation of the decisions taken in the previous year. The floor is open for about an hour, during which citizens express what has been taking place, possible disagreement with the administration, and what should be done in the region in the coming year. Participation in these meetings is crucial because they constitute the basis for participating in the remaining parts of the process. Participation is individual, but individuals throughout the registration process are required to demonstrate membership in voluntary associations. In 1999, about two-thirds of participants were involved in regional associations. Delegates are elected at the end of the first round of regional assemblies based on two criteria. The first is the total number of people attending the assembly. The formula to determine the total number of delegates in Porto Alegre is as follows: for "up to 100 people attending— 1 delegate for every 10 people, from 101 to 250—1 for every 20, from 251 to 400, 1 for 30, from 401 on, 1 for 40" (POA, 1999:6). For instance, in 1999 the first-round regional assembly in central Porto Alegre was attended by 520 people; thus, the region had 26 delegates (10 for the first 100 attendees, 8 for the next 150, 5 for the next 150, and 3 for the remaining 120). Belo Horizonte's process is similar. The administration opens each assembly with a statement of what was decided in the previous year and the current state of implementing these decisions. In the first round of regional assemblies, the administration explains the resources available for public works in the areas of pavement, sewage, housing, and so on. The main public works proposals in each sub-region (Belo Horizonte has thirty-seven sub-regions) are presented by the communities, initiating a process of negotiation among them.

Thus, the first round of regional assemblies in PB incorporates the practice of local assemblies introduced by neighborhood movements in Brazil in the late 1970s. PB draws on the alternative practice introduced by neighborhood movements in order to offset clientelism, particularism, and non-accountable technical personnel. It takes advantage of the fact that as a reaction to these, the population at the local level in Brazil rejects the presence of political mediators in the distribution of material goods and is inclined to negotiate this process in an open and public way. PB meets both criteria by transferring to a regional assembly the deliberation over which resources and/or public goods are needed by whom.

The second stage of PB is the so-called intermediary meetings in Porto Alegre or the establishment of criteria for distribution of public resources in Belo Horizonte. The intermediary assemblies in Porto Alegre have two responsibilities: ranking thematic priorities and deliberating over which public works the region will claim. Ranking is a process through which five out of twelve types of public goods (pavement, sewage, legalization of urban property, organization of the city, housing, education, health and social assistance, transportation, leisure, sports, economic development, and culture) are selected as priorities. These are then combined with two administratively determined criteria: the evaluation of the population's previous access to public goods and the classification of each of the city's regions according to population. Thus, three criteria are used in ranking. The first is previous access (and therefore present need). A table for classifying priorities assigns grades in inverse relation to previous access to a particular public good. According to the 1999 criteria, up to 80 percent of previous access to a public good leads to a grade of 1, up to 60 percent previous access, grade 2, and up to 20 percent, grade 5. The second criterion is the population of the region and the third the community's own ranking of its priorities, again on a scale of 1 to 5. At the end of this process, a region can reach up to 15 points if it previously had less than 20 percent access to a public good, chooses this good as a top priority, and has more than 120,000 inhabitants. In Belo Horizonte, instead of a second participatory stage, a set criterion for the distribution of resources is used in the first round of regional assemblies. The administration announces the resources available for each region using a formula that assigns resources in direct proportion to population and inverse proportion to average income:

$$PVR = popR$$
$$e \; 1/Y$$

Half of PB's resources are then evenly divided among the regions and half are allocated through this formula.[1]

The intermediary meetings in Porto Alegre and the formula for distribution of resources in Belo Horizonte show a second characteristic of participatory publics: how they deal with complexity. In Porto Alegre there is a direct connection between complexity and the public dimension. Unequal access to public resources is made public by a table of previous access to public goods; thus differential access to public goods is transformed in an objective criterion to be taken into account in the process of deliberation. In Belo Horizonte, differential access to public goods is instead made into a formula that predetermines the resources available to each of the city's regions. Both cases show that, contrary to the argument of the democratic elitist tradition, participatory designs are able to cope with complexity without reducing the scope of political participation. These participatory designs deal with complexity by transforming it into rules that predetermine characteristics of the participatory process (B. Santos, 1998).

In both Porto Alegre and Belo Horizonte, after the round of regional assemblies a council of delegates is elected. In Porto Alegre, the region elects councilors to the PB Council in the second round of regional assemblies. This process, which takes place in June, leads to the formation of a council composed as follows: two councilors from each of the sixteen regions (32); two from each of the five thematic assemblies (10); one from the UAMPA—the umbrella organization of neighborhood communities—and one from the public service trade union (2). The PB council thus has forty-four members. In Belo Horizonte there is instead a forum of regional priorities in which the delegates from each sub-region, having already visited other sub-regions, negotiate on the final format of the budget. The public works approved by the delegates are integrated into the budget proposal. Twenty percent of the delegates present at the regional forum become members of the Comforças, a monitoring body that follows the bidding for public works and can negotiate substitutions in case of technical problems.

Thus, the final element of PB is a set of deliberative or monitoring councils made up of popular representatives. In Porto Alegre the PB Council negotiates the final budget with Gabinete de Planejamento (GAPLAN). In Belo Horizonte, where the decisions taken by the forum of priorities are binding, the role of the council—Comforças—is to monitor the bidding and implementation. In both cases, the administration retains its administrative prerogatives but shares information with a deliberative body located at the public level.

A few elements of PBs should be pointed out in relation to democratization. In the first place, regional assemblies, the common element of PBs in Porto Alegre and Belo Horizonte, draw directly on preexisting practices introduced by neighborhood movements of the 1970s and 1980s. Community actors introduced the idea of local assemblies during this period, and they accordingly have a long experience of discussing community needs. PB draws on these preexisting practices to address pressing issues such as particularism and clientelism. In the second place, the fact that institutional innovation draws on actors who renovated the available stock of political practices leads to a pressure for renewing political practices. Thus, members of the PB Council in Porto Alegre or members of Comforças in Belo Horizonte entered politics during the democratization process and transformed their critique of existing practices into a new form of negotiating over the distribution of public goods. Last but not least, the new practices that emerged with PB implied transforming closed and obscure processes of decision-making into issues to be addressed publicly. Thus, PB provides an alternative way of understanding the process of democratization and its connection with institution building, one that in certain crucial respects can also be seen in the Mexican IFE.

The emergence of the IFE was similar to that of PB in Brazil. The IFE was the direct result of public action against electoral fraud. The Mexican authoritarian regime had long pursued a very particular electoral logic. Although fraud was widespread and the financing of the electoral process completely uneven, the regime always wanted to negotiate the rules with the opposition. A good analogy of the functioning of the Mexican political system would be an uneven soccer game.[2] It was a game in which one of the teams could have more players than the other and had a smaller goal. Yet the greatest worry of the stronger team was of a walk-out. To avoid this, the regime was eager to negotiate the rules. The better the other team played, more willing the stronger team was to make concessions on the rules. This is why there have been so many changes in the electoral law since the 1988 elections. Although the PRI regime held regular elections from 1929 on, it was only in the mid-1980s that the general public became aware of electoral fraud—in the 1985 elections in the state of Nuevo Leon, in the 1986 elections of Chihuahua, and then in the national elections of 1988.

The IFE and its *ciudadanización*—the process through which citizens took charge of the organization of elections and in which the high deliberative rankings of the institution were occupied by citizen councilors—differ from the Brazilian case because they were the result of a long process of negotiation in which an existing institution, which was supposed to assure the PRI government's control over the electoral process, became progressively more autonomous from the state and from the political parties until it ultimately took up the citizens' initiatives against fraud. The *ciudadanización* of the IFE was a two-track process in which two results were progressively achieved: on one hand, it broke the control of the powerful secretary of the interior (*governacion*) over the IFE and, on the other, it broke the connection between the councilors and the grassroots in order to deprive the PRI of its power to appoint ballot officers at the local and regional levels. Allow me to describe how the two processes together led to a second form of participatory public.

The IFE was created by the 1990 electoral law as a federation of government representatives, political parties, and citizens' representatives. The initial composition of the IFE General Council was as follows: a president (the secretary of the interior), two deputies, two senators, six magistrate councilors (who were supposed to play the role of independent members), representatives of the political parties with representation in Congress (4 PRI, 2 PAN, and 1 PRD), and representatives of registered parties without representatives in Congress. Although there were calls for the creation of an institution with political autonomy from the state, only in the so-called Chapultepec negotiations did this demand become pronounced.

The Chapultepec negotiations took place in 1995 and 1996. These negotiations were crucial in breaking the links between the IFE and the secretary of the interior. Civic associations such as the Movimiento Ciudadano por la Democracia (MCD), the Mexican Academy for Human Rights, and Alianza Cívica all demanded an autonomous electoral institution. The civic institutions proposed the following format for the IFE: "The IFE should have a General Council formed by citizens councilors proposed by the political parties and elected by the chamber of deputies. The General Council should also be integrated by delegates of political parties. Citizen councilors should have voice and vote and should have the prerogative to elect the general director of the institute. Delegates of political parties should only have voice. The IFE should have its own budget, thus guaranteeing its full autonomy" (Poder Ciudadano, 1995). Two of the civic associations' demands were key to the autonomy of the IFE. First, they wrested control of the electoral institution from the secretary of the interior, who used to be the president in the former structure. It was agreed that IFE councilors should be appointed by consensus, and it would be up to the councilors themselves to elect the general director. Second, the IFE should have an independent budget, freeing it from financial constraints imposed by the government. The 1996 electoral law led to the *ciudadanización* of the IFE.[3] The councilors became autonomous from the secretary of the interior, and the long-standing control of the electoral process by the government and the political parties was broken. According to the 1996 electoral law, the IFE consisted of a General Council, composed of a president councilor, eight electoral councilors, and an executive secretary. Political parties had councilors with voice but without a vote.

The new IFE General Council had the following powers:

- Appointing the executive administrators of the institute
- Appointing presidents of regional and local districts in national elections
- Registering political parties and national political groups
- Setting ceilings for campaign spending
- Approving the institute's annual budget
- Coordinating the vote counting in national elections

These powers show how the civic associations' agenda was transformed into a new public institution. Reform to the list of electors, ceilings on campaign spending, and independently appointed presidents of electoral districts had been the key demands of Mexican civic associations in the early 1990s. Not only did these become the responsibilities' of the new electoral institutions, but the carrying out of the responsibilities tasks incorporated citizens, showing again the importance of preexisting practices at the public level in the creation of the Mexican electoral institute.

Two prerogatives of the IFE were of central importance to its success in securing electoral reform. The first followed from the General Council's power to appoint the personnel in charge of regional and local districts. This triggered a so-called cascade process. In Mexico, electoral fraud took place mainly at the regional and local levels. The cascade consisted in the reproduction of the autonomy of the IFE at the local and regional levels. In each of the thirty-two states there were seven local councilors appointed as follows: the president of the IFE's General Council appointed the president of the local council, and the six other members were selected by the majority of the council. Thus, an autonomous IFE General Council was rapidly duplicated in the local and regional (*districtales*) councils. In a meeting on May 25, 1999, the IFE General Council defined the principle of *ciudadanización*: the 9 councilors in Mexico City appointed 224 state councilors, who in turn appointed 2,100 district councilors, who in turn placed 450,000 citizens in charge of organizing the elections. These 450,000 individuals were all subject to the same criteria: no previous membership in political parties and no links with the state administration.

The second key to establishing an impartial electoral system was the General Council's control over the IFE's six technical agencies, namely, the agencies in charge of voter registration, the approval of actions related to political parties, the organization of elections, the professionalization of the electoral process, civic education, and its own administration. Of the six agencies, three were of decisive importance: the voter registration agency, which established a public process of checking the accuracy of the electoral list; the agency in charge of civic education, which trained those who worked on election day; and the administrative agency, which established a professional process of reward and punishment of administrative personnel, creating a structure of disincentives for participating in electoral fraud.

Thus, *ciudadanización* in Mexico depended on a double logic: in order to be effective it needed to operate at both the top and grassroots levels, involving in each case different knowledge and practices. At the top level, citizens' councilors needed to acquire control over the electoral list, the access of political parties to the media, and the process of electoral organization. And at the grassroots level, *ciudadanización* required that social actors committed to clean elections oversee electoral districts to guarantee that fraud would not take place on the local level.

The logics of participation in Brazil and *ciudadanización* in Mexico are similar: they assume that there has been cultural renewal, or renewal in the practices of social actors. They thus locate renewal outside the structures of the state, and most of the time outside the political parties. With the help of one political party in Brazil (Workers Party), or the partial help of the opposition parties in Mexico (PRD and PAN), they propose new institutions in which new practices can be incorporated. In Brazil, local assemblies incorporated anti-clientelistic practices to reform the distribution of public goods. In Mexico, anti-fraud leaders at the top level of the IFE opened the way for the appointment of previous members of Alianza Cívica and other civic organizations to electoral districts, triggering a cascade in which networks of anti-fraud activists were placed in charge of organizing the elections. In both cases, cultural innovation led to both institutional innovation and insulating the new institution from well-established elite practices—clientelism in Brazil and electoral fraud in Mexico.

PARTICIPATORY PUBLICS: UNDERSTANDING THE TRANSFER
OF INNOVATION FROM THE
PUBLIC TO THE POLITICAL LEVEL

The emergence of participatory publics is linked to the action of multiple social actors and to effective experiences at the local level. I therefore now turn to the process through which each of these institutions was created.

Participatory budgeting in Brazil arose through the public action of many different actors. The contentious nature of the budget process was identified as a political issue by the community movements in Porto Alegre in the second half of the 1980s. In a meeting in 1986, the União das Associações de Moradores de Porto Alegre (UAMPA) first proposed a way of deciding on the allocation of city resources, which anticipates to-day's participatory budgeting: "[T]he most important aspect that

determines the actions of the city government is the definition of the allocation of public resources. We want to participate in the decisions on
investment priorities in each neighborhood, in each region and in the city
in general" (UAMPA, 1986). The idea of PB was launched by UAMPA,
which pointed out the centrality of budget issues and how new social
actors could participate in the process. Yet, for PB to emerge and acquire
an institutional format, much more was required: changes in national
legislation, which took place during 1988, as well as in local legislation;
negotiations among different actors on the institutional format; and elections in which the winning candidate embraced popular participation in
the city administration.

During the 1988 constitutional process in Brazil, social actors made
several proposals that led to a meaningful increase of popular participation in the political process. The 1988 Brazilian Constitution incorporated the new drive for political participation in article 14, which allows
popular initiative as one of the mechanisms to initiate congressional legislation. In article 29, on the organization of the cities, it required that each
city have a law forecasting its development and forms of administrative
organization. Such laws should incorporate the following principles: "the
cooperation of civic associations in city planning and the possibility of
popular initiative in legal projects of interest of the city population." In
Porto Alegre, where PB first arose, its city law forecast in article 1 "participatory and de-centralized democratic administration." Thus, the second element of the development of participatory publics is the incorporation of new cultural practices at the legal and institutional levels.

An institutional framework for the emergence of PB had been in place
since the approval of Porto Alegre's city law. Yet the law said nothing
about PB. PB emerged when the Workers Party (PT) candidate won the
mayoral election in 1988.[4] The PT had its first important victories in the
local elections of 1988, when it elected the mayors of São Paulo and Porto
Alegre, among other cities; in some cases, like that of São Paulo, it decided to practice something similar to its proposed workers councils.
Even in Porto Alegre, the conception that prevailed during the first year
of PT administration was deeply influenced by the idea that politics always involves the representation of particular interests and that the PT
should only change the particular interests that prevailed within local
administration (Utzig, 1996:211). Thus, the second moment in the formulation of PB was the negotiations among neighborhood communities,
the PT, and the city administration on the format of the deliberative
process.

The political decisions on PB were made in an overlapping way during
the first year of PT administration in Porto Alegre. From its inauguration,
the Olívio Dutra administration tried to increase participation in general.

TABLE 6.1
Original Proposal and Final Design of the PB

	Original Proposal	Form of Deliberation	Final Design
Neighborhood Associations	local assemblies and control of the population on budget decisions	based on direct deliberation at the local level	neighborhood associations proposal prevailed at the local level
Legal change	1988 Constituent Assembly introduces a general principle of participation	based on the cooperation of civic associations	Porto Alegre city law incorporates the idea of participatory administration and creates the legal conditions for PB
Workers Party	Workers councils and a mechanism for the election of city councils	based on delegates electing new delegates	Workers Party proposal prevailed at the intermediary level (municipal budget council)
Local administration	inversion of priorities on the city process of decision-making; concentration of claims at the level of the CRC	based on a combination of participation and administration	administration proposal kept the connection between participation and the operation of administrative institutions (GAPLAN, CRC)

In the first year, most of the secretaries introduced some participatory elements into their health, education, and planning proposals. At the same time, in its first thirty days the Dutra administration made the crucial decision of charging the Coordination of Relations (CRC) with the responsibility of centralizing all of the community's claims. The CRC thus became central to the PB process. Although it had existed prior to 1989, the CRC's role had been to provide city associations with tax-exemption certificates (*atestado de utilidade pública*). Thus, four steps toward PB overlapped in the beginning of the Dutra administration: the concern of urban social movements with budgetary control and with direct participation at the local level; the emphasis the party placed on participation and councils; the decentralizing initiative of several secretaries, including the planning secretary, to encourage popular participation; and the idea, which emerged in the first thirty days, to centralize participation in the CRC. Table 6.1 summarizes the initiatives that led to the introduction of the elements of participatory budgeting.

Thus, PB involves the four elements characteristic of participatory publics. The initiative emerged from social actors at the public level, who first proposed democratization of the budget through the transfer of budgetary powers from the state to social actors. The second element is a capacity for institutional innovation, which, in the case of PB, involved an expansion of participation at the local level approved in the Constituent Assembly and later incorporated into city law. The third element is a connection between the public and the political system, which furnished the political will to create a new institutional design. In Porto Alegre, this element is represented by the Workers Party mayor, a member of a party that favored participation, although on a somewhat different model from that advocated here. The fourth element is a process of negotiation, which proposes participatory designs based on preexisting practices at the local level. Thus, in Porto Alegre the proposal of local assemblies already practiced by neighborhood associations was central to the viability of the experiment. Comparing the Porto Alegre experience with the creation of the IFE in Mexico reveals some commonalities.

The *ciudadanización* of the IFE was also linked to the action of multiple social actors. The Mexican regime had always been eager to negotiate rules of the electoral process. Electoral reforms took place in 1986, 1989–90, 1993, 1994, and 1996, an almost constant process of change of the electoral law. Yet, the actions leading to the creation of an autonomous IFE were linked to specific negotiations with either political or civic actors as a result of specific cases of electoral fraud.

The first frauds that led to political conflicts were against the PAN in Nuevo Leon in 1985 and Chihuahua in 1988. The latter led to the first public actions: blockades of bridges and hunger strikes. This was also the first time the Church took a stand against electoral fraud. Archbishop Talamaz Escandari and Almeida declared that he would not officiate masses on Sunday in protest against the fraud. At the same time, intellectuals with very different political positions, such as Octavio Paz and Carlos Fuentes, participated in public demonstrations against fraud (Cantun, 2000). Electoral fraud in the 1988 presidential election took place against the backdrop of these demonstrations, leading to still more protests and the initial lack of legitimacy of the presidency of Salinas De Gortari. It was at this moment that the first negotiations between the government and the opposition took place, leading to the creation of the IFE.

In the 1989 negotiations, all parties converged around one important institutional change: the basis of electoral regulations in article 41, on the sovereignty of the people, instead of article 60, on the organization of the national congress (Becerra, Salazar, and Woldenberg, 2000:227). This was the first step in acknowledging that it was up to citizens and not political society to organize the electoral process. Yet, the most important discussion in the 1989 negotiations was about the format of an institution in charge of organizing elections. At this point, the PRD defended the autonomy of the electoral institute from the state and political parties. It proposed the creation of an autonomous electoral institution with a council composed of one representative from each political party. The

1990 law created the IFE as an institution that was at the same time a federation of representatives of the state and political parties and with six independent representatives called magistrate councilors. Thus, the democratization of Mexican electoral law involved simultaneous actions from three directions: public demonstrations by citizens against electoral fraud; different actions by the two opposition parties, insisting that elections acknowledge the people's sovereignty; and the creation of an institution, the IFE, which at that point was still completely controlled by the secretary of the interior.

The second important moment in the formation of the IFE as a participatory public took place between 1991 and 1994. After the election in San Luis de Potosi in 1991 and the electoral fraud against Dr. Nava, multiple political actors again converged. For the first time the idea of an electoral institution *ciudadanizada* (constituted only by citizens) emerged. The fraud was so obvious and the protests so forceful that the elected governor never managed to govern and resigned. A new governor was nominated, though not Dr. Nava. This process led to the creation of the MCD. When new elections took place in Nuevo Leon in 1993, the electoral institution was made up solely of citizens, without any government-appointed members. Thus, the idea of *ciudadanización* emerged and was practiced at the local level before it appeared nationally.

The third moment of the *ciudadanización* of the IFE took place in 1994, a contentious year in Mexican politics. On January 1, the Zapatista uprising shook the whole political system. In March, the PRI candidate for president, Donaldo Coloso, was murdered. Following the logic of the Mexican political system, new negotiations between the PRI and the opposition were set up and again the structure of the IFE changed. The IFE that emerged from the 1995–96 negotiations corresponded to the demands of several civic associations, among them, Alianza Cívica, the MCD, and the Mexican Academy for Human Rights. All proposed an organizational structure for the IFE that would not include the secretary of the interior. However, in the 1995–96 negotiations, PAN resisted the idea of *ciudadanización*, in particular the idea of excluding the interior secretary from the IFE's General Council, though PAN itself introduced the principle of *ciudadanización* in the electoral system of Baja California, where it won elections in the early 1990s. At the end of the 1996 negotiations, the IFE had a different structure: only citizens' councilors were included in its executive institutions; the cascade principle was incorporated, with the reproduction of the citizens' councilors principle at the state and local levels during presidential elections; and the administrative organs were subordinated to the IFE General Council (Becerra, Salazar, and Woldenberg, 2000). Thus, the principle of *ciudadanización* was already in place, although owing to time constraints it could not

TABLE 6.2
Original Proposal and Final Design of the IFE

	Original Action	Final Design
Social actors	protest against electoral fraud; proposal by civic associations of an electoral institute formed by citizens	in the Chapultepec negotiations the proposal of an electoral institute autonomous from the state emerges
Political parties	protest against electoral fraud; PAN creates an electoral institute with the participation of citizens in Baja California; PRD proposal of *ciudadanizacion* at the federal level	political parties accept their presence in the IFE having only voice but not vote; PRI accepts the exclusion of the secretary of the interior from the IFE's General Council
Institutional actions	creation of an autonomous IFE (*ciudadanizado*) with eight citizen councilors	citizen councilors propose the cascade process as an action to broaden the element of *ciudadanization*

become fully operational in time for the 1997 elections. For the 2000 elections, the IFE General Council in a resolution issued on May 25, 1999, adopted the principle of full control by the citizens (*ciudadanización*), with preliminary lists of councilors made at the local level and approved by the General Council.

This analysis of the dynamic of the IFE's *ciudadanización* shows, as in the case of PB in Brazil, a process coordinated by multiple actors, among them the social actors who protested against fraud in Chiuhuahua, San Luis de Potosi, Guanajuato, and other states, and against the fraud in the presidential election of 1988. Civic organizations were formed as a result of the fraud and started to act against it at the local and national levels. The MCD, the Mexican Academy for Human Rights, and Alianza Cívica were among the first to propose the idea of citizens' control. The opposition political parties also exerted their influence in two ways: by introducing the practice of *ciudadanización*, which PAN pioneered, and by proposing to extend it, the PRD's position. The negotiation in the Castillo de Chapultepec was of central importance in the constitution of a General Council for the IFE. And finally, it was up to the IFE General Council to introduce the cascade principle, which extended the idea of *ciudadanización* from the top to the grassroots level. Table 6.2 summarizes the development of our second case of a participatory public, the IFE *ciudadanizado*.

Thus, some characteristics of the institutional creation of PB in Brazil and the IFE in Mexico are similar. First, the contentious issue in each case—the centrality of the budget, the necessity of an independent electoral institute—was identified by social actors at the public level. Second, the institutional proposal that resulted involved the direct participation of citizens. In Brazil, citizens participate in the elaboration of the budget in local assemblies, thereby transferring practices at the local level in social movements to the institutional level. In Mexico, a similar process takes place: citizens who used to participate in the monitoring of elections become presidents of electoral districts and work to prevent fraud. Yet the design of participatory institutions is complex and emerges as a result of different proposals made by social, political, and institutional actors at different moments of the process. In Brazil, neighborhood associations argued that all budgetary decision-making should take place at the local level. It was up to the PT to introduce the PB Council, and it was up to the city administration to introduce institutions that could elaborate the budget and make decisions at the local level compatible with the timetable of a complex administration. In Mexico, citizens' control (*ciudadanización*) was proposed by civic associations and found its institutional form in the IFE, whose initial design made it subject to the government. In the 1995–96 negotiations, the format of a thoroughly autonomous institution emerged. Yet an autonomous IFE was initially rejected by PAN at the federal level (Becerra, Salazar, and Woldenberg, 2000), even though it was the first party to organize an election through an electoral institute fully controlled by citizens. It was up to the IFE's General Council, made up of eight citizens' councilors, to reproduce its structure from the top to the bottom of the electoral system. This involved many social actors from Alianza Cívica and other civic organizations who had previous monitoring experience and could serve as electoral district presidents and secretaries. In the next two sections of this chapter I will describe the success of PB in generating cultural innovation in the distribution of public goods at the local level and the similar success of the IFE *ciudadanizado* in ensuring fair elections.

PARTICIPATORY BUDGETING IN BRAZIL: LOCAL PARTICIPATION, JUSTICE, AND ADMINISTRATIVE EFFICIENCY

Participatory budgeting connects in a singular way increased participation and the establishment of criteria of justice. Participation in PB in Porto Alegre and Belo Horizonte takes place mainly at the regional level in local or intermediary assemblies. An evaluation of the participatory characteristics of PB in Belo Horizonte and Porto Alegre shows that participation is directly linked to the credibility of the process and the creation of public rules for action. Participation in PB assures a form of deliberation that is public and makes available information on the access to public goods. Table 6.3 shows the levels of participation in Porto Alegre.

Some characteristics of participation in PB should be stressed. First, initial participation in Porto Alegre's PB was low. In the first year, it was low in most regions and very low in those without any previous tradition of social organization, such as Restinga, Glória, Ilhas, and Humaitá

TABLE 6.3
Number of Participants in the Regional Assemblies in Porto Alegre

	1990		1991		1992		1993		1994		1995		1996		1997		1998	
Ilhas	14	80	33	90	32	132	148	129	58	77	195	103	131	72	246	104	271	113
Navegan-tes	5	10	15	32	37	128	68	337	112	227	273	136	215	75	476	91	498	126
Leste	52	100	90	705	125	385	235	467	166	409	243	229	214	409	204	195	591	119
Lomba	24	40	44	119	55	514	207	419	124	551	823	827	679	294	792	362	129	509
Norte	34	50	47	97	90	511	208	224	209	141	240	380	175	317	339	489	538	386
Nordeste	5	28	NA	363	55	221	604	668	323	388	485	283	396	286	530	184	696	210
Partenon	22	53	74	264	174	922	210	569	270	826	595	205	638	171	500	216	465	340
Restinga	NA	36	NA	181	66	303	144	206	196	768	404	480	589	174	834	311	922	426
Glória	10	20	55	142	104	206	127	226	164	350	299	70	321	151	251	133	234	120
Cruzeiro	91	90	101	128	62	235	293	345	59	423	283	283	426	223	430	132	399	205
Cristal	6	10	NA	81	80	388	107	252	157	215	195	74	240	98	278	290	251	81
Centro-Sul	49	52	44	458	89	502	320	1,268	156	1,051	108	293	1,159	354	1,571	239	1,162	299
Extremo-Sul	16	25	64	80	118	569	485	397	238	484	380	420	403	251	542	247	749	257
Eixo da Baltazar	0	28	23	152	97	455	304	405	127	517	376	563	352	391	287	189	528	332
Sul	14	0	NA	29	85	378	119	501	219	390	654	449	492	155	553	424	282	306
Centro	6	6	18	165	173	319	181	562	60	183	329	171	147	153	350	119	669	305
Total	976		3,694		7,610		10,735		9,638		10,848		10,151		11,908		12,518	

(where only 36, 20, 80, and 10 people respectively participated in the second round of regional assemblies). The low level of participation in almost all regions was probably linked to doubts about the capacity of the process to deliver public goods. In the second year, however, there was a huge change in the pattern of participation. On the one hand, the effectiveness of the first year's deliberations was a strong incentive in those regions with a tradition of community organization, such as the Leste (east region), where 705 attended the second regional assembly, or Partenon, where 264 people attended the second regional assembly. On the other hand, participation remained very low in regions without a tradition of participation or community organization. These regions, which are among the poorest, had low levels of participation for some years. Thus, again we can note how preexisting practices at the societal level predetermine the effectiveness of the process. In the first years of PB in Porto Alegre, the feasibility of a form of broadened participation depended on those actors who already shared a tradition of local assemblies at the regional level. It was only after such a tradition became an acknowledged form of claiming public goods that it was generalized to the city as a whole.

A second element worth noting is how participation is directly linked to deliberation. If we look into the pattern of participation during the first five years, participation in the second regional assembly is larger than in the first. Throughout this period, the deliberative moment was the second round of regional assemblies, when the councilors were elected. Beginning in 1996, delegates were elected in the first round of regional assem-

TABLE 6.4
Participation in Belo Horizonte's PB

	First Round	Second Round	Third Round	Regional Forum	Total
93/94	3,671	4,215	6,202	1,128	15,216
94/95	5,796	5,323	14,461	1,243	26,823
95/96	5,801	11,796	17,597	1,314	36,508
96/97	2,938	9,586	17,937	1,334	31,795
97/98	3,416	3,081	11,871	1,050	19,418
99/2000	stage suppressed	2,905	16,323	1,947	21,175

Source: Planning secretary.

blies, making them more deliberative. Attendance in the first round then became higher than in the second (in 1996, 6,577 people attended the first round of regional assemblies and 3,574 people attended the second round). This tendency persists to this day, demonstrating the capacity of the population to identify the deliberative moment and to participate in a rational way.

The most important aspect of the participatory process in Porto Alegre is the continuous increase in participation despite the fact that the fora of participation have changed. Participation increased each year with few exceptions (1994 and 1996). The almost continuous increase in participation can be attributed to confidence that the deliberative process would continue due to the political hegemony of the Workers Party in the city. In this sense, the pattern of participation in Porto Alegre can be contrasted with that in Belo Horizonte, where city politics has been more contentious. Table 6.4 shows the variations in participation in Belo Horizonte.

Participation in Belo Horizonte shows more variation due to stronger doubts about the continuation of the process. In the first year, participation in Belo Horizonte was already high due to the demonstration effect of the Porto Alegre experience—the population had good reason to assume that it was participating in an effective process. Participation increased even more once the effectiveness of the process at the city level became clear. In the second year of PB, participation rose more than 50 percent over the previous year, but then decreased in 1996–97 with the emergence of doubts regarding PB's future. In that year's city elections, there were serious doubts that the PT candidate would win and thus that PB's decisions would be implemented. Participation decreased again in 1997–98 because, despite the fact that the new, non-PT administration promised to continue the PB process, social actors doubted that it would implement the decisions. However, once it become clear the deliberations would be respected, participation grew again. Participation in PB thus varies according to two factors: previous traditions of association and the perceived effectiveness of the process. Participation shows rational characteristics, particularly in relation to social actors' willingness to participate in collective and public forms of deliberation.

A second important element is that in both Porto Alegre and Belo Horizonte the participatory process is connected to criteria of justice. In Porto Alegre, those critera are determined by the table of previous access to public goods, which has to be harmonized with the participatory process. In Belo Horizonte, they are determined by the formula that distributes resources to the regions. In Porto Alegre, in each of the twelve areas in which decisions are going to be taken in the intermediary meetings, a table of previous access to public goods by the different regions predetermines the deliberative process. This predetermination allows us to see why the PB process does not become merely particularistic, as some of the literature on democratic theory argues (Arendt, 1958; Schumpeter, 1942; Sartori, 1987). Participation in PB is connected to rules for the access to public goods. In Porto Alegre, the city's sixteen regions are differentiated according to previous access to the good in question. In some regions, such as Centro, previous access to pavement has led to the paving of more than 99 percent of the streets. In other regions, such as Extremo-Sul and Lomba do Pinheiro, almost 80 percent or 55 percent of the streets, respectively, were unpaved. In contrast to decision-making by a bureaucracy pressed by particular interests, PB incorporates criteria of justice into the deliberative process by combining three elements: previous access to a public good, population of the region, and popular deliberation in intermediary assemblies. For each of these criteria, a region is evaluated and given a ranking from 1 to 5. Thus, the regions with the most need for one public good and whose populations are larger have a greater chance of getting this public good. On the other hand, a region that already has this good or a region with a small population is not going to accumulate as many points, according to these criteria.

Thus, participatory budgeting is capable of broadening popular sovereignty while dealing with issues of justice. This combination contradicts the democratic elitist conception of democracy, which works with a narrow and individualistic conception of interest representation that is used to justify reducing the scope of popular sovereignty. According to authors such as Schumpeter (1942), Downs (1956), and Elster (1989), among others, the problem with broad participation is that it operates in individualistic settings in which it is very difficult to define the common good. As an alternative to broader participation, democratic elitism therefore combines decentralized forms of interest representation with electoral competition. It is then up to the electorate to choose the dominant articulation of interests. Although the literature in general argues for enhancing particular interests through this form of representation (Lowi, 1969), it does not recognize participatory democracy as an alternative because of what it sees as the rationality problems involved in participation.

The case of PB is instructive in seeing how broadened forms of participatory, democratic deliberation might be able to shed new light on this problem. Despite being a broadened form of popular sovereignty, PB does not leave the whole decision-making process on the allocation of public goods to participatory institutions. It introduces rules as a device to partially predetermine decision-making. By doing this, it offers two innovations in terms of democratic practices. First, it sets limits on particularism, limits that have been historically lacking in the practice of both representative and participatory democracy. These practices thereby change the terms of the democratic debate, as I argued in chapter 2. Second, interests considered legitimate in the PB process must be justified and must overlap with the two criteria of justice outlined above. Thus, the connection between participation and rules in PB re-actualizes the role of broadened forms of participation and democratic deliberation. Participation in PB does not mean that any decision can be made. In this sense, PB represents a new way of harmonizing participation and institutionalization, a way in which democratic practices arising from new forms of collective action are connected with rules for decision-making.

A second area in which PB innovates is in popular control over the implementation of decisions concerning city investments. PB has produced significant results in terms of the control of the administrative personnel through broadened forms of monitoring, which are in two forms. In Porto Alegre, the PB Council is responsible for monitoring budget implementation. This is accomplished through the tension between two administrative arenas, GAPLAN and the CRC, and the PB Council. Thus, administrative officials are in charge of implementation, but their autonomy is not absolute; they are required to explain choices to a body of representative delegates. Belo Horizonte has a special monitoring body, Comforças. According to Faria (1996), the aims of the Comforças are:

1. checking and supervising the schedule of implementation of the budget (timetable, expenses, and accountability)
2. supervising substitutions or re-dimensioning when choices made by the community face technical opposition
3. presenting the community's point of view before a technical decision is made
4. demanding explanations for controversial issues during implementation
5. organizing meetings with the community to explain the administration's point of view on certain issues

6. appointing two representatives to the commission that supervises
7. participating in the organization of the regional forum
8. investigating abuses of power and the appearance of special interests in the deliberative process (103–4).

Thus, PB incorporates the autonomous organization of the citizens in
order to establish a system of local monitoring that allows the population
to control the internal operation of the administration. In this way, the
connection of decisions taken by the popular assemblies with the way
these decisions are translated into administrative orders is subject to popular control.

PB also introduces a new conception of administrative accountability
by transforming monitoring into a permanent feature of the administrative process. Forms of monitoring instituted by the PB Council in Porto
Alegre or by the Comforças in Belo Horizonte represent the integration of
local participatory structures with administration. PB anticipates the administration's lack of responsiveness to popular demands by giving the
people a permanent and institutional presence in monitoring bodies. This
reduces irregularities in public bidding—an endemic problem in Brazil—
and at the same time forces the administration to adapt to popular participation in technical questions.

The monitoring institutions introduced by PB show how deliberation
can be separated from implementation without giving technicians exclusive access to administrative arenas, a feature of the elitist conception of
democracy. PB instituted a public body in charge of presenting the community's point of view within the administration. This solution overcomes the disadvantages of elitist designs by giving a more democratic,
less particularistic solution to the link between technical knowledge and
exclusive access to administration. Monitoring bodies generate groups of
active participants who acquire a greater understanding of technical issues. These groups can convey technical details to the general population
and debate technical issues with administrative bodies. In seven years of
PB in Belo Horizonte, 1,428 people participated in the PB monitoring
bodies. Asked if participating in Comforças led them to understand better
the problems of their sub-regions, 88.5 percent of Comforças members
in the center-south of the city and 76.9 percent in the Barreiros region
answered positively (Faria, 1996:126). Thus, an attractive aspect of monitoring institutions is that they differentiate between deliberation and implementation, yet at the same time respond better to technical considerations by making technical bodies more accountable.

Monitoring bodies also challenge a second aspect of the democratic
elitist conception of democracy, namely, that complex decisions require
specialized knowledge and therefore a specialized body to deal with such

issues in a routinized way. PB challenges the universal application of these rules in two ways. First, it shows that the role of technicians in decision-making bodies should not give them exclusive power to make decisions. Popular access to decision-making bodies in Brazil reduces corruption in bidding processes and also applies pressure to the implementation process, as the case of Belo Horizonte demonstrates. Second, PB also shows that the problem of knowledge can be tackled in a more democratic way. Although the people of Porto Alegre and Belo Horizonte knew little about the administrative process, after one or two years in a monitoring body their knowledge was enhanced. This shows that the transfer of complex knowledge from technicians to bodies of popular representatives of the population is not impossible, as the elitist conception of democracy has argued. In addition, the presence of a monitoring body makes it easier to address conflicts between technicians and the population. Thus, PB opens space for an intermediate conception between Weber's position on the exclusive access of technicians to decision-making bodies and participatory democracy's call for enhanced participation at the administrative level. It shows the feasibility of what was proposed in chapter 2—an intermediate position in which the popular supervision of administrative decision-making and a dynamic tension between technicians and monitoring bodies leads to the democratic control of processes previously considered out of bounds. In this case, the extension of popular sovereignty and democratic deliberation is made compatible with rational administration.

IFE: Participation, the Struggle against Fraud, and Administrative Efficiency in Electoral Organization

The IFE connects in a singular way the participation of citizens in the organization of the electoral process with the control of fraud. Beginning in the early 1990s, civic associations in Mexico singled out three areas of contention regarding the morality of the electoral process: a fair and objective list of the electorate; minimal equality of access to the media for different political parties; and administrative reform to identify the sources of electoral fraud (which were many) and replace corrupt officers with citizens committed to electoral fairness. Citizen participation in a new institutional design helped to tackle all these issues.

After the experience of fraud in the 1988 presidential election, one of the issues raised by civic associations in Mexico was the reliability of the list of the electorate. It was a major source of fraud. Traditionally, Mexican elections featured two well-known groups, the so-called *rasurados* and the *fantasmas*. *Rasurados* were electors who were eliminated from the voters list for no apparent reason and *fantasmas* were electors added on election day who did not appear on the electoral list. The creation of fair electoral lists thus became a priority for the opposition parties and civic associations. Although a nominal list of electors was introduced in the 1990 electoral reform (Becerra, Salazar, and Woldenberg, 2000), electoral frauds occurred in 1991 in Potosi and Guanajuato and there were no guarantees of the reliability of the electoral list. Civic associations made three demands regarding the *padron electoral* (electors list):

- a reliable list of electors that would guarantee just one electoral document per person (the list should be a public and unchangeable document ready three months before the elections)
- a monitoring institution to evaluate the precision of the list
- the publication of reports on electoral accuracy in the media (MCD, 1993)

The 1994 elections were the first to take place with a reliable list of electors and mechanisms to inhibit generalized fraud. The final list of electors was reached using a method involving three steps: all electors were registered, leading to the formation of a general bulletin of electors (*Catalogo General de Electores*); an electorate list was compiled from this bulletin; and election credentials were issued from the list (PNUD, 1997:15). The first demand of civic organizations was that the electoral list be made public. They established, as in PB in Brazil, a tension between the public and the technical personnel in charge of making the list by introducing monitoring.

For the 1994 elections a public process of verifying and monitoring the electoral list was introduced according to the demands of civic associations and political parties. An evaluation of the 1988 electoral list found that there were errors associated with half of the names (wrong addresses, birthdates, etc.). In the 1991 elections, inconsistencies declined to 12 percent of the cases, despite well-known cases of fraud. And in the 1994 elections, inconsistencies decreased to 2.5 percent as a result of monitoring. The final list of electors had 3.5 million fewer people than the initial one. In addition, a monitoring group audited the electoral list for two months, concluding that 96.4 percent of its data were reliable (Becerra, Salazar, and Woldenberg, 2000:337). Thus, the Mexican case shows again that insulation of administrative personnel can be an obstacle to democratizing political practices. It was precisely the transformation of an administrative matter into a public issue controlled by citizens that led to a reliable electoral list. The Mexican case shows, like the Brazilian, that broader participation challenging the insulation of technical personnel can help tackle political issues in new democracies. The Mexican re-

TABLE 6.5
Reliability of the Electoral List and Participation in Mexican Elections

	Number of Electors	Inconsistencies in the Electoral List (%)	Number of Voters
1988	38,740,000	50	19,910,000
1991	39,239,000	12	24,320,000
1997	53,220,000	3.6	29,771,000
2000	59,584,000	3.6	37,600,000

Source: IFE.

sponse to electoral fraud shows that the institutionalized presence of social actors in monitoring institutions can anticipate the administration's lack of responsiveness to public demands. In fact, contrary to many assumptions, incorporating social actors into monitoring bodies can generate more efficiency and accountability by increasing participation.

It is interesting to note that there is a close relation among the civic associations' demand for a reliable electoral list, the political parties' proposal of a specific institutional format, and the number of participants in Mexican elections, as table 6.5 shows. As the electoral process becomes controlled by citizens, more electors are registered. At the same time, as the reliability of the electoral list increases, more people take the time to vote. Thus, the relationship between morality and politics is restored by an institutional process controlled by citizens.

The second issue on which civic associations' action led to new institutions was the access of political parties to financing and the media. The media have historically been a major obstacle to the democratization of the electoral system in Mexico. In the 1988 elections, they ignored open and generalized fraud. In addition, the distribution of media time and access to the different campaigns were completely uneven. In the 1988 presidential election, the campaign of the PRI candidate, Salinas De Gortari, received three times more written press coverage and more than seven times more television coverage than did the Cardenas campaign (Adler, 1993:154).[5]

Mexican civic associations publicly thematized the issue of more democratic access to the media in the political campaigns and started monitoring the media. In 1993 the MCD proposed equal media time for all political candidates, as well as public media monitoring (MCD, 1993). In the beginning of 1994, after the explosion of the Chiapas rebellion, the Mexican Academy for Human Rights started to monitor media coverage of the uprising, and on January 1, 1994, *Alianza Cívica* started monitoring seventy different media outlets in twenty states, documenting many cases of media bias in the coverage of the 1994 presidential election (Aguayo, 1996:164). After this monitoring, the IFE General Council

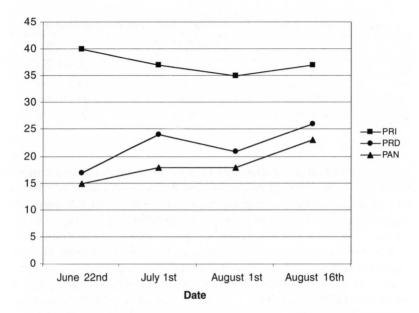

Fig. 6.1. Access to television by Party in the 1994 Presidential Election in
Mexico, reprinted, by permission, from Becerra, Salazar, and
Woldenberg, *La mecanica del cambio politico em Mexico.*

(then controlled by the secretary of the interior) issued a set of unofficial
guidelines tackling the issue of media access for the first time. Figure 6.1
shows the changes in media coverage during the 1994 presidential campaign after the issue was publicly raised by Alianza Cívica and addressed
by the IFE General Council.

Access to the media was then part of the 1995–96 negotiations, which
agreed on the following: setting economic limits in the acquisition of television time; introducing random monitoring by the IFE for the evaluation
of television coverage; and initiating public debates among the candidates
(Becerra, Salazar, and Woldenberg, 2000:409).

After its *ciudadanización*, the IFE incorporated some of the institutional features demanded by civic associations regarding the monitoring
of media access. The General Council issued a resolution for 2000 in
which it incorporated three demands of civic associations and political
parties. According to this resolution:

1. Each mass media outlet was asked to comply with the resolutions
   regarding citizens' right of access to information.
2. The IFE General Council introduced on its own initiative a process
   of monitoring the main radio and television news programs, issuing

a report on the coverage of the presidential elections every two weeks. On the basis of these reports, it would issue recommendations to media owners, asking them to make the elections coverage more even.

3. The IFE, the political parties, and the government agreed that the advertising of the two major government social programs— Pronasol and Procampo—would be suspended twenty days before the elections. (IFE, 2000)

IFE monitoring shows a little more balance in the 2000 elections than in the first period of the campaigns of 1996 or 1988, although the coverage of the PRI candidate's campaign still received more time on private television than did those of the other candidates.

Thus, creating equal access to the media also involved transferring preexisting practices from the public to the institutional level. Media monitoring was first introduced by civic associations, such as Alianza Cívica and the Mexican Academy for Human Rights. They were able to politicize the issue and to place it on the public agenda. In the 1995–96 negotiations, these demands were taken up by the IFE. Again, in this regard, Mexican democratization shows that the transfer of available democratic potentials from the public to the institutional level can play a decisive role in institutional innovation.

The third issue on which the IFE made changes concerned the composition of its administrative personnel. In Mexico, elections personnel have often been responsible for fraud. Although the creation of the IFE in 1989 was an important advance in developing an institutional way to introduce an autonomous process of electoral organization, its first administrative format was prone to fraud. The fact that the secretary of the interior was the chair of the institution gave him a lot of leeway in nominating those in charge of training electoral officers. The fraud in San Luis de Potosi in 1991, for example, was largely due to the organizers of the election. One common form of fraud came from the designation of electoral precinct personnel by the state governments or the PRI, instead of the IFE.

After the *ciudadanización* of the IFE in 1996, many of those in intermediary positions, such as the director of electoral qualification and the administrative director, were replaced.[6] In the first IFE General Council nominated after the 1996 reform, only one person from the old structure remained, Felipe Soliz, who left the IFE a year later. This led to the replacement of the six executive directors in charge of areas such as media control, electoral organization, and electoral qualification.

The change at the top led to changes in the administrative structure. During 1996 and 1997, the IFE General Council elaborated a new constitution for the electoral service. It included entrance through public examination instead of political appointment and incentives to reward professionalism, so that the struggle against fraud became a sine qua non condition for a position in the IFE. The IFE also introduced punishments for personnel involved in fraud. These became guiding principles for a highly successful reform that, in the end, created an administrative agency with a professional ethos. Thus, a third element in the constitution of a participatory public was present in the IFE: the capacity of citizens' councilors to neutralize electoral fraud by disciplining or replacing electoral personnel. Again, citizens at the grassroots level were essential to discovering the most common forms of fraud and using this knowledge administratively at the upper levels to design anti-fraud mechanisms. As in Brazil, the Mexican case shows how knowledge obtained by common citizens can be connected with a participatory form of deliberation. It shows that the democratic elitist tradition completely misses how practices and information obtained by social actors can be essential to the success of democratic institutions. Again, in Mexico as in Brazil, the process of democratization works when there is renewal of elites and a transfer of new cultural potentials to the institutional level. Preexisting practices were essential to the IFE's success in organizing clean and legitimate elections.

PUBLIC DELIBERATION, PARTICIPATION, AND DEMOCRATIZATION IN BRAZIL AND MEXICO

Participatory publics simultaneously addresses a major concern associated with democratization in Latin America—the gap between continuity in elite culture and renovation in public culture—and another associated with the postwar debate that led to the consensus on democratic elitism—the ostensible impossibility of attaining administrative rationality without narrowing the scope of political participation. PB in Brazil and the IFE in Mexico provide the Latin American democratic debate with an example of public deliberation that directly addresses what have been acknowledged as the three main obstacles to democracy in the region: the nature of its political elites; the hybridization of its democratic practices; and the lack of institutional mechanisms capable of either expanding the public culture or responding to the specific problems of building democracy in the region. Allow me to explain the theoretical possibilities for democratization opened by the PB and the IFE in each of these areas.

PB and the IFE are excellent examples of why theories of democratization should not bind themselves to analyzing elites, especially where there has been a renovation of the political culture at the public level. Harnessing democratic potentials by transforming informal publics into deliberative publics, it is possible to locate an alternative source of democratic values to those suggested by democratic elitism and transition theory. This alternative is based on a different connection among social actors, democratic practices, and institutional designs. Once democratic values become available within the public culture, it is possible to transfer them to the deliberative level through innovative institutional designs.[7] In the Brazilian case, a non-clientelistic and non-particularistic approach to the distribution of public goods was institutionalized. In the Mexican case, the fight against electoral fraud and equal access to the media acquired an institutional format in the IFE. Thus, a theory of democratization can give a completely different response to the problem of ambiguity within elite culture—an answer which, however, requires jettisoning democratic elitist assumptions in the analysis of democratization. This answer is to broaden the stock of democratic practices by institutionalizing them in non-party forms at the public level.

PB and the IFE show why the aggregation of majorities is not the only strategy available at the political level for new democracies. PB addresses the problem of deliberative inequality by introducing criteria for equalizing participation and by taking measures to replace political mediators with the direct participation of social actors. The two elements together offset a hybrid and hierarchical tradition because they impose costs on both the disempowerment of social actors and the persistence of non-participatory local structures. By reducing the role of political mediators in the access to public goods and by reducing the connection between political brokers and the system of representation, PB helps overcome deliberative inequality and fosters public discussion. By publicizing the access of each sector of the population to public goods and establishing a rotation principle, PB weakens the capacity of brokers to control their clienteles. The IFE plays a similar role in electoral organization in Mexico. By keeping political mediators out of the organization of elections, the IFE offsets the hybridization of political structures. It imposes costs on administrative personnel involved in fraud and incorporates social actors who had been struggling against fraud into the electoral process. By publicizing cases of fraud, by publicizing the unequal access to the media, and by brokering agreements to reduce government advertising, the IFE transformed an unequal game of political competition into a fair one. Thus, the two cases show that local public deliberation and citizen involvement in institutions help turn a vicious cycle into a virtuous one: the public procedure introduced by PB shows citizens who want to use autonomous political strategies how to pursue full deliberative equality, while the IFE shows those who favor the reconnection of politics and morality how they can act in public to enhance full political equality.

These two arguments point in the direction of another issue of particular importance for democratization theory, namely, how to address the relationship between cultural tradition and institutional innovation. In chapters 2 and 3, I pointed out the capacity of the public sphere to challenge elements within a given cultural tradition by publicly thematizing them and limiting their non-democratic components through institutional design. In this view, the first step of democratization is identifying practices within the public culture capable of offsetting undemocratic practices and traditions. Thus, the emergence and consolidation of new democracies is no longer understood as the outcome of singular characteristics of a homogeneous culture but as a cultural dispute at the center of which lies the possibility of introducing and consolidating democratic practices. According to this perspective, the challenge of democratic engineering is strengthening those forms of renovation within the public culture that address its undemocratic tendencies and then transforming them into new institutional practices.

PB and the IFE show that institutional designs involving social actors can address a contradictory element within the public culture, namely, existing deliberative inequalities. By acting as institutional fora for the negotiation of material and political demands, PB and the IFE act on two fronts. First, they offer institutional and material incentives for those within the hybrid tradition to aspire to full deliberative equality. These incentives are both direct and emulative, as in cases where the material gains of those who have begun to participate actively and autonomously provoke those who remain inactive to do the same, or where those who knew about fraud but did nothing have a chance to act against it. At the same time, they foster the deliberative and participatory activity of those already active by integrating them into public deliberative institutions, such as PB councils, monitoring bodies, or electoral districts. Participatory publics thereby reconnect three dimensions that have remained separate in democratic elitist approaches to democratization: the cultural, the public, and the institutional. They begin by diagnosing the existing public culture and its forms of innovation; they identify innovation in the public thematization of contentious issues; and they give institutional form to the problem of unequal deliberative capabilities by creating both incentives for participation and disincentives for political intermediation by brokers. They thereby provide a solution to a specific problem within the existing culture through a particular institutional design.

CHAPTER SEVEN

⨕

Concluding Remarks on the Democratizing Role of Participatory Publics

This book is based on a critique of the democratic elitist tradition and the analysis of democratization it has inspired. I defined the democratic elitist tradition based on its three main concerns: the reduction of the scope of politics to the activities of government; its defense of the concentration of politics in the hands of active minorities; and its fear of the pressure caused by mass mobilization and collective action on the operation of political institutions. I took issue with this tradition by showing that its attempt to transform the problems that led to the democratic breakdown in Europe during the first wave of democratization—undifferentiated mass mobilizations—and the response that led to the consolidation of democracy in Europe during the second wave of democratization—restriction of sovereignty to electoral competition among political elites—could not be transformed into a general theory of democratization. I criticized this framework by showing that democracy in third-wave countries has not been threatened by undifferentiated forms of political mobilization as it had been in Europe during the interwar period. I maintained that the central problem faced by democracy in these countries is a narrow stock of democratic practices. Thus, in these cases, institutionalization ceases to be the opposite of mobilization, which also changes its form to collective action at the public level. Institutionalization in such a condition has to assume a different meaning, namely the connection between new collective forms of occupation of the public space with new institutional designs. I assumed that this new framework could give a response to two issues approached in this work: the anti-democratic nature of Latin American elites and pro-democratic forms of collective action.

The problem of the nature of the Latin American elites permeates this entire work. It was introduced in connection with the idea that since the second wave of democratization Latin American countries have been struggling with the fact that rule by elites in the region has been equivalent to attempts to reverse political results ex post, with lack of respect for human rights and with the strengthening of mechanisms contradictory with deliberative equality. The theory of transition to democracy made an early attempt to address this issue by revising the idea of a positive role played by the elites and introducing a differentiation between what it called *blandos* and *duros*, or soft-liners and hard-liners. But this is insufficient to solve the problem of the nature of the elites because it bypasses the fact that those in favor of the restoration of political competition need not be in favor of other practices essential to the strengthening of democracy, such as the organizational autonomy of society or the enforcement of the rule of law. I showed how the stock of available practices at the level of Latin American political societies is ambiguous in that they do not hesitate to return to hierarchical mechanisms and further deliberative inequalities in the cases in which such mechanisms are instrumental to enhance the formation of political majorities. At this level, the analysis presented in this work is not much different from the "delegative democracy" diagnosis, which also assumes a strong continuity at the level of political elites. My analysis differentiates itself from the "delegative democracy" perspective in another aspect, namely in the refusal to accept the elites/masses dichotomy and the proposal of substituting it for a search of types of practices predominant at the public level.

I proposed an alternative framework for the study of democratization that I call participatory publics. This framework is based on four elements. First, it involves the stress on transformations at the public level as a starting point of democratization. It is my contention that transformations in forms of occupation of the public sphere such as getting rid of political mediators in the process of distribution of public goods and the development of a tradition of free and autonomous voluntary associations were central to the recent Latin American democratization processes by introducing the possibility of horizontal social relations at the public level. The second element is the capacity to renovate at the public level problematic elements within the public culture. I argue that in the Latin American case this problematic element is a hierarchical culture that disempowers social actors and uses non-public means to decide on the deliverance of public goods. These are the problems that a process of democratization should address to create horizontal forms of deliberation. The third element is the capacity at the political level to create new institutional designs through which informal publics assume deliberative capacity on precisely those issues that the majoritarian culture is ambiguous. In the Latin American case, I argued that the hegemonic culture remained ambiguous in relation to three issues: human rights; distribution of public goods; and stability of the rules of the political game. The fourth element is the idea that institutional designs that bind new elements within the public culture with specific solutions to each of the above-mentioned dilemmas are a central feature for the completion of Latin American democratization.

I approached the formation of a democratic public sphere in Latin America as a reaction to the weight of the specific path of cultural formation and nation building in the region. I argued that there are non-elitist possibilities for overcoming a tradition of hybridization and the forms of deliberative inequality it generates, through the formation of common language for expression at the public level, or through the creation of an egalitarian space for the presentation of common identities, or through the emergence of a tradition of organizational autonomy from the state. However, the new practices at the public level do not lead to a homogeneity of practices. Moreover, the restoration of democracy might lead to an aggregative conception of politics centered on both the rule of elites and the restoration of competition within political society. The logic of aggregation of majorities, which is proper to political society, points in the direction of bypassing differences between practices and finding the utilization of clientelism instrumental in the creation of electoral majorities. Such a diagnosis led me to show a conflict between a new public culture and the reorganization of political society in the new Latin American democracies. Such a conflict if not processed adequately might in the end endanger democracy itself.

Participatory budgeting in Brazil and the IFE *ciudadanizado* in Mexico might represent a way out of the dilemma faced by third-wave democracies for two reasons: they build directly on the elements of the local culture that have been renovated through a structure of incentives and disincentives, and they draw on the critique of clientelism and the tradition of political mediators, proposing a structure of public deliberation that gives incentives to participation and imposes costs to disempowerment. They also give a consistent response to the problem of complexity, an issue that has been in the background of the whole democratic discussion during the twentieth century. PB does not conflate deliberation with administration, thus becoming one of the first proposals for democratic deliberation in third-wave countries that breaks at the same time with two traditions: the tradition of not providing an institutional response to cultural drawbacks within the specific culture, a trend that has characterized the proposals which draw on democratic elitism; and the tradition of not taking into account the drawbacks involved in direct administration of political proposals by social movements or social actors, a problem involved in most of the proposals of a more republican type of democracy. The IFE shows similar characteristics; it provides an institutional response to specific drawbacks in the public culture and incorporates new actors in the process of electoral organization without losing sight of the complexity issue. It also keeps a differentiation between the operation of a complex administrative body and forms of making information and data available to social actors. In this sense, both PB and the IFE respond well to cultural problems inside the elite's culture and to the theoretical debate on democratic participation that took place during the whole century by standing midway between participation and complex administration. The question that remains is: Can this framework provide a response to other drawbacks in third-wave democracies such as human rights violations and constant changes in the rules of the political game?

Any answer to this question has to be partial. The strength of the participatory publics is, as I have shown, their capacity to act as a problem-solving public addressing specific drawbacks of the local culture through innovative institutional designs. Their extension, however, requires the availability of actors and practices that may not be available everywhere as the experience of extending forms of local participation in Mexico has shown. In addition, in the case of human rights it has been more difficult to generate participatory publics than in the case of deliverance of public goods. Human rights groups in all three new democracies have been unable to propose an institutional design capable of binding security and human rights, in spite of the presence of human rights activists in all three countries. A public design involving the communities, social movements activists, and the state has to emerge in order to make feasible forms of participatory publics dealing with the human rights issue. The specific form of the design cannot be anticipated due to the lack of a grounding experience, which points in the direction of experimental, problem-solving publics (Sabel and Fung, 1999). In this case, the public dimension of deliberation assumes an experimental character due to the unavailability of guiding experiences. What can be expected of these publics is the introduction of institutional innovations that might lead to renovations in human rights policies for the poor. The commitment to new values and practices needs in this case to be translated into an institutional design, which might emerge from multiple and simultaneous practices. Again, it is more likely that innovation will emerge from these publics than from the practices of political society, although some kind of support for innovation will have to come from sectors within the political system, as has been the case for PB and the IFE.

The most complicated issue facing the new Latin American democracies is related to the rules for the relationship between actors at the public level and political society. There is no doubt that problems such as constant changes in the rules of the political game and difficulties in establishing accountability are still present in the new Latin American democracies in a similar fashion to those during the second wave of democratization. It is, however, also true that democracy this time showed itself more resistant to these changes. Social action in the public space, as in Mexico and Brazil, played an important role in curbing power abuses by political society. Monitoring movements (such as Alianza Cívica) or forms of occupation of the public space (the movement for the impeachment of Collor de Mello in Brazil) played an important role in curbing a tradition of disregard for the rules of the political game. Yet, the characteristics of monitoring and defensive actions by informal publics show their limitations: they generally have a better chance of curbing undesirable practices than of introducing a new pattern of relation between the public and the political levels. Again, the issue of a stronger form of public deliberation is raised.

It is worthwhile to point out that in the last decade many forms of citizens participation and deliberation emerged in the new Latin American democracies. The forms of democratic participation were broadened not only in countries such as Brazil and Mexico, for which we have pointed out the sources of the movement for broader forms of participation, but also in countries such as Colombia and Nicaragua, which passed through different forms of transition to democracy. In Brazil, forms of citizen participation were acknowledged by its National Constituent Assembly and became standard in areas of health policies, social assistance, and urban policies. Article 204 on the organization of social assistance of the Brazilian 1988 Constitution demands the participation of the population through its organized associations in the formulation of policies as well as in the monitoring of their implementation. In its chapter on the organization of the health system a similar demand was made, which was then implemented through Law 8.142 introducing health councils with citizen participation at the local level. Today there are more than two thousand health councils and about the same number of social assistance councils in Brazilian cities (Tabagiba, 2002). A similar phenomenon took place at the local level in Mexico with the institution of a law on citizen participation. Two such laws were instituted in Mexico City, one in 1995 and the other in 1988 when the city mayor was Cuatemoc Cardenas, a member of the opposition party, the PRD. The 1988 law on citizen participation instituted a horizontal form of representation of Mexico City's 1,270 neighborhoods. In the election, 572,000 people participated, 8,410 of whom were representatives who are now members of Mexico City neighborhood commissions, introducing a more horizontal form of claiming material goods and negotiating their deliverance with local authorities (San Juan, 2002). Again, it is possible to see in the case of Mexico and Brazil, as well as in other Latin American countries, that sectors of political society are moving toward releasing part of the power concentrated in their hands and transferring it to institutions that incorporate citizens and try to establish new public patterns of relationship between state and society. The possibility of transferring from the political to the public level the process of deliberation on public policies can provide the new democracies with a generalizing element that might slow down particularism and provide a solution to one of the central problems faced by second-wave democracies. Participatory publics can provide a generalizing element to help overcome the current conflict between the public and the political dimensions. Again, if this is the direction in which these new democracies will evolve, it will imply the transformation of an informal public opinion into a deliberative, decision-making body.

The three issues tackled in this work point in the same direction, namely toward introducing stronger deliberative devices as the result of political renovation. A conception of political renovation changes the terms of the democratic debate, which is still bounded by the opposition between mobilization and institutionalization. Political innovation points in a different direction, namely that the transfer of institutions and problems from the political setting outside their original core does not lead to institutionalization. It leads instead to the establishment of a double pattern of behavior: along with nonbinding institutions new democracies develop non-institutional and binding mechanisms. Only a change in strategy can lead to a different perspective according to which the institutional problem ceases to be solved by following the first postulate of the democratic elitist tradition, the narrowing down of politics to the activities of government. As long as the democratic impulses in Latin America remain insulated at the societal level, democratization strategies are bound to fail. Democratic designs in the new Latin American democracies are dependent on their capacity to move democracy from a societal practice into a form of public deliberation. By associating social actors' self-understanding of democracy with the dilemmas of democratization theory, I have pointed out a different path that bets on the possibility that new democratic patterns of interaction might one day become the dominant form of state and society relations in the region. This remains a hope to be fulfilled by the same social actors whose practices inspired the democratic designs upon which this work draws.

NOTES

ↄↄ

1. I am defining wave of democratization in an empirical way as "a group of transitions from non-democratic to democratic regimes that occur within a specified period of time and that significantly outnumber transitions in the opposite direction during that period of time" (Huntington, 1991:15).

2. On the idea of the public sphere, see Habermas, 1989, 1992; Cohen and Arato, 1992; Calhoun, 1992; Thompson, 1995; Melucci, 1996.

Chapter 1
Democratic Theory and Democratization

1. The concept of sovereignty made its way into political theory before the emergence of modern democratic theory. Hobbes and Bodin introduced the idea of sovereignty into modern political thought, understanding it as an attribute of the state. Yet, it was Rousseau who transferred the concept from the state to the people. For Rousseau, sovereignty is linked to the formation of the general will and, thus, with the citizens' expression of preferences and its incorporation into a political body. In this sense, he is the precursor of democratic theory understood as a theory of the sovereignty of the people. See Hobbes, 1968; Rousseau, 1968.

2. Norberto Bobbio is one of the authors who most clearly grasps this contradiction. He comments: "As societies gradually change from a family economy to a market economy and from a market economy to an economy which is protected, regulated and planned, there is an increase in the number of political problems whose solution requires technical expertise. Technical problems require experts, an expanding team of specialized personnel. . . . Technocracy and democracy are antithetical: if the expert plays a leading role in industrial society he cannot be considered as just any citizen" (Bobbio, 1987:37).

3. The link between politics and rationality precedes democratic theory. Thomas Hobbes (1968) associated his conception of politics with rationality in his solution to the issue of why individuals should join the social contract. For him, rationality is associated with individuals' drive for self-preservation, which he links to the justification of the legitimacy of sovereign rule. Only for Rousseau is rationality linked to the formation of the general will and thus with democracy.

4. Hannah Arendt and the young Habermas mistakenly identified this process with what they called "the societalization of politics." For Arendt, the entrance of issues belonging to the realm of necessity in the political arena leads to the loss of the specificity of politics as an action performed in public aiming at the public good: "[T]he term 'public' signifies the world itself, in so far as it is common to all of us and distinguished from our privately owned place in it" (Arendt, 1958:47). For Arendt as well as Habermas, the entrance of social issues into politics meant

the replacement of the public formation of rationality with the blind defense of particular interests. See Arendt, 1958:47; Habermas, 1989. Both authors failed to perceive the possibility of constructing a public sphere in which particular interests might represent the point of departure for a public debate on the general interest. Habermas revised his conception of the societalization of politics as a sign of the decay of the public. See Habermas, 1992.

5. This leads to the dissociation of elitism and democracy typical of the interwar period. Authors such as Pareto, Michels, and Gasset sided with anti-democratic political proposals in this period because of their belief that elites would automatically prevail in any form of government.

6. I have in mind here the different contributions to the justification of formal or procedural ethics made by authors such as Rawls, Apel, and Habermas. They agree on the impossibility of reaching a substantive notion of the common good. It is from this shared point of view that each proposes elements for reconstructing a formal or procedural conception of ethics. See Rawls, 1971; Apel, 1988; Habermas, 1990.

7. Robert Dahl located such a consensus at the level of each individual's capacity for autonomy. "[T]o live under the law of one's own choosing and thus to participate in the process of choosing those laws facilitates the personal development of citizens as moral and social beings" (1991:91).

8. It is worth calling attention to the changes the Weberian concept of rationality has to pass through to become a utilitarian evaluation of costs and benefits. First, Weber distinguished between an action based on the evaluation of means and ends and an action based on values and beliefs (Weber, 1978, 1:24–5). This differentiation disappears in Downs's approach. Second, Downs narrows the idea of evaluating means to a utilitarian calculation of costs and benefits, equating economic rationality with rationality per se.

9. It is worth situating the work of Robert Dahl within the postwar democratic debate. In one sense, Dahl's work fits into the democratic elitist tradition due to his willingness, at least in his *Preface to Democratic Theory*, to limit democracy to electoral competition between political groups. However, another aspect of Dahl's work differentiates him from democratic elitism: his search to improve the conditions for competition through the introduction of what he calls the maximization principle (1956:132). Dahl stands between the elitist and non-elitist traditions. I will come back to Dahl's position on the role of the public space in chapter 2.

10. I am drawing here on Samuel Huntington's concept of reverse "waves" of democratization. According to Huntington, a reverse wave of democratization is a group of transitions from democratic to non-democratic regimes that occur within a specified period of time and that significantly outnumber transitions in the opposite direction during that period of time (1991:15).

11. There is a huge bibliography on populism in Latin America, which approaches in different ways the main characteristic of the phenomenon, namely, the direct relation between the state and the masses. The classic work on Latin American populism was written by Argentinean sociologist Gino Germani. He showed the contradiction between two categories, modernization and institutionalization, in order to propose a contrast between European and Latin American

modernization. In the case of Europe, the modernization of the state led to the creation of institutions for political mediation. This preceded a later period of mobilization and integration of demands by the existing political institutions. In Latin America, this temporal gap did not exist. Germani's work gave birth to a huge debate on the rational or anti-rational characteristics of populist forms of mobilization. It is, however, worth noting that the common framework of the debate is a shared understanding of the relationship between mobilization and incorporation. See also Weffort, 1979; Laclau, 1978.

12. The features of these theories are reproduced in some of the recent attempts to systematize empirically the characteristics of democratic and non-democratic countries. In a recent article, Przeworski et al. establish an empirical correlation between socioeconomic development and democracy: "[O]nce a country has a democratic regime, its level of economic development has a very strong effect on the probability that democracy will survive. Poor democracies, particularly those with annual per capita income of less than $1,000 are extremely fragile. . . . Above $6,000, democracies are impregnable and can be expected to live forever: no democratic system has ever fallen in a country where per-capita income exceeds $6,055 (Argentina's level in 1976)" (1996:41). Despite the usefulness of the authors' systematization, an analytical question proper to the field of democratic theory immediately arises: what conditions allow democracy to survive in a poor country (India) and lead to its breakdown in one of the wealthiest countries in the world (Argentina in 1954)? Therefore, even if the empirical correlation holds above a certain economic level, it is of no use in the many cases that fall below that level, including most of those of the so-called third-wave democracies.

13. According to Linz and Stepan, democratic regimes at one point had "a reasonable chance to survive and become fully consolidated but . . . certain characteristics and actions of relevant actors—institutions as well as individuals—decreased the probability of such development" (1978:10).

14. The type of mass participation varied widely in the different processes of democratization in Latin America. In Chile, there were several episodes of mobilization between 1983 and 1986, yet the sharp divide between mass mobilization and the existing political system did not lead to negotiations which could have led to some form of liberalization. Mexico saw an endless process of negotiation between elites. However, due to its disconnection from the formation of an independent civil society, full democratization was achieved very late through the electoral process. In the case of Brazil, the internal process of negotiation among elites led to democratization only when it was articulated with intense mass mobilizations during the so-called *diretas* campaign. See Martins, 1986; Smith, 1991; Oxhorn, 1995; Olvera, 1995; Avritzer, 1995.

15. A very good example of the mistakes involved in the process of institution building was the recent discussion of forms of government in Latin America. Political scientists introduced parliamentarianism from the perspective of institution building, whereas politicians understood it as a good opportunity to change the rules of the game in their own favor. This was the case, again, in the introduction of presidential reelections, which power-holders approved for their own benefit. See Lamounier, 1992; Liphart, 1992.

16. O'Donnell's break with the teleology of the democratic consolidation argument is also a self-critique, since the idea of a second transition also involved the teleological assumption of a move from a democratically elected government to a democratic regime. The actors or processes that could lead from one moment to the next have never been identified. See O'Donnell, 1992:26.

CHAPTER 2
DEMOCRATIC THEORY AND THE FORMATION OF A PUBLIC SPHERE

1. In *The Theory of Democracy Revisited*, Giovanni Sartori attempts to recast Dahl's theory in democratic elitist language: "Dahl's basic strategy is to reserve the word democracy for the ideal 'system' and to use 'polyarchy' as its real world approximation. I accept instead 'democracy' for the real world, but divide its meaning in two halves: the prescriptive (normative) and the descriptive (denotative)" (1987, 1:154). The difference between the two authors is made clear, though underestimated by Sartori: the conceptual definition of democracy provides an arrival point in relation to which democratic practice can be measured.

2. Dahl proposes a distinction between democracy and polyarchy. For him, polyarchies "are regimes that have been substantially popularized and liberalized, that is, highly inclusive and extensively open to public contestation" (Dahl, 1971:8). Though this definition could have influenced early definitions on transitions, it did not play a role in the discussion on democratization until the completion of the processes of transition to democracy. See O'Donnell, 1994; 1998.

3. Critical theory is a twentieth-century development within the Marxian tradition of social thought. Its idea of social criticism is derived from a remark by Karl Marx in a letter to Rouge, where he defined his understanding of philosophy as follows: "Philosophy has now become secularized and the most striking proof of this can be seen in the way that philosophical consciousness has joined battle not only outwardly but inwardly too. If we have no business with the construction of the future or with organizing it for all time there can still be no doubt about the task confronting us at present: the ruthless criticism of the existing order." Marx's intention not to deal with the future but to criticize the existing social order was somehow lost in his thought as well as in the trajectory of Marxian social theory until it was recovered in the early twentieth century by what became known as the Frankfurt School. Here I use the term critical theory only to refer to this tradition.

4. I will use the term publicity as the English translation for *Offentlichkeit*. Publicity became the standard English word for the term since the translation of Habermas's *The Structural Transformation of the Public Sphere*. Since the standard use of the word in English has a different meaning, I will use publicity only to refer to the concept and will reserve the terms public space and public sphere to describe the sphere between the market and the state in which free interaction takes place.

5. This dual conception leads to a new understanding of modernity. Both Marx and Weber based their theories of modernity on analyses of the impact of emerging specialized subsystems on the arenas of social interaction. Marx under-

stood the emergence of the capitalist economy as the detachment of the process of material reproduction from an interactive arena. Phenomena such as objectification and reification were understood as the side effects of substituting systemic dynamics for interactive logics. See Marx and Engels, 1858; 1871. Weber based his understanding of modern societies on an analysis of a similar process by showing how formal criteria had replaced substantive criteria in morality, science, and art. At the political level, this process led to the formation of an order of bureaucrats whose action is oriented by formal rules. Again, the result is the substitution of action coordination by the rules of a self-regulating subsystem for interactive forms. See Weber, 1930; 1978. The first generation of the Frankfurt School radicalized both Weber's and Marx's understanding of the emergence of autonomous subsystems by making their systemic forms of rationality—what Adorno and Horkheimer called instrumental rationality—the only possible kind of rationality. Thus, by introducing a dual understanding of social action within modernity, Habermas is breaking with all these traditions.

6. Many express concern that Habermas has taken the distinction between systemic and non-systemic forms of action too far. Thomas McCarthy argues that applying this distinction to the political realm may prevent further democratization: "[I]f self-determination, political equality, and the participation of citizens in decision-making are the hallmarks of true democracy, then a democratic government cannot be a political system in Habermas's sense, that is, a domain of action differentiated from other parts of society and preserving its autonomy in relation to them" (McCarthy, 1991:170–71). McCarthy is right to point out that Habermas concedes too much by considering systemic arenas very large parts of the political system such as parliament and political parties. However, it is possible to consider parties and parliament media connecting the public sphere to the administrative system. In the last part of this chapter I will propose an extension of democracy based on this dual framework.

7. Nancy Fraser tried to transform these empirical criticisms into a theoretical critique by making the empirical problem caused by the homogeneous nature of bourgeois publics into an heuristic problem. Habermas assumes, she argues, that confinement of public life to a single public sphere is a positive state of affairs. Fraser fails to acknowledge that the counterpublics formed by women and blacks in response to the homogeneity of the bourgeois publics were in communication with the other publics. Thus, her attempt to transform an empirical critique of exclusion into an alternative conception of the public space has no empirical foundation (Fraser, 1997: 94–76).

8. Good examples of the role played by deliberation in building consensus are the recent peace negotiations in the Middle East and Northern Ireland. In both cases, it was possible to establish a consensual framework for the peace process because both parties deliberated on a minimal agenda. If the parties had pursued their objectives within a more Habermasian framework they would have had to wait for the unlikely eventuality of agreement on all major issues. Thus, in this case at least, the role of deliberation in forging consensus is clear. In the recent peace accord in Northern Ireland another feature played a very important role: the establishment of a deadline for reaching a minimal consensual agenda. This

showed that consensus could be forged under different deliberative conditions, which need not make it less binding after agreement has been reached. The case also shows that a previous consensus on the form of institutional deliberation—a national referendum—can facilitate consensus on more substantive points.

CHAPTER 3
DEMOCRACY AND THE LATIN AMERICAN TRADITION

1. In a recent essay, Seyla Benhabib corroborated this idea by claiming that there are culture-transcending validity claims. In her view, democracy as a form of practical reason "has become the collective and anonymous property of cultures, institutions and traditions as a result of the experiments and experiences both ancient and modern" (1996:69). This feature of both the democratic idea and democratic practices can be seen as one of the reasons for the appeal of democracy in non-democratic political settings as well as in non-Western cultures.

2. It is very difficult to evaluate the analytical significance of dependency theory. Most of the theoreticians who worked with the dependency framework have since switched to other analytical paradigms more in tune with contemporary Latin American societies. Nevertheless, a few have engaged in a serious effort of self-criticism of the analytical flaws of the dependency enterprise. Among those who have changed paradigms we can certainly include Cardoso himself, although he never revisited the assumptions of his own theory but instead criticized the most epiphenomenalist versions of the dependency approach (Cardoso and Serra, 1979). A fair verdict on dependency theory should probably note the greater theoretical sophistication of Cardoso and Faletto's version while pointing out the uselessness of this sophistication in light of the empirical flaws in its assumption of a contradiction between center and periphery, based on the latter's insertion in the international economic system—a flaw that has remained with dependency theory from the very beginning.

3. I am grateful to Alberto Olvera for his comments that led to this remark.

4. Inglehart's theory of modernization makes the identical mistake in the analysis of non-Western societies (1997). The author sees a link between culture and economic development, which leads him to place different countries on a continuum and to argue for a teleological conception of culture and politics. The author seems to have completely missed the entire debate on institution building and political learning and instead relies on an empiricist approach to modernization.

5. Many authors have stressed the rejection of liberalism and individualism in the political thought of seventeenth-century Spain (Bernice, 1963; Morse, 1982). All showed how, at both the philosophical and political levels, Spain remained tied to Aristotelianism and tried to build from this perspective an alternative view to Western modernity. Richard Morse has attempted to construct a conception of Ibericism based on its rejection of rationalism and science. Yet, his attempt fails insofar as he reduces Western rationality to instrumental rationality and rather naively tries to recover alternative forms of rationality. For a critique, see Schwartzman, 1988. Iberianism has also been recently criticized for the lack of an

attempt to associate ideas and institutions and to show which institutions, in the Latin American case, were reponsible for the reproduction of the Iberian elements in the region (Souza, 2000).

6. Brazil should be distinguished from other Hispanic American countries due to its much more conservative path to independence. Two factors might explain the more conservative Brazilian independence: the fact that the country hosted the Portuguese royal family during the Napoleonic Wars; and the temporal moment of the independence of Brazil. According to W. G. dos Santos, the Brazilian elites watched the main events of the Hispanic American independences and agreed to sacrifice republicanism in order to maintain the country as a national unit. This has led it to sacrifice not only the republican element of national liberation, but also the idea of civil equality. Brazilian independence allowed the Portuguese royal family to remain in power. It also attempted to reconcile liberalism with slavery. These compromises led to a general crisis in the second half of the nineteenth century but guaranteed the territorial integrity of the nation-state (W. Santos, 1977). Nevertheless, the Brazilian regime was identified by the country's elites with liberalism.

7. On the critique of the approach of popular culture, see Thompson, 1995. The author shows how the encounter between local and Western cultures was much more complex than authors such as Schiller had assumed, involving adaptation, selective appropriation, and incorporation depending on the different cases. He also criticizes the conception of an originally untainted culture, as have recent feminist and black studies. See Thompson, 1995; Escobar and Alvarez, 1992.

8. In an earlier essay, Damatta analyzed the function of citizenship in what he called a "relational universe." In a relational society individuals reject the universality of the law and attempt to humanize it by introducing a particularistic component. Damatta illustrated this phenomenon with the attempts of Brazilians to connect themselves to someone at the level of public administration in order to be treated with "attention," "tolerance," and "respect." The author's example exemplifies the flaws of his theory: he naively transforms what is clearly an elite or middle-class attempt to circumvent law into a generalizable attitude toward the state. The huge lines in Brazilian social security and health offices seem to prove that Damatta's strategy for avoiding the universality of the law is not available to all Brazilians, who pay a high price for the existence of a relational universe in the country. See Damatta, 1975:72.

9. Adam Przeworski has recently renewed such a conception under a rational choice cover. He maintains that "he is not claiming that normative commitments to democracy are infrequent or irrelevant, only that they are not necessary to understand how democracy works" (1991:24). He argues that uncertainty and the individual's need to reduce it are sufficient to explain the operation of democracy, but he is unable to explain the survival of democracy using only this framework. As a matter of fact every rational choice theory smuggles at one point or another a normative element into its analysis in order to explain the survival of democracy. In Przeworski's case, this element derives from individuals' fear that uncertainty might undermine their autonomy, leading them normatively to opt for political systems that guarantee it. For the relation between individual autonomy and normativity, see Dahl, 1991.

CHAPTER 4

THE TRANSFORMATION OF THE LATIN AMERICAN PUBLIC SPACE

1. The break with electoral competition assumed different forms in different Latin American countries. In Brazil, the authoritarian regime never completely ruled it out, but chose only to impose institutional limits on elections for high administrative positions such as the presidency. It also limited the freedom of political organization, predetermining the number of political parties. In Chile and Argentina, the breakdown of electoral competition was sharper. In Chile, elections were abolished, but a plebicitary form of governmental approval was kept. Eventually, this primeval electoral device helped complete the transition to democracy. In Argentina, the authoritarian regime never allowed election; when electoral competition reappeared, it signaled the end of authoritarianism.

2. There is a huge literature on liberalization, most of it produced with the framework of transition theory. The most important references are Cruz and Martins (1983), Martins (1986), and Mainwaring (1986) on Brazil, and Smith (1990) and O'Donnell (1990) on Argentina. Most of the literature discusses issues related to the relinquishing of power or the relationship between authoritarian power-holders and political society. The main issues include: the initiative of the transition; electoral law; and the necessity of pacts between authoritarian power-holders and the democratic opposition. Two characteristics of this literature are important to bear in mind: the influence of the elites/masses dichotomy, which led it to pay attention to issues such as the initiative of the process of liberalization, which transition theory assigns to the authoritarian regimes; and its focus on pacts and electoral law, which implies the possibility of intra-elite pacts between authoritarian power-holders and the democratic opposition.

3. The paradigmatic cases are Brazil and Mexico. In both cases the authoritarian regimes were represented in elections by a political party that was benefited by the electoral laws. The aim of the opposition was also similar in both cases—to win elections in spite of the unfair rules for competition. Chile might be considered a radicalization of the model that transformed electoral competition in yes or no referenda. Again, Argentina is the exception. Due to the Peronists' high levels of support, authoritarianism was not associated with any form of election.

4. It is unclear whether transition through collapse, where the authoritarian regime is defeated by an external enemy, involves a process of liberalization. It can be argued, however, that Argentina was already liberalizing at the time of the Malvinas War. Nevertheless, it is clear that the war greatly accelerated democratization in Argentina.

5. I understand identity not as a communitarian redefinition of the nature of belonging, as Sandel (1984) and other neo-communitarian authors do, but as a process of self-reflection on existing societal norms and structures of domination. In this sense, the new democratic identity constructed in many Latin American countries involved less reinterpreting the bonds of community than a move toward a more democratic political culture in which democratic social norms are incorporated into the process of collective action.

6. Guerra shows clearly how this process worked in the late nineteenth century, when a great many independent voluntary associations were established in

Mexico in places such as San Luis de Potosi. Liberal clubs were formed, and there was the possibility of the constitution of an autonomous social space. Yet, the autonomy of the clubs could not resist the domination of Mexican politics by political parties and the military (Guerra, 1988, 2:21).

7. The method for arriving at the composition of associations in the total universe was slightly different in the two cities. In Belo Horizonte all associations that seek registration in the city notary were included in the universe. For São Paulo, due to the size of the universe, some procedures were taken to reduce the number of associations to be searched. All the associations included are the ones registered in the downtown notary of the city, which has also other three notaries for the registration of associations. We decided not to count religious or recreational associations in São Paulo because they did not fit exactly with the idea of either civic associations or form of collective action. Yet, the data on the decreasing representation of recreational associations in the total universe was already available (W. Santos, 1993). For a definition of associations utilized, see Diamond 1994.

8. Gay (1994) has studied the relationship between continuity and change in societal practices in Brazil. His study of two neighborhood associations in Rio de Janeiro shows how each pursued a completely different form of social action: one drew heavily on clientelism, whereas the other expressed social movements' reaction against political mediators. More important than establishing typologies of social action, however, is pointing out that the number of autonomous neighborhood organizations increased sharply in Brazil throughout the liberalization period. I return to this point in chapter 5.

9. Alain Touraine has completely missed this point in his analysis of social movements in Latin America. For him, the fragmentation of the social world and the subordination of collective action to a statist logic continue to be the main factors orienting social action in Latin America. Touraine commits the serious mistake of conflating pluralization with fragmentation. He also fails to distinguish between different relations with the state. The fact that social movements such as urban ones no longer consented to integration into the state is more important than the fact that they directed their claims for services and resources to the state (Touraine, 1988:130–31).

10. There are also important human rights movements in Chile and Mexico, which for the aims of this book I have chosen not to discuss. Garreton's (1996) study of the Chilean human rights movement shows how it has been oriented by cognitive and cultural values. He also shows how these values remained in tension with political society's pragmatism during the Chilean transition.

11. The religious institutions eager to play the role of umbrella to human rights claims differed from country to country. In Brazil, the Catholic Church was already reevaluating its relationship with the state when the human rights issue emerged and was thus willing to raise the issue and protect human rights associations (Bruneau, 1974; Casanova, 1994). In Argentina, the Catholic Church sided for a very long time with the institutions that decided to ignore the so-called dirty war. Jewish institutions, however, played an important role in defending human rights in Argentina (Brysk, 1994; Roeniger and Sznajder, 1999).

12. The most important were: Asamblea Permanente por los Derechos Huma-

nos; Liga Argentina por los Derechos del Hombre; Movimento Ecumenico por los Derechos Humanos; Madres de Plaza de Mayo; Abuelas de Plaza de Mayo; Comision de Familiares de Desaparecidos y Presos por Razones Politicas; and Servicio de Paz y Justicia; Centro de Estudos Legales y Sociales (Leis, 1989:14–17).

13. I am not denying the existence of a tradition of instrumentalizing rights in Argentina. Peruzzotti (1993) has shown how the instrumentalization of law by Yrigoyen and by the Peronists precluded the possibility of a regarding law as a moral, consensual device. Nevertheless, I maintain that instrumentalization in Brazil was more severe because it involved denying the civil rights of common citizens.

14. Two important episodes were addressed by human rights movements in Brazil: the state-sanctioned murder of a São Paulo public television journalist, and a series of bombings that killed an administrative officer of the Bar Association. In both episodes, members of the regime's repressive apparatus were directly involved, and the government responded in both cases by denying responsibility. In the case of the murdered journalist, the cause of the death was denied; the inquiry into the cause of the bombing became a legal farce. In both cases, a conflict over the truthfulness of the regime's account was the central element of human rights groups' political actions.

15. The level of electoral fraud differs between the two countries; it is much lower in Brazil due to Vargas's electoral reform in the 1930s. Getulio Vargas, a former governor of Rio Grande do Sul who seized power by force in 1930 after being defeated in a fraudulent presidential election, proposed a complete overhaul of the Brazilian electoral system. He transferred authority over elections from political society to highly educated individuals, hoping to draw on their professional ethos. He also transferred control over procedures from political society to the judiciary by creating a system of electoral courts. The level of electoral fraud in Brazil has been low ever since. See Gomes, 1985.

16. This aspect has only been tangentially approached in the literature. In his work on the Brazilian Constituent Assembly, Rodrigues (1987) showed that there were more representatives that had belonged to the authoritarian regime's former political party than to the opposition party. Democratization in Brazil saw continuity in practices such as party change, the exchange of votes for material benefits by parliament members, and utilizing administrative resources to create clientelistic machines. See also Hagopian, 1996.

17. This argument, which applies better to Mexico than to Brazil or Argentina, has been defended by many authors and has received its most consistent formulation in an influential article by Sergio Zermeno (1996).

CHAPTER 5
DEMOCRATIZATION IN LATIN AMERICA

1. Phillip Schmitter has most clearly insisted on this point. He argues that democratization should involve only the restoration of electoral competition and not issues such as social justice or the rule of law. For him, the connection of democracy with these two issues was merely episodic, the Anglo-Saxon case having connected democracy with a preexisting tradition of rule of law and some

European cases having connected it with a tradition of social justice. In Latin America, where none of these traditions was internal or previous to democratization, Schmitter argues, they establish external constraints on democracy itself. Schmitter's argument conflates two completely different dimensions: the rule of law and social justice. It is clear that the latter is external to democracy, although the existence of democracy might facilitate its existence. The rule of law, however, is intrinsic to the democratic tradition. It is not an episodic coincidence that democratic breakdown has been less common in the Anglo-Saxon world than elsewhere, and it is not a coincidence that the democratic systems consolidated during the first and the second waves of democratization incorporated the rule of law into their traditions in the cases where it had not been available before. See Schmitter, 1998.

2. Joshua Cohen rightly criticizes the idea that innovation might necessarily emerge in the periphery of the political system:

> Habermas thinks it suffices to make the case for autonomous influence flowing from the periphery, under conditions of crisis. But once that case for possibility is on hand, we can ask whether there are other forms of citizen participation that would more fully achieve the radical promise. Those forms would need to meet three conditions: they must permit and encourage inputs that reflect experiences and concerns that may not occupy the current agenda (sensors, rooted in local experience and information); they must provide disciplined assessment of proposals through deliberation that encompasses fundamental political values; and . . . they [must] also provide more institutionalized, regularized occasions for citizen participation in collective decision-making. (1998:37).

I will come back to these three issues as I discuss participatory innovation at the local level in Brazil in chapter 6.

3. It is, however, important to understand that the post-democratization electoral defeat of the party linked to the authoritarian regime in Brazil, the PDS, did not affect the composition of political society. First, during the negotiation of the transition to democracy a split in the PDS led to a second party, which participated in the negotiations. Second, in the two years between the transition and the first congressional elections, members of the PDS moved to other parties in order to preserve their electoral viability. Thus, the electoral defeat of the PDS did not mean a change in practices within political society. See Avritzer, 1998.

4. It is beyond the aims of this work to discuss the Uruguayan case. However, the solution found in Uruguay in order not to prosecute the military is instructive due to both the moral formula achieved and the use of deliberative mechanisms. During the Uruguayan transition, the military did not demand any kind of amnesty, arguing that it had commited no crimes. In 1985, the first year of democratic rule, relatives of the disappeared presented evidence to the courts and a conflict emerged between the military, which refused to testify, and the civilian courts. Confronted with a military veto of further investigation, in December 1986 the government proposed a law acknowledging its de facto incapacity to punish certain crimes. Thus, with Law 15.848 the Uruguayan state acknowledged its inability to punish the military without granting them amnesty. The law was

later submitted to a referendum and ratified by 58 percent of the voters. See Zala-quett, 1996a:28–30.

5. The second moment of the Argentinean democracy, in which the Peronistas returned to power with Menen, makes the argument of the ambiguities of political society even stronger. The ambiguities of the Peronistas in relation to human rights were strong due to their collectivist and organicist conception of society. Their return to power sharpened the dissociation between human rights movements and political society. See Roeniger, 1998.

6. Only during the Cardoso government did the Brazilian state start a process of indemnifying the families of the dead and missing. This process was conducted by a commission nominated by the president. Despite acknowledging the responsibility of state forces in the death of members of the political opposition to authoritarianism, it did not make any of its members responsible for that. The special commission on death and disappearance created by Law 9.140 of 1995 involved representatives of the executive (foreign ministry and armed forces), Congress, sectors of the judiciary, and civil society. It decided to indemnify all the missing and all those who died within state institutions. The most contentious cases involved members of the armed opposition (136) supposedly killed in action. All state agents responsible for deaths continue to be covered by the 1979 amnesty.

7. It is important to distinguish the support of Brazilian public opinion for the criminalization of human rights abuses from the support of Argentinean public opinion for the same issue. The level of consensus on human rights in Argentina is much higher than it is in Brazil. Yet, most military police actions that lead to serious human rights violations are opposed by Brazilian public opinion. This opposition did not translate into strong actions to change the law, making human rights organizations politically isolated in this respect. On human rights organizations in Brazil, see Pinheiro, 1996b.

8. A good example of the ambiguity of Brazilian courts in relation to human rights violations against the poor was the different sentences arising from the Carandiru massacre—an episode in which São Paulo's police was called to put an end to a prison rebellion and ended up killing 111 inmates. Some judges criticized the police action in their sentences whereas others denied indemnification in cases where the inmates were not killed by firearms (Dimenstein, 1996:109).

9. The net gains are as follows: in the north of Brazil, Amapá and Acre increased their representation in Congress from one to eight MPs. The northeastern states had a net gain of sixteen MPs. Together the north and northeastern states had a net gain of thirty-three MPs. See Avritzer, 1998.

10. The Mexican Academy for Human Rights is one of the civic associations which formed Alianza Cívica. It was created in 1980 around a broad human rights agenda. In the early 1990s it decided to center its agenda on political rights and, in particular, on the issue of electoral monitoring.

11. The decision of the IFE's General Council was made four votes to three. The argument for not granting APN status to Alianza Cívica was made by the PRI representative in the IFE (parties had representatives without voting prerogatives). The decision came at a very delicate moment in which the IFE was acquiring autonomy vis-à-vis the all powerful secretary of government.

12. Two different examples are very instructive in this respect. One is the loss of autonomy of neighborhood associations which previously fought for autonomy. This has taken place in some areas of Brazil, Rio de Janeiro in particular, a city in which the strengthening of traditional politics and organized crime go hand in hand with the weakening of the movements that fought for autonomy (Gay, 1994). A second good example is given by Abers (1998), who shows how incentives to get rid of clientelism created effective forms of partici pation in the case of Porto Alegre in the south of Brazil. Thus, my argument is that the problem is less how wide in scope new democratic practices are and more how the continuity at the political level of old clientelistic practices hinders emerging forms of social autonomy.

13. There is a theoretical problem in the way O'Donnell interprets both republican and liberal traditions. O'Donnell stresses in republicanism "the severe view of obligation of rulers" and in liberalism "the commitment to freedoms in society." In the former case, anti-corruption legislation would be derived from the idea of public virtues, and in the latter the capacity to enforce rights would be derived from the need to protect the private domain. However, it is not clear that O'Donnell exhausts the array of possibilities by raising the connection between the traditions and the issues he has in mind. For instance, corruption has been historically low in countries such as Germany and Britain, which have a weaker republican tradition. It has been higher in Italy, which has a stronger republican tradition than both countries. In general, rights have been strong in the Anglo-Saxon tradition due to its capacity to enforce the law and not only because of a strong tradition of privacy. See O'Donnell, 1998:118.

14. See also Fox, 2000.

15. This was the result of a very fertile discussion on accountability that took place in Buenos Aires in May 2000. For the results, see Peruzzotti and Smulovicz, 2002.

CHAPTER 6
PARTICIPATORY PUBLICS IN BRAZIL AND MEXICO

1. PopR is the regional population, PVR is the virtual population, Y is the regional average income, and e is a constant with a value of 2.7182818.

2. I am grateful to Jean-François Proud'homme for suggesting this analogy.

3. It is worth noting that although the 1996 legislation gave the IFE's General Council full autonomy in the organization of the elections, there was not enough time to fully implement the idea of *ciudadanización*. The IFE's new councilors assumed their position on October 31, 1996, and had only two months to appoint the president and secretaries of the electoral precincts for the 1997 elections. Thus, only 30 percent of these councilors were appointed by the IFE's General Council.

4. The Workers Party is a left-wing party created in Brazil in the last phase of the democratization process. It advocated a participatory form of grass roots organization based on local councils, and the election of city councilors by local councilors. In its 1988 program for the city of Porto Alegre, the Workers Party did not include the idea of participatory budgeting but only that of popular councils.

On the overlap between the Workers Party and urban social movements in the early 1980s in Brazil, see Doimo, 1995; Dagnino, 1994; and Avritzer, 1998.

5. Written press coverage was measured by column inches given to each candidate in an average article. The average article on Salinas was 98.5 inches, while Cardenas received only an average of 30.1 inches. Television coverage was measured by the number of stories on each candidate and total time each candidate got in a nightly news program. Salinas had 74 stories and 141 minutes of coverage, while Cardenas had 10 stories and almost 9 minutes of coverage. See Adler, 1993:152–55.

6. It is important to keep in mind that one major source of electoral fraud in Mexico was the nomination of uneducated people to organize electoral districts. Although there were guidelines mandating well-educated people as district presidents, it was common to change the levels of education in the registration of electoral officials in order to change the district presidents on election day.

7. Institutional designs in this perspective are part of what Domingues (1996;1999) calls active citizenship.

REFERENCES

❦

Abers, Rebeca. 1996. From ideas to practice: The P.T. and participatory governance in Brazil. *Latin American Perspectives.* 23, no. 4:35–53.

———. 1998. From clientelism to cooperation: Local government, participatory policy, and civic organizing in Porto Alegre, Brazil. *Politics and Society* 26, no. 4:511–537.

Adler, I. 1993. *The Mexican case: The media in the 1988 presidential election.* In *Television, politics and the transition to democracy in Latin America,* ed. T. Skidmore, 1945–73. Baltimore: Johns Hopkins University Press.

Adorno, T. W. 1951. *The authoritarian personality.* New York: American Jewish Committee.

———. 1973. *Negative dialectics.* New York: Seabury Press.

Aguayo, S. 1996. A Mexican milestone. *Journal of Democracy.* 6 (April): 157–67.

Alianza Cívica. 1995a. *Tramite legal para el escrito de peticion.*

———. 1995b. *Petition to Mexico's President Ernesto Zedillo.* March 28, 1995.

———. 1996a. *Habeas corpus petition to rotating district judge.* N.p.

———. 1996b. *The privileges of Mexican presidents.* June.

———. 1997a. *Alianza Cívica: Agrupacion politica nacional.* January 24, 1997.

Almond, G. A., and S. Verba. 1963. *The civic culture: Political attitudes and democracy in five nations.* Princeton, Princeton University Press.

Alvarez, Sonia, Evelina Dagnino, and Arturo Escobar, eds. 1998. *Culture of politics/politics of culture.* Boulder: Westview Press.

Apel, K. O. 1988. *The transformation of philosophy.* Milwaukee: Wisconsin University Press.

Apter, D. 1973. *Political change.* London: F. Cass.

Apter, D. E. 1965. *The politics of modernization.* Chicago: University of Chicago Press.

Arato, A. 1981. Civil society against the state: Poland 1980–1. *Telos* 47:23–47.

Arato, A., and J. Cohen. 1988. Civil society and social theory. *Thesis Eleven* 1:40–64.

Arendt, H. 1951. *The origins of totalitarianism.* Cleveland: World Publishing Company.

———. 1958. *The human condition.* Chicago: University of Chicago Press.

Assies, William. 1994. Urban social movements in Brazil. *Latin American Perspectives.* 21 no. 81:81–105.

Auyero, J. 1997. *Estudios sobre clientelismo politico contemporaneo:* Buenos Aires: Losada.

Avritzer, L. 1994. *Sociedade civil e democratização.* Belo Horizonte: Del Rey.

———. 1995. Transition to democracy and political culture: An analysis of the conflict between civil and political society in post-authoritarian Brazil. *Constellations* 2, no. 2:242–67.

———. 1996. *A moralidade da democracia.* São Paulo: Perspectiva.

Avritzer, L. 1997. Um desenho institucional para o novo associativismo. *Lua Nova* 1, no. 38:149–74.

———. 1998. Modernization and political culture: An analysis of the impeachment of Collor de Mello. In *Corruption and political reform in Brazil*, ed. K. Rosenn and R. Dows, 119–38. Miami: North South Center.

———. 1999a. Diálogo y reflexividad: Acerca de la relación entre esfera pública e medios de comunicación. *Metapolítica* 3, no. 9: 79–94.

———. 1999b. Teoria critica e teoria democratica: Da impossibilidade da democracia ao conceito de esfera pública. *Novos Estudos Cebrap* 1, no. 53: 167–88.

———. 2000. Democratization and changes in the pattern of association in Brazil. *Journal of Interamerican Studies and World Affairs* 42, no. 3: 59–76.

Azevedo, Sérgio, and Antônio Augusto Prates. 1991. *Planejamento participativo, movimentos sociais e ação coletiva*. Ciências Sociais Hoje. São Paulo: Anpocs-Vértice.

Bachrach, P. 1967. *The theory of democratic elitism: A critique*. Boston: Little Brown.

Baierle, Sergio. 1998. The explosion of experience. In *Politics of culture/culture of politics*, ed. S. Alvarez, E. Dagnino, and A. Escobar, 118–38. Boulder: Westview Press.

Baily, S. 1982. Las sociedades de ayuda mutua e el desarollo de al comunidad italiana en Buenos Aires. *Desarollo Economico* 21, no. 84: 22–32.

Banck, G., and A. Doimo. 1988. Between utopia and strategy: A case study of Brazilian urban movments. In *Urban social movements in the third world*, ed. F. Schuurman and T. Naerssen, 125–50. London: Routledge.

Barber, B. R. 1984. *Strong democracy: Participatory politics for a new age*. Berkeley: University of California Press.

Barbero, J. M. 1987. *Dos Meios as Mediações*. Barcelona, Gilli.

Barcelos, C. 1992. *Rota 66*. Rio de Janeiro: Editora Globo.

Barros, R. 1986. The left and democracy in Latin America. Telos 68:49–70.

Barry, B. M. 1970. *Sociologists, economists and democracy*. London: Collier-Macmillan.

Becerra, R., P. Salazar, and J. Woldenberg. 2000. *La mecanica del cambio politico em Mexico: Elecciones, partidos y reforma*. Mexico D. F.: Ediciones Cal y Arena.

Benhabib, S. 1992. Model of the public space: Hannah Arendt, the liberal tradition and Jürgen Habermas. In *Habermas and the public sphere*, ed. C. Calhoun, 73–98. Cambridge, MA: MIT Press.

———. 1996. Toward a deliberative model of democratic legitimacy. In *Democracy and difference*, 67–94. Princeton: Princeton University Press.

Bernice, Hamilton. 1963. *Political thought in sixteenth century Spain*. Oxford. Oxford University Press.

Blum, Robert. 1997. The weight of the past. *Journal of Democracy* 8. no. 4: 28–42.

Bobbio, N. 1987. *The future of democracy: A defense of the rules of the game*. Minneapolis: University of Minnesota Press.

Bohman, J. 1996. *Public deliberation: Pluralism, complexity and democracy.* Cambridge, MA: MIT Press.

Boschi, C. 1986. *Os Leigos e o Poder.* São Paulo: Atica.

Boschi, Renato. 1987. *A arte da associação.* Rio de Janeiro: Vértice.

Boxer, C. R. 1962. *The golden age of Brazil, 1695–1750: Growing pains of a colonial society.* Berkeley: University of California Press, in cooperation with the Sociedade de Estudos Históricos Dom Pedro Segundo.

Bruneau, T. C. 1974. *The political transformation of the Brazilian Catholic Church.* New York: Cambridge University Press.

Brysk, A. 1994. *The politics of human rights in Argentina.* Stanford: Stanford University Press.

Burke, P. 1978. *Popular culture in early modern Europe.* New York: New York University Press.

Calhoun, C. J. ed. 1992. *Habermas and the public sphere.* Cambridge, MA, MIT Press.

Camin, A. 1990. *Despues del Milagro.* Mexico. D. F.: Cal y Arena.

Cammack, P. 1990. Brazil: The long march to the new republic. *New Left Review* (190): 21–58.

Cantun, Jesus. 2000. Interview by Leonardo Avritzer and Alberto Olvera. Mexico D. F., July.

Cardoso, F. H., and E. Faletto. 1979. *Dependency and development in Latin America.* Berkeley: University of California Press.

Cardoso, F. H., and J. Serra. (1979). *As desventuras da dialéctica da dependência.* Princeton: Institute of Advanced Studies.

Casanova, J. 1994. *Public religions in the modern world.* Chicago: University of Chicago Press.

Cohen, Jean L. 1985. Strategy or identity: New theoretical paradigms and contemporary social movements. *Social Research* 52, no. 4: 663–716.

———. 1996. The public sphere, the media and civil society. In *Rights of access to the media*, ed. A. Sajo, 29–50. The Hague: Kluwer.

Cohen, Jean. L., and A. Arato. 1992. *Civil society and political theory.* Cambridge, MA: MIT Press.

Cohen, Joshua. 1997. Deliberation and democratic legitimacy. In *Deliberative democracy.* ed. J. Bohman and W. Rehg, 67–92. Cambridge, MA: MIT Press.

———. 1998. *Reflections on Habermas on democracy.* Florence: European University Institute.

Cohen, Joshua, and J. Rogers. 1995. *Associations and democracy.* London: Verso.

Cohen, Joshua, and Charles Sabel. 1997. Direct-deliberative polyarchy. *European Law Journal.* 3, no. 4: 313–42.

Collier, D., and Joint Committee on Latin American Studies. 1979. *The new authoritarianism in Latin America.* Princeton: Princeton University Press.

Comparato, F. K. 1998. The impeachment process and the constitutional significance of the Collor Affair. In *Corruption and political reform in Brazil*, ed. K. Rosenn and R. Dows, 73–85. Miami: North South Center.

Conniff, M. 1975. Voluntary associations in Rio: 1870–1945. *Journal of Interamerican Affairs* 17, no. 1: 64–82.

Constitucion politica de los Estados Unidos Mexicanos. 2000. Mexico D. F.: Editorial Ista.

Cooke, M. 1994. *Language and reason: A study of Habermas's pragmatics.* Cambridge, MA: MIT Press.

Cornelius, W. A. Craig, and D. Fox, eds. 1994. *Transforming state-society relations in Mexico.* La Jolla: University of San Diego Press.

Costa, Sérgio. 1994. Esfera Pública, sociedade civil e movimentos sociais no Brasil. *Novos Estudos* 38: 38–52.

———. 1997. Contextos da construção do espaço público no Brasil. *Novos Estudos* 47:179–92.

Coutinho, C. N. 1982. *A democracia como valor.* Rio de Janeiro: Paz e Terra.

Cruz, Sebastião Velasques, and Carlos Estevam Martins. 1983. De Castelo a Figueiredo: Uma incursão na pre-historia da abertura. *Sociedade e política no Brasil pós-64,* ed. B. Sorj, and M. H. de Souza, 13–61. São Paulo: Brasiliense.

Dagnino, E. 1994. *Anos 90: Política e Sociedade no Brasil.* São Paulo: Brasiliense.

———. 1988. Culture, citizenship and democracy: Changing discourses and practices of the Latin American left. In *Culture of politics/politics of culture,* ed. Sonia Alvarez, Evelina Dagnino, and Arturo Escobar, 33–63. Boulder: Westview Press.

———. ed. 2002. *Sociedade civil e espaços públicos.* Campinas: Editora da Unicamp.

Dahl, R. A. 1956. *A preface to democratic theory.* Chicago: University of Chicago Press.

———. 1971. *Polyarchy: Participation and opposition.* New Haven: Yale University Press.

———. 1991. *Democracy and its critics.* New Haven: Yale University Press.

Damatta, R. 1975. *Carnavais, malandros e heróis.* São Paulo: Brasiliense.

———. 1985. *A casa e a rua: Espaço, cidadania, mulher e morte no Brasil.* São Paulo: Brasiliense.

Diamond, L. 1994. Toward democratic consolidation. *Journal of Democracy* 5, no. 3: 4–18.

Diamond, L. J., J. Linz, and S. Lipset. 1989. *Democracy in developing countries.* Boulder: Lynn Rienner.

Dias-Barriga, M. 1996. Necessidad: Notes on the discourse of urban politics in the Ajusco foothills of Mexico City. *American Ethnologist* 3:2.

Dimenstein, Gilberto. 1988. *A república dos Padrinhos.* São Paulo: Brasiliense.

———. 1996. *A democracia em Pedaços.* São Paulo: Brasiliense.

Doimo, A. M. 1995. *A vez e a voz do popular.* Rio de Janeiro: Relume Dumara.

Domingues, J. Maurício. 1996. *Sociological theory and collective subjectivity.* London: MacMillan.

———. 1999. *Criatividade social, subjetividade coletiva e a modernidade brasileira contemporânea.* Rio de Janeiro: Contracapa.

Downs, A. 1956. *An economic theory of democracy.* New York: Harper.

Dresser, Denise. 1991. *Neo-populist solutions to neo-liberal problems.* La Jolla: University of San Diego Press.

———. 1994. Bringing the poor back in: Solidarity as a strategy of regime legitimation. In *Transforming state-society relations in Mexico*, ed. W. Cornelius, A. Craig, and Fox, 143–165. La Jolla: University of San Diego Press.

Dunn, J. 1979. *Western political theory in the face of the future*. Cambridge: Cambridge University Press.

———. *Democracy: The unfinished journey, 508* BC *to* AD *1993*. New York: Oxford University Press.

Eisenstadt, S. N. 1966. *Modernization: Protest and change*. Englewood Cliffs, NJ: Prentice-Hall.

———. 1970. *Readings in social evolution and development*. New York: Pergamon Press.

———. 1973. *Tradition, change, and modernity*. New York: Wiley.

Eisenstadt, S., and W. Schluchter. 1998. Path to early modernities: A comparative view. *Deadalus* 127, no. 3: 1–18.

Elster, J. 1989. *Foundations of social choice theory*. Cambridge: Cambridge University Press.

Escobar, Arturo, and S. Alvarez. 1992. *The making of new social movements in Latin America: Strategy, identity and democracy*. Boulder: Westview Press.

Faria, Claudia. 1996. O orçamento participativo em Belo Horizonte. Master's dissertation, UFMG, Belo Horizonte.

Fausto, B. 1983. *Trabalho urbano e conflito social (1890–1920)* São Paulo: Difel.

Fedozzi, Luciano, S. Baierle, and R. Abers, 1995. *Orçamento participativo: Pesquisa sobre a população que participa da discussão do orçamento público junto à Prefeitura Municipal de Porto Alegre* . Porto Alegre.

Finley, M. I. 1973. *Democracy ancient and modern*. New Brunswick, NJ: Rutgers University Press.

FSP. 1996. *Folha de São Paulo*. São Paulo: Editora Folha da Manha.

Forment, C. 1991. Dimensiones socio-institutionales dela sociedad politica y bases culturales de la pratica politica. In *Transiciones a la democracia en Europa e America Latina*, ed. Carlos Barba Solano, 39–57. Mexico D. F.: Flacso.

Foweraker, J., and Ann Craig, eds. 1990. *Popular movements and political change in Mexico*. Boulder: Lynn Rienner.

Foweraker, J., and T. Landman. 1997. *Citizenship rights and social movements: A comparative and statistical analysis*. New York: Oxford University Press.

Fox, Jonathan. 1993. *The politics of food in Mexico: State power and social mobilization*. Ithaca: Cornell University Press.

———. 2000. *Civil society and political accountability: Propositions for a discussion*. Paper presented at the Hellen Kellog Institute for International Studies, Notre Dame. May.

Franco, Maria Sylvia de Carvalho. 1974. *Homens livres na ordem escravocrata*. São Paulo: Atica.

Frank, A. G. 1970. *Latin America: Underdevelopment or revolution*. London: MR Press.

Fraser, N. 1989. *Unruly practices: Power, discourse and gender in contemporary social theory*. Minneapolis, University of Minnesota Press.

———. 1997. *Justice interruptus: Critical reflections on the postsocialist condition*. London: Routledge.

Fukuyama, F. 1995. Trust: The social virtues & the creation of prosperity. New York: Free Press.

Gamson, J. 1989. Silence, death and the invisible enemy: AID's activism and social movement newness. *Social Problems* 36: 351–67.

García Canclini, N. 1993. *Transforming modernity: Popular culture in Mexico.* Austin: University of Texas Press.

———. 1995a. *Consumidores y ciudadanos: Conflictos multiculturales de la globalización.* México D.F.: Grijalbo.

———. 1995b. *Hybrid cultures: Strategies for entering and leaving modernity.* Minneapolis: University of Minnesota Press.

Garreton, M.A. 1996. Human rights and democratization processes. In *Constructing democracy: Human rights, citizenship and society in Latin America,* ed. E. Jelin and E. Herschberg, 39–56. Boulder: Westview Press.

Gasset, Ortega y. 1930. *La rebelión de las massas.* Madrid: Revista de Ocidente.

Gay, R. 1994. *Popular organization and democracy in Rio de Janeiro.* Philadelphia: Temple University Press.

Geertz, C. 1973. *The interpretation of cultures: Selected essays.* New York: Basic Books.

Germani, G. 1971. *Política y sociedad en una época de transición: De la sociedad tradicional a la sociedad de masas.* Buenos Aires: Paidós.

———. 1981. *The sociology of modernization: Studies on its historical and theoretical aspects with special regard to the Latin American case.* New Brunswick, NJ: Transaction Books.

Gomes, A. M. 1985. Confronto e compromisso no processo de constitucionalização. In *História geral da civilização Brasileira.* ed. S. B. Holanda, 9–85. São Paulo: Difel.

Guerra, X. F. 1988. *Mexico: Del antiguo regimen a la revoluccion.* 2 vols. Mexico D. F.: Fondo de Cultura.

Gunther, R., N. Diamandouros and Puhle, H. 1996. O'Donnell's illusions: A rejoinder. *Journal of Democracy* 7, no. 4: 151–59.

Habermas, J. 1975. *Legitimation crisis.* Boston: Beacon Press.

———. 1984. *The theory of communicative action.* 2 vols. Boston: Beacon Press.

———. 1987. *The philosophical discourse of modernity.* Cambridge, MA: MIT Press.

———. 1989. *The structural transformation of the public sphere: An inquiry into a category of Bourgeois society.* Cambridge, MA: MIT Press.

———. 1990. *Moral consciousness and communicative action.* Cambridge, MA: MIT Press.

Habermas, J. 1992. Further reflections on the public sphere. In *Habermas and the public sphere.* ed. C. Calhoun., 421–60. Cambridge, MA: MIT Press.

———. 1995. *Between facts and norms.* Cambridge, MA: MIT Press.

Habermas, J., and F. Hagopian. 1992. The compromised consolidation: The political class in the Brazilian transition. In *Issues in democratic consolidation: New South American democracies in comparative perspective,* ed. S. Mainwaring, G. O'Donnell, and A. Valenzuela, 243–93. Notre Dame: Hellen Kellog Institute.

————. 1996. *Traditional politics and regime change in Brazil*. New York: Cambridge University Press.

Hahner, J. E. 1986. *Poverty and politics: The urban poor in Brazil, 1870–1920*. Albuquerque: University of New Mexico Press.

Hall, J. 1994. *Civil society: Theory, history and comparison*. Cambridge: Polity Press.

Held, D. 1987. *Models of democracy*. Cambridge: Polity Press.

Hobbes, T. 1968. *Leviathan, 1651*. Baltimore: Penguin Books.

Hobsbawm, E. 1987. The age of empires. London: Weidenfeld and Nicolson.

Horkheimer, M. 1947. *Eclipse of reason*. New York: Seabury Press.

Horkheimer, M., and T. W. Adorno. 1946. *Dialectic of enlightenment*. New York: Herder and Herder.

Human Rights Watch. 1997. *Police brutality in Brazil*. Washington: Human Rights Watch.

Huntington, S. P. 1969. *Political order in changing societies*. New Haven: Yale University Press.

————. 1991. *The third wave: Democratization in the late twentieth century*. Norman: University of Oklahoma Press.

————. 1996. *The clash of civilizations*. New York: Simon and Schuster.

Ianni, O. 1970. *Crisis in Brazil*. New York: Columbia University Press.

————. 1975. *O colapso do populismo no Brasil*. Rio de Janeiro: Civilização Brasileira.

Inglehart, R. 1990. *Culture shift in advanced industrial society*. Princeton: Princeton University Press.

————. 1997. *Modernization and postmodernization: Cultural, economic, and political change in 43 societies*. Princeton: Princeton University Press.

Inglehart, R., M. Basáñez and A. Menendez. 1998. *Human values and beliefs: A cross-cultural sourcebook: Political, religious, sexual, and economic norms in 43 societies: Findings from the 1990–1993 world value survey*. Ann Arbor: University of Michigan Press.

Jacobi, P. 1986. *Políticas públicas de Saneamento Básico e Reivindicaçõe Sociais no município de São Paulo*: São Paulo: Cortez.

Jelin, E. 1994. The politics of memory. *Latin American Perspectives*. 81, no. 21:38–58.

Jelin, E., and A. Abós. 1987. *Movimientos sociales y democracia emergente*. Buenos Aires: Centro Editor de América Latina.

Jelin, E., and E. Hershberg. 1996. *Constructing democracy: Human rights, citizenship, and society in Latin America*. Boulder: Westview Press.

Kaase, M. 1990. *Social movements and political innovation*. In *New social movements*, ed. R. Dalton and M. Kuechler, 123–47. Cambridge: Polity Press.

Kant, I. 1959 (1781). *Foundations of the metaphysics of morals, and what is enlightenment?* New York: Liberal Arts Press.

Keane, J. 1988a. *Democracy and civil society: On the predicaments of European socialism, the prospects for democracy, and the problem of controlling social and political power*. New York: Verso.

Keane, J. 1988b. *Civil society and the state*. New York: Verso.

Kinzo, M. D. A. G. 1988. *Legal opposition politics under authoritarian rule in Brazil.* New York: St. Martin's Press.

Knight, A. 1990. *Historical continuities in social movements.* In *Popular movements and political change in Mexico,* ed. Joe Foweraker and Ann Craig, 78–102. Boulder: Westview Press.

Kornhauser, W. 1959. *The politics of mass society.* Glencoe, NY: Free Press.

Laclau, E. 1978. *Politics and ideology in Marxist theory: Capitalism, fascism, populism.* London: Verso.

———. 1985. New social movements and the plurality of the social. In *New social movements and the state in Latin America,* ed. D. Slater, 27–42. Amsterdan: Cedla.

Lamounier, B. 1992. *Parlamentarismo x presidencialismo.* São Paulo: IDESP.

Landes, J. B. 1990. *Woman and the public sphere in the age of the French Revolution.* Ithaca: Cornell University Press.

———. 1995. The public and the private sphere: A feminist reconsideration. In *Feminists read Habermas,* ed. J. Meehan, 91–116. London: Routledge.

Leal, V. N. (1946). *Coronelismo, enxada e voto.* 6th ed. São Paulo: Alfa-Omega.

Leis, H. R. 1989. *El movimento por los derechos politicos y la politica argentina.* Buenos Aires: Centro Editor de America Latina.

Linz, J. 1973. *The future of an authoritarian situation or the institutionalization of an authoritarian regime: The case of Brazil.* In *Authoritarian Brazil,* A. Stepan, 233–254. New Haven: Yale University Press.

———. 1994. *Presidential or parliamentary democracy: Does it make a difference?* In *The failure of presidential democracy,* ed. Juan Linz and A. Valenzuela, 3–87. Baltimore: Johns Hopkins University Press.

Linz, J., and A. Stepan. 1978. *The breakdown of democratic regimes.* Baltimore: Johns Hopkins University Press.

———. 1996. *Problems of democratic transition and consolidation.* Baltimore: Johns Hopkins University Press.

Liphart, A. 1992. *Parliamentary versus presidential government.* Oxford: Oxford University Press.

Lipset, S. M. 1959. Democracy and working-class authoritarianism. *American Sociological Review,* 24, no. 4; 482–501.

———. 1960. *Political man: The social bases of politics.* Garden City, NY: Doubleday.

Lowi, T. 1969. *The end of liberalism: Ideology, policy and the crisis of public authority.* New York: W. W. Norton.

Luhmann, N. 1990. *The differentiation of society.* New York: Columbia University Press.

Mainwaring, S. 1986. Transition to democracy in Brazil. *Journal of Interamerican Studies and World Affairs* 28: 149–179.

———. 1990. *Clientelism, patrimonialism and economic crisis: Brazil since 1979.* Washington: Latin American Studies Association.

Mainwaring, S., and T. Scully. 1995. *Building democratic institutions: Party systems in Latin America.* Stanford: Stanford University Press.

Mainwaring, S., and M. S. Shugart. 1997. *Presidentialism and democracy in Latin America*. New York: Cambridge University Press.

Mainwaring, S., and E. Viola. 1985. New social movements, political culture and democracy: Brazil and Argentina in the 80's. *Telos* 61 (Fall): 17–52.

Mainwaring, S., A. Valenzuela, and J. Linz. 1998. *Politics, society, and democracy*. Boulder: Westview Press.

Mansbridge, Jane. 1990. *Beyond self-interest*. Chicago: University of Chicago Press.

Martins, L. 1986. The liberalization of authoritarian Brazil. In *Transitions from authoritarian rule*, ed. G. O'Donnell, P. Schmitter, and L. Whitehead, 2:72–94. Baltimore: Johns Hopkins University Press.

Marx, K., and F. Engels. 1848. *Manifesto of the Communist Party*. New York: International Publishers.

———. 1976 [1871]. Preface and introduction to *A contribution to the critique of political economy*. Peking: Foreign Languages Press.

Mattelart, A. 1986. *La communicacion masiva en el proceso de liberacion*. Mexico D. F.: Siglo XXI.

McCarthy, J. D., and M. Zaid. 1977. Resource mobilization and social movements: A partial theory. *American Journal of Sociology* 82: 1212–41.

McCarthy, T. A. 1981. *The critical theory of Jürgen Habermas*. Cambridge, MA: MIT Press.

———. 1991. *Ideals and illusions*. Cambridge, MA: MIT Press.

McConnell, S. 1998. *Global citizens, national politics*. Chicago: Latin American Studies Associations.

Mello Moraes, J. 1982. *História do Brasil reino e do Brasil império*. Belo Horizonte: Itatiaia.

Melucci, Alberto. 1980. New social movements: A theoretical approach. *Social Science Information*. 19, no. 2: 199–226.

———. 1985. The symbolic challenge of contemporary movements. *Social Research* 52, no. 4: 789–816.

———. 1989. *Nomads of the present: Social movements and individual needs in contemporary society*. Philadelphia: Temple University Press.

———. *Challenging codes: Collective action in the information age*. New York: Cambridge University Press.

Melucci, A., and L. Avritzer. 2000. Complexity, cultural pluralism and democracy: Collective action in the public space. *Social Science Information* 39 no. 4:507–28.

Moisés, J. A. 1995. *Os Brasileiros e a democracia*. São Paulo: Ática.

Mommsen, W. J. 1984. *Max Weber and German politics, 1890–1920*. Chicago: University of Chicago Press.

Morse, R. M. 1964. The heritage of Latin America. In *The founding of new societies*, ed. L. Hartz, 123–77. New York: Harcourt.

———. 1982. *El espejo de próspero: Un estudio de la dialéctica del Nuevo Mundo*. Mexico D. F., Siglo Veintiuno.

———. 1989. *New world soundings: Culture and ideology in the Americas*. Baltimore: Johns Hopkins University Press.

Munck, G. 1990. Identity and ambiguity in democratic struggles. In *Popular movements and political change in Mexico*, ed. J. Foweraker, and A. Craig, 23–42. Boulder: Lynn Riener.

O'Donnell, G. A. 1973. *Modernization and bureaucratic-authoritarianism; Studies in South American politics*. Berkeley: Institute of International Studies, University of California.

———. 1990. *Análise do autoritarismo burocrático*. Rio de Janeiro: Paz e Terra.

———. 1992. Transitions, continuities and paradoxes. In *Issues in democratic consolidation: New South American democracies in comparative perspective*, ed. S. Mainwaring, G. O'Donnell, and A. Valenzuela, 17–56. Notre Dame: Hellen Kellog Institute.

———. 1994. Delegative democracy. *Journal of Democracy*: 5, no. 1: 55–69.

———. 1995. *Another institutionalization: Latin America and elsewhere*. Taipei: International Forum for Democratic Studies.

———. 1996. Illusions about consolidation. *Journal of Democracy* 7, no. 2:34–51.

———. 1998. Horizontal accountability in new democracies. *Journal of Democracy*. 9 no. 3: 112–26.

O'Donnell, Guillermo, and Phillip Schmitter. 1986. *Transitions from authoritarian rule*. Vol. 4., *Tentative conclusions about uncertain democracies*. Baltimore: Johns Hopkins University Press.

O'Donnell, G., P. Schmitter, and L. Whitehead, eds., 1986. *Transitions from authoritarian rule, vol. 2, Latin America*. Baltimore: Johns Hopkins University Press.

Offe, Claus. 1985. New social movements: Challenging the boundaries of institutional politics. *Social Research* 52, no. 4:817–67.

Olvera, A. 1995. *Regime transition, democratization and civil society in Mexico*. New York: New School for Social Research.

———. 1997. Civil society and political transition in Mexico. *Constellations* 4, no. 1:105–23.

———. 2002. Civic alliance: Pro-democratic social movements, civil society and the public sphere. In *Sociedad civil, espacios publicos y democratizacion en Mexico: Los contornos de un proyecto*, ed. Alberto Olvera. Mexico D. F.: Fondo de Cultura.

Oxhorn, P. 1995. *Organizing civil society: The popular sectors and the struggle for democracy in Chile*. University Park: Pennsylvania State University Press.

Parsons, T. 1949. *The structure of social action: A study in social theory with special reference to a group of recent European writers*. Glencoe, NY: Free Press.

———. 1951. *The social system*. New York: Free Press.

Parsons, T., and J. Toby. 1977. *The evolution of societies*. Englewood Cliffs, NJ: Prentice-Hall.

Pasquali, A. 1962. *Comunicacion y cultura de massas*. Caracas: Monte Avila Editores.

Pateman, C. 1970. *Participation and democratic theory*. Cambridge: Cambridge University Press.

Pereira, A. 1998. Persecution and force: The origins and transformation of Brazil's political trials. *Latin American Research Review* 33, no. 1:43–63.

Peruzzotti, Enrique. 1993. The Weimarization of Argentinian democracy. *Thesis Eleven* 34: 126–40.

———. 1997. Democratizing democracy: Political culture, public sphere and collective learning in post-dictatorial Argentina. Guadalajara: Latin American Association.

Peruzzotti, Enrique, and Catalina Smulovitz. 2002. *Enforcing the rule of law: The politics of societal accountability in Latin America*. Pittsburgh: Pittsburgh University Press.

Pinheiro, P. S. 1981. Violência e cultura. In *Direito, cidadania e participação*, ed. B. Lamounier, F. Weffort, and V. Benevides, 31–60. São Paulo: Queiróz.

———. 1985. *Política e trabalho no Brasil*. Rio de Janeiro: Paz e Terra.

———. 1996a. O passado não está morto: Ném passado é ainda. In *A democracia em pedaços*, eds. G. Dimenstein, 7–45. São Paulo: Brasiliense.

———. 1996b. *Popular responses to state-sponsored violence*. ed. D. Chalmers, 261–80. In *The new politics of inequality in Latin America*. New York: Oxford University Press.

———. PNUD. 1997. *Analisis del sistema electoral mexicano*. New York: United Nations Report.

POA, 1999. *Regimento do orçamento participativo*. Porto Alegre.

Poder Ciudadano. 1995. *Reforma electoral*.

Przeworski, Adam. 1988. *Democracy as a contingent outcome of conflicts*. In *Constitutionalism and Democracy*, ed. J. Elster and R. Slagtad, 59–80. Cambridge: Cambridge University Press.

———. 1991. *Democracy and the market: Political and economic reforms in Eastern Europe and Latin America*. New York: Cambridge University Press.

Przeworski, A., and S. Stokes. 1999. *Democracy, accountability and representation*. Cambridge: Cambridge University Press.

Przeworski, A., and Group on East-South Systems Transformations. 1995. *Sustainable democracy*. New York: Cambridge University Press.

Przeworski, Adam, M. Alvarez, J. Chelbub, and F. Limongi. 1996. What makes democracy endure. *Journal of Democracy*. 7:39–55.

Putnam, R. D. 1973. *The beliefs of politicians: Ideology, conflict, and democracy in Britain and Italy*. New Haven: Yale University Press.

———. 1993. *Making democracy work: Civic traditions in modern Italy*. Princeton: Princeton University Press.

Quijano, A. 1971. *Nationalism and capitalism in Peru*. New York: Monthly Review Press.

Ramirez, J. M. 1990. Urban struggles and their political consequences. In *Popular movements and political change in Mexico*, ed. J. Foweraker and A. Craig, 234–236. Boulder: Lynn Riener.

Rawls, J. 1971. *A theory of justice*. Cambridge, MA: Belknap Press of Harvard University Press.

Reis, Elisa. 1995. Desigualdade e solidariedade: Uma releitura do familismo amoral de Banfield. *Revista Brasileira de Ciências Sociais* 10, no. 29:35–48.

Rodrigues, L. M. 1987. *Quem è quem na constituinte: Uma análise sócio-política dos partidos e deputados*. São Paulo: OESP, Maltese.

Roeniger, Luis. 1989. *Hierarchy and trust in modern Mexico and Brazil*. New York: Praeger.

——. 1998. Discursos globales y radicacion local: El caso de los derechos humanos en el cono sur. *Cuadernos Americanos Nueva Epoca* 6, no. 66:105–29.

Roeniger, L., and G. Ayata. 1994. *Democracy, clientelism and civil society*. Boulder: Lynn Rienner.

Roeniger, Luis, and M. Sznajder. 1999. *The legacy of human rights violations in the Southern Cone*. Oxford: Oxford University Press.

Rivera, L. 1998. *Entre redes y actores*. Xalapa: Instituto de Investigaciones Historico Sociales.

Rosenn, K. 1971. The Jeito. *American Journal of Comparative Law* 19: 514–49.

Rostow, W. W. 1960. *The stages of economic growth: A non-Communist manifesto*. Cambridge: Cambridge University Press.

Rousseau, J.-J. 1968. *The social contract*. Baltimore: Penguin Books.

Rustow, D. 1970. Transition to democracy. *Comparative Politics* 2, no. 2: 337–63.

Sabel, Charles, and A. Fung. 1999. After backyard environmentalism: Towards a new model of information-based environmental regulation. *The New Democracy Forum. http://www-polisci.mit.edu.*

Sader, E. 1989. *Quando novos personagens entraram em cena*. São Paulo: Paz e Terra.

Sandel, M. 1984. *Liberalism and the limits of justice*. New York: Cambridge University Press.

San Juan, Carlos. 2002. Experiencias de una ciudad en transicion. In *Sociedad civil, espacios publicos y democratizacion en Mexico: Los contornos de un proyecto*, ed. Alberto Olvera. Mexico D. F.: Fondo de Cultura.

Santos, Boaventura de. 1998. Participatory budgeting in Porto Alegre: Towards a redistributive justice. *Politics and Society*. 26, no. 4:461–510).

Santos, W.G. dos. 1977. *Liberalism in Brazil: Theory and praxis*. In *Terms of Conflict*, P. Blachman, 1–38. Philadelphia: Institute for the Study of Human Issues.

——. 1979. *Cidadania e justiça: A política social na ordem brasileira*. Rio de Janeiro: Editora Campus.

——. 1993. *As Razões da desordem*. Rio de Janeiro: Rocco.

Sartori, G. 1987. *The theory of democracy revisited*. 2 vols. Chatham: Chatham House Publishers.

Schiller, H. I. 1969. *Mass communications and American empire*. New York: A. M. Kelley.

Schluchter, W. 1989. *Rationalism, religion, and domination: A Weberian perspective*. Berkeley: University of California Press.

Schmitt, C. 1923 [1988]. *The crisis of parliamentary democracy*. Cambridge, MA: MIT Press.

Schmitter, Phillip. 1971. *Interest conflict and political change in Brazil*. Stanford: Stanford University Press.

———. 1995. Transitology: The science or the art of democratization? In *The consolidation of democracy in Latin America*, ed. J. Tulchin and B. Romero, 11–41. London: Lynn Rienner.

———. 1998. *Reflections on the allegedly poor quality of neo-democracy in Latin America and Europe*. Caxumbu: Anpocs.

Schumpeter, J. A. 1942. *Capitalism, socialism, and democracy*. New York: Harper.

Schwartzman, S. 1988. Uma crítica a R. Morse. *Estudos Cebrap* 22:185–92.

———. 1989. *Bases do autoritarismo Brasileiro*. São Paulo: Foresnse Universitária.

Smelser, N. 1962. *The theory of collective behavior*. New York: Free Press.

Smith, W. 1990. *Authoritarianism and the crisis of the Argentine political economy*. Stanford: Stanford University Press.

———. 1991. State, market and neo-liberalism in post-transition Argentina: The Menem experiment. *Journal of Interamerican Studies and World Affairs* 33, no. 4: 46–82

Souza, Jesse. 2000. *A modernização seletiva: Uma interpretação do dilema Brasileiro*. Brazil: UNB.

Stepan, A. 1986. Paths toward redemocratization: Theoretical and comparative considerations. In *Transitions from authoritarian rule*, ed. G. O'Donnell, P. Schmitter, and L. Whitehead, 3:64–84. Baltimore: Johns Hopkins University Press.

———. 1988. *Rethinking military politics*. Princeton: Princeton University Press.

Swidler, A. 1995. *Cultural power and social movements*. In *Social movements and culture*, ed. H. Johnston and B. Klandermans, 25–40. Minneapolis: University of Minnesota Press.

Tabagiba, L. 2002. Os conselhos gestores e a democratiza ção das políticas públicas no Brasil. In *Sociedade civil e espaços públicos*, ed. Evelina Dagnino. Campinas: Editora da Unicamp.

Tarres, M. L. 1992. *La voluntad de ser: Mujeres en los noventa*. Mexico: El Colegio de Mexico.

Taylor, C. and A. Gutmann. 1992. *Multiculturalism and "the politics of recognition": An essay*. Princeton: Princeton University Press.

Thompson, J. 1990. *Ideology and modern culture*. Cambridge: Polity Press.

———. 1995. *Media and modernity*. Cambridge: Polity Press.

Thompson, J. B., and D. Held. 1982. *Habermas critical debates*. Cambridge, MA: MIT Press.

Tiano, S. 1986. Authoritarianism and political culture in Argentina and Chile in the mid-60's. *Latin American Research Review* 21, no. 1: 73–98.

Tilly, C. 1986. *The contentious French*. Cambridge, MA: Belknap Press.

———. *Coercion, capital, and European states, AD 990–1990*. Cambridge: Blackwell.

Tocqueville, A. de. 1966. *Democracy in America*. New York: Harper & Row.

Touraine, Alain. 1988. *Palavra e sangue*. Campinas: Editora da Unicamp.

UAMPA. 1986. *A participação popular na administração municipal*. Porto Alegre.

Unger, R. M. 1998. *Democracy realized: The progressive alternative.* New York: Verso.

Uricochea, F. 1984. *The patrimonial origins of the Brazilian state.* Berkeley: University of California Press.

Utzig, J. E. 1996. Notas sobre o governo do orçamento participativo em Porto Alegre. *Novos Estudos* 45:209–22.

Véliz, C. 1981. *The centralist tradition of Latin America.* Princeton: Princeton University Press.

Verba, S., K. L. Schlozman, and M. Brady. 1995. *Voice and equality: Civic voluntarism in American politics.* Cambridge, MA: Harvard University Press.

Wallerstein, I. M. 1979. *The capitalist world-economy: Essays.* New York: Cambridge University Press.

Weber, M. 1930. *The Protestant ethic and the spirit of capitalism.* New York: Scribner.

———. 1958. *From Max Weber.* New York: Oxford University Press.

———. 1978. *Economy and society,* 2 vols. Berkeley: University of California Press.

Weffort, F. C. 1979. *O populismo na política brasileira.* Rio de Janeiro: Paz e Terra.

———. 1989. *Why democracy?* In *Democratizing Brazil,* ed. A. Stepan, 327–50. New York: Oxford University Press.

Williams, R. 1981. *Culture.* Glasgow: Fontana.

Young, I. M. 1996. Communication and the other: Beyond deliberative democracy. In *Democracy and difference,* ed. S. Benhabib, 120–35. Princeton: Princeton University Press.

Zalaquett, J. 1996a. Confronting human rights violations committed by former governments: Principles applicable and political constraints. In *Transitional justice: How emerging democracies reckon with former regimes,* ed. Neil Kritz, 3–31. Washington, DC: United States Institute for Peace.

———. 1996b. The dilemma of new democracies confronting past human rights' violations. In *Transitional justice: How emerging democracies reckon with former regimes,* ed. N. Kritz, 203–7. Washington, DC: United States Institute of Peace.

Zermeno, Sergio. 1996. *La sociedad derrotada.* Mexico: Siglo XXI.

INDEX

Accountability, 4, 6, 104–106, 116, 124, 126, 129; short and long cycle of, 107, 112, 131–32, 135; societal, 133; vertical and horizontal, 132

Alfonsin, Raul, 109, 111

Alianza Cívica, 4, 124–29, 159–60, 169, 182n.10; adote um funcionário, 124–26; creation of, 97–98; and the IFE, 128, 137, 138, 143–45, 149, 150; monitoring in 1994 elections, 97; National Political Association Campaign, 126–28

Almond, Gabriel and Sidney Verba, 24, 58, 62. *See also* Political culture

Alvarez, Sonia, 58, 94, 98

Amnesty: in Brazil, 91; the military self-amnesty in Argentina, 109

Apathy, in democratic theory, 20

Arato, Andrew and Jean Cohen, 46–47

Arendt, Hannah, 14, 171–72n. 4

Argentina, 3–10, 86; Alfonsin, Raul, 109–11; authoritarianism in, 24; human rights social movements in, 87–90, 109–12; Nunca mas, 110; Menen, Carlos Saul, 112, 182n.5

Associations in Latin America: during the colonial period, 73–74; during the period of democratization in Brazil, 84–86. *See also* Neighborhood associations

Azevedo, Sérgio and Antônio Augusto Prates, 100

Belo Horizonte, 84–86; participation in PB in, 153; participatory budgeting in, 137–38, 153–56; voluntary associations in, 93

Benhabib, Seyla, 176n.1

Bicudo, Hélio, 115

Boschi, Renato, 93

Bohman, James, 38

Brazil, 3–10, 24, 90–92, 96, 99, 105, 137, 169; authoritarianism in, 112, 178n.1; Cardoso government, 122; Collor, 121–22, 131, 169; Constituent Assembly, 113, 119, 148, 180n.16; democratization, 106–107, 117–23; Diretas já movement, 4, 96, 173n.14; 1998 Constitution, 113, 146, 169; Sarney government, 119–21

Brazilian Bar Association, 91, 180n.14

Breakdown of democracy, 24, 78, 86

Bobbio, Norberto, 171n.2

Bureaucratization: critique of the Weberian conception, 47; Weberian conception of bureaucratization, 12

Brysk, Alison, 87, 88, 109, 110

Canclini, Nestor Garcia, 57, 63–68, 69

Cardoso, Fernando Henrique and Enzo Faleto, 60–61, 64; Cardoso government, 122. *See also* Dependency theory

Cardenas, Cuauhtemoc, 97, 184n.5

Catholic Church. *See* Church

Chiapas rebellion, 119